LOFT CONVERSION

PROJECT GUIDE

CONSTRUCTION PRODUCTS ASSOCIATION

Complies with 2010 revisions to the Building Regulations

RIBA ⊞ **Publishing**

construction
products association

© Construction Products Association, 2010

Published by RIBA Publishing, 15 Bonhill Street, London EC2P 2EA

ISBN 978 1 85946 357 4

Stock code 70564

British Library Cataloguing in Publications Data
A catalogue record for this book is available from the British Library.

Commissioned by John Tebbit, Construction Products Association
Written by Chris Derzypilskyj BSc (Hons), MBEng, ICIOB, Construction Products Association
Publisher: Steven Cross
Commissioning Editor: Lucy Harbor
Designed and typeset by Liaison Design
Printed and bound by Polestar Wheatons, Exeter

RIBA Publishing is part of RIBA Enterprises Ltd.
www.ribaenterprises.com

FOREWORD

I am delighted, as the Minister with responsibility for the Building Regulations, to provide the opening words to the first update of this Guide.

This Guide, produced by industry working collaboratively to help achieve compliance with the Building Regulations, has now been updated to reflect changes to the requirements of those Regulations.

The Guide brings together guidance from the Approved Documents and industry literature in a document aimed to help smaller builders and interested consumers, in particular, better understand the requirements of the Building Regulations and to help improve compliance. It will also be of use to building control professionals.

The Construction Products Association, with its partners from across industry, are all to be congratulated for producing and updating this guide. The Loft Conversion Project Guide is available as a free download from the Construction Products Association (CPA) website, and in hard copy from RIBA Bookshops (www.ribabookshops.com).

I would like to extend my thanks to all the partners in the team who put in their time, expertise and resources to make this Project Guide a reality. I hope that industry finds it useful and a valuable aid to building better loft conversions.

Andrew Stunell

Andrew Stunell
Parliamentary Under-Secretary of State,
Communities and Local Government

PREFACE AND
ACKNOWLEDGEMENTS

The origins of this guide lie in the Future of Building Control Consultation 2008, in which the government recognised the need to do more to help the public, industry and Building Control Bodies to better understand and comply with the Building Regulations. The view proposed was that additional guidance in the form of 'Project Guides' was needed to complement the Approved Documents.

Please note: Although the Department responsible for compliance with Building Regulations, Communities and Local Government, supports the issuing of this guide, it has not been approved by the Department. As a result, although the document aims to be as comprehensive as possible, even following the guidance exactly cannot ensure building work complies with building regulations. To check whether work will comply with building regulations, anyone proposing to carry out work covered by the guide must contact a Building Control Body. This should be done **before** starting work.

> "We will work with industry and other stakeholders to produce project guides in areas where there is a high volume of projects taking place, levels of compliance with the standards are thought to be low and work is generally carried out by those who do not encounter the Building Regulations on a day-to-day basis."
>
> Source: **The Future of Building Control Consultation**, Communities and Local Government, 2008

In response, in June 2008 the Construction Products Association took the initiative and began researching how these guides might become a reality. It became clear that no public funding would be available until the Project Guides were established as viable, so the Association committed its own resources to seeing whether such guides could be produced and whether they would be seen as being of benefit.

A survey was conducted through structured interviews with nine key institutions and an on-line survey with Building Control Bodies. The web-based survey was backed by Local Authority Building Control and circulated to all local authority Building Control Bodies in England, Wales and Northern Ireland. Despite a short time period for comment, over 100 responses were received, indicating a high level of interest in the guides. Overwhelmingly the highest interest (69%) was for a guide on loft conversions. These results matched those of a survey carried out in 2007 as part of the Future of Building Control Consultation.

The Association's survey also highlighted the lack of guidance and information readily available from local authority Building Control Bodies. Only 26% of the respondents published guidance on loft conversions, of which much was out of date and plagiarised, giving further support to the need for a guide.

The Association established a Project Guide Steering Group 'to be proactive in the selection, content, design and implementation of Project Guides'. The Steering Group agreed that loft conversions should be the subject of the first guide, and Chris Derzypilskyj of the Construction Products Association was tasked with developing the guide.

The Steering Group members consisted of representatives and observers from:

Association of Consultant Approved Inspectors

LABC Local Authority Building Control

NHBC National House Building Council

FMB Federation of Master Builders

energy saving trust Energy Saving Trust

Thanks are due to the following organisations (other than those mentioned above) for contributions during the development of the guide:

- British Plastics Federation
- British Woodworking Federation
- Celotex Insulation
- Communities and Local Government
- Kingspan Insulation
- Knauf Insulation
- Saint-Gobain
- West Midlands Fire Service

The Association would also like to thank all those who contributed through the consultation stage of this document.

The following organisations have supplied diagrams, tables and pictures, for which the Association is grateful:

- ADM Systems Limited
- Applied Energy Products Limited
- Blackdown Horticultural Consultants Limited
- British Standards Institute
- British Woodworking Federation
- Building Research Establishment
- Building Act 1984
- E A Higginson & Co. Limited
- Celotex Insulation
- Communities and Local Government
- Dream Lofts
- Dunelm Geotechnical and Environmental
- Elecsa
- Healthy Homes UK
- Home Living
- I D Steel Wrought Iron
- Jablite Limited
- Kingspan Insulation
- Knauf Insulation
- L. K. Goodwin Co.
- Local Authority Building Control
- Loft Shop
- Monodraught
- National House Building Council
- One Project Closer
- Passivent Ltd
- Thermap Limited
- Timber Research and Development Association
- Universal Forest Products
- Velux Company Limited
- Jablite Limited
- Web Dynamics

ABOUT THE GUIDE

The guide is produced by the Construction Products Association, in collaboration with the Association of Consultant Approved Inspectors (ACAI), Local Authority Building Control (LABC), National House Building Council (NHBC), Federation of Master Builders (FMB) and the Energy Saving Trust (EST).

As noted in the preface, Communities and Local Government has not approved the guide. As a result, even following the guidance exactly does not ensure building work complies with building regulations. **Therefore, anyone proposing to carry out work covered by the guide should contact a Building Control Body before starting work to check that their proposals comply with Building Regulations.**

The purpose of the guide is to simplify the Building Regulations process, assist in compliance and, where applicable, offer solutions to achieve minimum, good and best standards for construction. It is intended as an easy-to-use guide designed to bring together solutions offered in the current Approved Documents and third-tier guidance such as industry literature. It is not possible to, nor is it intended that this guide should cover every aspect of the design. Primarily, its purpose is to highlight the basic design considerations which need to be addressed. The guide is not a statement of law.

The guide does not include guidance on the following:

- Any dwelling where the current number of storeys (or once converted number of storeys) exceeds four (including basements).

- Modular units.

- Unusual or unorthodox design and construction.

For all of these, your chosen Building Control service provider should be approached for additional guidance.

The guide has been structured as follows:

Chapter 1: Before the project starts

This chapter provides information on the key policies and issues associated with a loft conversion. The homeowner will be able to determine whether the proposal will be subject to planning permission and, if so, the necessary documentation and the course of action required. The route to Building Regulations Approval is explained via local authority or approved inspector, with additional information detailing the types of applications available and their processes. Advice is also given on the Party Wall Act 1996, covenants, the CDM Regulations 2007 and regulations concerning bats.

Chapter 2: Existing structure

This chapter provides information on the feasibility of converting a loft area into a habitable space. It takes into account applicable parts of the Building Regulations and how they relate to establishing a design for a loft conversion. It also details fundamental areas inspected when surveys are undertaken to ensure that satisfactory in-service performance for the design life of the building is likely to be achieved.

Chapter 3: Proposed structure

This chapter provides information on how a loft conversion will alter and affect the existing structure. It discusses the four main types of roof design that are found within existing dwellings and how converting this space can have an effect on the wall construction below. Guidance has been included on how to notch and drill roof members when installing wiring and pipework.

Chapter 4: Stairs

This chapter provides information on the importance of the new stairs location when carrying out a loft conversion. It highlights the four types of stairs available for use, the stair construction, minimum headroom requirements and guidance for creating the stairwell opening.

Chapter 5: Windows and doors

This chapter provides information on minimum, good and best U-values and energy ratings for windows and external doors. Protection from falling through new windows and external doors is covered, including the need for safety glazing in critical locations and their cleanability. Guidance is included on how to install a roof window within the roof structure, as well as the use of sun pipes where borrowed light is needed.

Chapter 6: Drainage

This chapter discusses above-ground drainage work only. It has been assumed that an additional or relocated bathroom or room containing a WC will connect directly into the existing system without the need to carry out any work below ground.

Chapter 7: Fire safety

This chapter covers the fire safety information relevant to three dwelling types. Areas within this chapter include: fire detection and fire alarm systems, means of escape, compartmentation, the building fabric and load-bearing elements. Building Control providers have varying views as to which of the technical solutions for Fire Safety described in this chapter they are willing to approve. It is therefore very important to check fire safety issues with the particular building control provider at the earliest opportunity for any given project.

Chapter 8: Insulation

This chapter provides information on the seven main insulation products that are widely used when converting a loft. It also describes many other products that are readily available. It gives minimum, good and best U-values for generic construction details using the seven main insulation products. The generic construction details consist of an external wall, separating wall, flat roof and pitched roof.

Chapter 9: Sound

This chapter provides information on the need to prevent sound transmission through areas which include the existing structure, separating wall, new floor and new internal walls.

Chapter 10: Ventilation

This chapter provides good practice techniques and information on the need to provide ventilation to areas including the converted roof, habitable rooms and wet rooms.

Chapter 11: Heating, electrical and lighting

This chapter provides information on the dwelling's heating system whether gas-fired, oil-fired, electric or solid fuel. Guidance is given for electrical and lighting installations including the minimum allowable light fittings and socket outlets per room.

Chapter 12: Sustainability

This chapter provides advice and directs the homeowner to tools and guidance currently available that offer support to those wishing to improve the energy efficiency of their existing home and contribute to a low carbon economy, as well as mentioning biodiversity and other sustainability issues.

Chapter 13: Other items

This chapter provides information and a useful list of necessary documentation that must be obtained or considered when carrying out a loft conversion.

CONTENTS

1. BEFORE THE
PROJECT STARTS

1.0 INTRODUCTION

1.0.1 This chapter provides information on the key policies and issues associated with a loft conversion. The homeowner will be able to determine whether the proposal will be subject to planning permission and, if so, the necessary documentation and the course of action required. The route to Building Regulations approval is explained via local authority or approved inspector, with additional information detailing the types of applications available and their processes. Advice is also given on the Party Wall Act 1996, covenants, the CDM Regulations 2007 and regulations concerning bats.

1.1 Because of the complexities of loft conversions and the necessary structural alterations, it is normally necessary to obtain professional advice from an architect, surveyor or structural engineer.

1.2 PLANNING

1.2.1 Planning seeks to guide the way our towns, cities and countryside develop. This includes the use of land and buildings, the appearance of buildings, landscaping considerations, highway access and the impact that the development will have on the general environment. In simple terms, planning determines whether the proposed work can be done. It is advisable for the homeowner to obtain in writing from the local authority confirmation of whether or not planning permission is required.

1.2.2 A loft conversion is considered to be permitted development, not requiring an application for planning permission. This is because the effect of this type of development on neighbours or the environment is likely to be small, and the government has issued a general planning permission to authorise loft conversions subject to the following limits and conditions:

- A volume allowance of 40m³ for terraced houses.

- A volume allowance of 50m³ for detached and semi-detached houses.

- No extension beyond the plane of the existing roof slope of the principal elevation that fronts the highway.

- No extension to be higher than the highest part of the roof.

- Materials to be similar in appearance to the existing house.

- No verandas, balconies or raised platforms.

- Side-facing windows to be obscure-glazed; any opening to be 1.7m above the floor.

- Roof extensions not to be permitted development in designated areas, e.g. conservation areas, world heritage sites or areas of outstanding natural beauty, a National Park or in the Broads.

- Roof extensions, apart from hip to gable ones, to be set back, as far as practicable, at least 200mm from the eaves.

Examples of planning restrictions are provided in Figure 1.1.

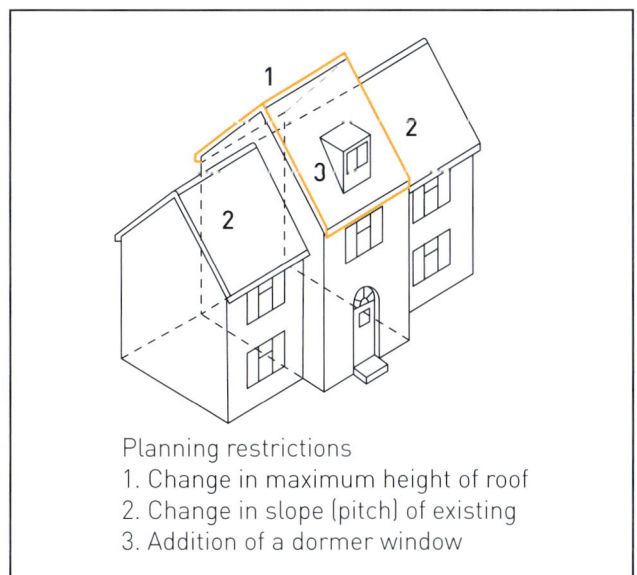

Planning restrictions
1. Change in maximum height of roof
2. Change in slope (pitch) of existing
3. Addition of a dormer window

Fig 1.1: Planning restrictions

1.2.3 If unsure, it is advisable for the homeowner to arrange a meeting with their designated case officer at the local planning office, who will discuss and inform accordingly whether planning permission is required for the proposals. If planning permission is necessary, a one-off fee will be required and the following information must be submitted together with a Full (detailed) Planning Application Form. This form can be filled out on paper or online at www.planningportal.gov.uk.

1.2.4 At least three copies of the following documents and application form are required with the submission:

- Existing layout – scale of 1:20, 1:50, 1:100 or 1:200.

- Proposed layout – scale of 1:20, 1:50, 1:100 or 1:200.

- Existing elevations –scale of 1:20, 1:50, 1:100 or 1:200.

- Proposed elevations – scale of 1:20, 1:50, 1:100 or 1:200.

- Location plan – scale not less than 1:1250.

- Site plan – scale of 1:500 or greater.

1.2.5 The planning process takes approximately eight weeks. Within this time frame the homeowner will be provided with a designated case officer who will visit the site, inform neighbours by letter of the proposed work, allowing them to object if they so wish, and place the application on the planning register, which allows anyone to view the application. A neighbour may object to the application if they feel the work overlooks their property, as shown in Figure 1.2.

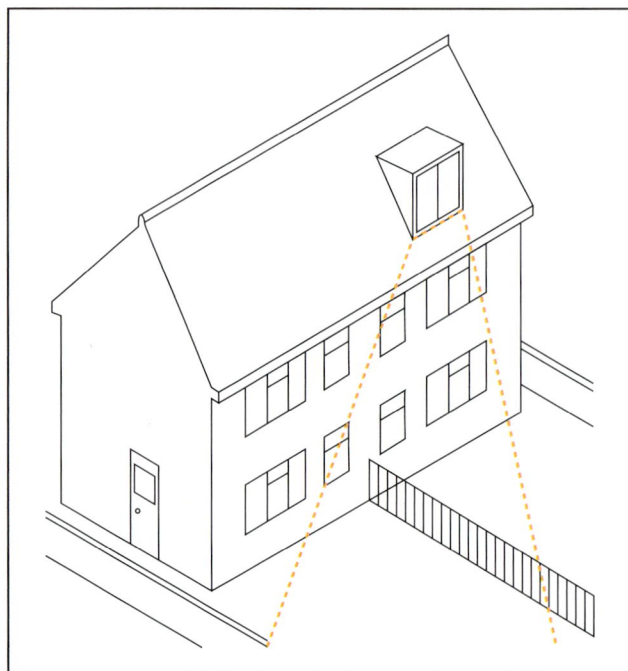

Fig 1.2: Overlooking neighbours

1.2.6 The case officer will consider whether the proposals are within the development plan for the area, and will normally ask for minor amendments to be made within the eight-week time frame to prevent a resubmission being required. At the end of the period the homeowner will receive one of the following:

a. **An approval** – the plans are deemed satisfactory. The approval will usually come with a number of conditions, the most common being that work must start within three years of the approval date.

b. **A refusal** – when this occurs it will come with a detailed list of issues outlining the decision to reject. There is no need for the homeowner to panic initially, however, as they are allowed to resubmit free of charge within 12 months of the rejection notice, and if the guidance within the 'detailed list' is followed they should be able to receive an approval at the second attempt. If the homeowner feels that resubmission is not appropriate, an alternative approach would be to appeal. Further information on this process is available from the local planning office.

1.3 BUILDING REGULATIONS

1.3.1 Building Regulations set standards for the design and construction of buildings to ensure the safety and health of people in or about those buildings. They also include requirements to ensure that fuel and power are conserved and facilities are provided for people, including those with disabilities, to access and move around inside buildings. Put simply, Building Regulations determine how the proposed work is done.

1.3.2 The Building Regulations are made under powers provided in the Building Act 1984, and apply in England and Wales. The current editions of the regulations are The Building Regulations 2000 (as amended) and The Building (Approved Inspectors etc.) Regulations 2000 (as amended), and the majority of building projects are required to comply with them. The Building Regulations contain various sections dealing with definitions, procedures and what is expected in terms of the technical performance of building work.

1.3.3 Loft conversions require Building Regulations approval if:

- They are to provide extra living accommodation.

- Roof windows are installed.

- They are to form a permanently accessible floored storage area.

- Structural members are to be removed or modified.

1.3.4 Where the intended use is only for lightweight storage such as of suitcases, general household items, etc. the provision of loose boarding is normally satisfactory. An application would not be required in such circumstances provided the access to the area is only by a removable/retractable ladder.

1.3.5 To achieve compliance with the regulations, the homeowner is required to use one of two types of Building Control service:

- Local authority Building Control service.

- An approved inspector's Building Control service.

1.3.6 Each local authority in England and Wales (Unitary, District and London Boroughs in England; County and County Borough Councils in Wales) has a Building Control section. It is their duty to see that building work complies with the Building Regulations except where it is formally under the control of an approved inspector. Individual local authorities coordinate their services regionally and nationally via an organisation called Local Authority Building Control (LABC). LABC has also developed an online service for creating and submitting building control applications. Homeowners can apply to most local authorities in England and Wales using this service at: **www.submit-a-plan.com**. Further information is available from the LABC website: **www.labc.uk.com**.

1.3.7 Approved inspectors are private-sector companies or practitioners and are approved for the purpose of carrying out Building Control services as an alternative to the local authority. Approved inspectors can provide a service in connection with work to existing buildings, including loft conversions. All approved inspectors are registered with the Construction Industry Council (CIC), who can provide a list of members. Some approved inspectors have an online service for creating and submitting Building Control applications. Further information regarding approved inspectors can be found on the Association of Consultant Approved Inspectors website: **www.approvedinspectors.org.uk/home.asp**.

1.3.8 The way to obtain approval will depend on whether the homeowner chooses to use the Building Control service of a local authority or an approved inspector.

1.3.9   If using a local authority, the procedures are set out in the Building Regulations. Some of these relate to pre-site procedures and others relate to procedures once work is under way on site. Two types of application for approval can be made.

1. **Full plans:** An application deposited under this procedure needs to contain plans and other information showing all construction details, preferably well in advance of when work is to start on site. The local authority will check the plans and consult the appropriate authorities (e.g. fire and sewerage). They must complete the procedure by issuing a decision within five weeks or, if agreed, a maximum of two months from the date of deposit.

   If the plans comply with the Building Regulations, the homeowner will receive a notice stating that they have been approved. If the local authority is not satisfied, they may ask the homeowner to make amendments or provide more details. Alternatively, a conditional approval may be issued. This will specify further information which must be deposited on revised plans. The local authority may only apply conditions if they have been requested to do so or if the homeowner has consented to them doing so. A request or consent must be made in writing. If plans are rejected, the reasons will be stated in the notice.

   A full plans approval notice is valid for three years from the date of deposit of the plans, after which time the local authority may send a notice to declare the approval of no effect if the building work has not commenced.

2. **Building notice:** Plans are not required with this process so it is quicker and less detailed than the full plans application. It is designed to enable some types of building work to get under way quickly, although it is perhaps best suited to small work.

If the homeowner decides to use this procedure they need to be confident that the work will comply with the Building Regulations; otherwise they will risk having to correct any work carried out if the local authority requests this. In this respect, the homeowner does not have the protection from the prosecution process provided by the approval of 'full plans'. If before the start of work, or while work is in progress, the local authority requires further information such as structural design calculations or plans, the homeowner must supply the details requested.

A 'building notice' is valid for three years from the date when the notice was given to the local authority, after which time it will automatically lapse if the building work has not commenced.

1.3.10   The Building Control service will make inspections as the work progresses to ensure compliance with the Building Regulations and other allied legislation. If building work is carried out, the homeowner is required, under the Building Regulations, to give the local authority notice of when the work has reached a particular stage. The local authority will explain about the notification procedures that the Regulations require to be followed at various stages of the work. When these stages are reached, the work should pause to give the authority time to make an inspection. They will advise the homeowner if the work does not comply with the Building Regulations. If the local authority is not informed of relevant stages of work for inspection it may, by notice in writing, require the work to be opened up for inspection so that whether or not the work complies with the Building Regulations may be ascertained. When the work is complete, the Building Control service will issue a final or completion certificate provided they are content that the completed work complies with the Building Regulations. For further information on the inspection regime, see Chapter 13.

1.3.11 If the homeowner chooses to engage an approved inspector, they should confirm with them the terms on which they wish to do so. The homeowner and inspector should jointly notify the appropriate local authority that the inspector is carrying out the Building Control function for the work. This notification is called an Initial Notice, and the local authority has five working days in which to raise any objections. Once this notice has been accepted by the local authority, the responsibility for planchecking and site inspection will be formally placed on the approved inspector.

An approved inspector will:

- Advise you on how the Building Regulations apply to the work.

- Check the plans.

- Issue a plans certificate (if requested).

- Inspect the work as it progresses.

- Issue a final or completion certificate.

1.3.12 There is a charge for these applications, which may vary between local authorities and approved inspectors. The homeowner should contact their local authority or approved inspector for details of these charges.

1.3.13 Both Building Control services will generally request two copies of the following documents with the submission:

- Existing layout – scale of 1:20, 1:50, 1:100 or 1:200.

- Proposed layout – scale of 1:20, 1:50, 1:100 or 1:200.

- Existing elevations – scale of 1:20, 1:50, 1:100 or 1:200.

- Proposed elevations – scale of 1:20, 1:50, 1:100 or 1:200.

- Location plan – scale not less than 1:1250.

- Site plan – scale of 1:500 or greater.

- Section though proposed building – scale of 1:20, 1:50.

- A full set of specification notes (unless detailed on the working drawing).

- Engineers design and details (where structural works are involved).

1.3.14 Where planning permission is required, it is advisable that this is obtained prior to making a Building Regulations application. If planning permission is refused and both applications were submitted with fees collectively, the homeowner will not receive a refund on the Building Regulations application.

1.3.15 Unauthorised loft conversions are illegal and may still be subject to both planning permission and Building Control after the project is completed. This is likely to make a property difficult to sell on in the future.

1.3.16 Where works are carried out without an application having been made, the owner may be prosecuted. However, to facilitate people who wish to have work approved, Building Control introduced in 1999 a new process called regularisation. A regularisation application is a retrospective application relating to previously unauthorised works – that is, works carried out without Building Regulations consent – started on or after 11 November 1985. The purpose of the process is to regularise the unauthorised works and obtain a certificate of regularisation. Depending on the circumstances, exposure, removal and/or rectification of works may be necessary to establish compliance with the Building Regulations. The homeowner should contact their local authority Building Control service to discuss their individual circumstances before submitting a regularisation application. Approved inspectors cannot carry out this function.

1.3.17 Examples of a local authority application form and an Initial Notice are provided in Chapter 13.

1.4 PARTY WALL ACT 1996

1.4.1 The Party Wall Act 1996 places certain obligations on homeowners intending to carry out work that involves the party wall/separating wall to a semi-detached or terraced property. The party wall/separating wall is illustrated by the dotted line in Figure 1.3.

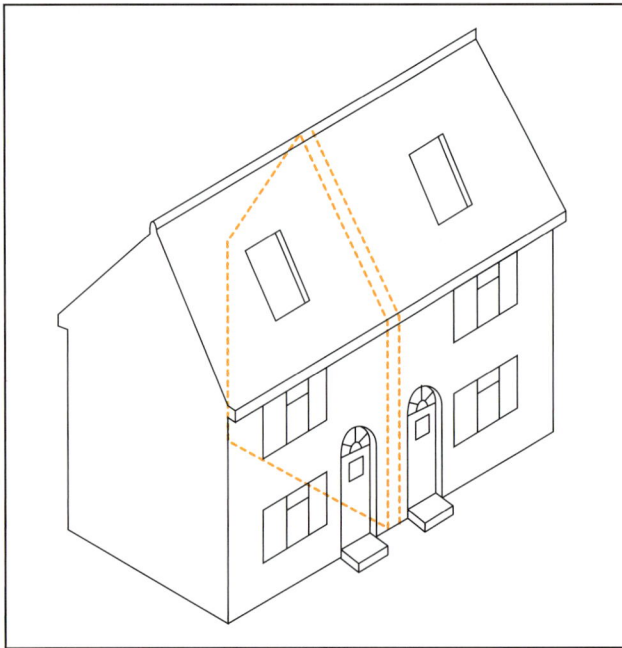

Fig 1.3: Party wall

1.4.2 Homeowners must determine whether the works fall within the scope of the Act, and where this is the case must arrange to serve statutory notice on all those defined by the Act as adjoining owners. They may wish to seek clarification through professional advice. Further details and the latest guide to the Party Wall Act are available on the Communities and Local Government website.

1.5 COVENANTS

1.5.1 Covenants are restrictions placed on a property by a previous owner or a landlord, if the property is rented or there is a lease. A covenant may also be related to historic rights. In all cases, the homeowner should consult a lawyer before proceeding, as a covenant may affect what work may be carried out.

1.5.2 If any other person's permission is required for the proposed conversion, this must be obtained before any plans are finalised or planning permission applied for.

1.6 THE CONSTRUCTION (DESIGN AND MANAGEMENT) REGULATIONS 2007

1.6.1 If the homeowner is carrying out, or having construction or building work done, they may need to notify the Health and Safety Executive (HSE) and may also have other duties under the Construction (Design and Management) Regulations 2007 (CDM 2007). Although a domestic client does not have duties under CDM 2007 and does not have to notify, those who work for them on construction projects do.

1.6.2 The CDM 2007 Regulations apply to most common building, civil engineering and engineering construction work. The homeowner must notify HSE of the site if the construction work is expected to either:

- last longer than 30 days; or
- involve more than 500 person days of construction work.

1.6.3 HSE should be notified in writing before construction work starts. Form F10 can be used, and the notification should be sent to the HSE office nearest to the proposed site.

1.6.4 Further information on the Construction (Design and Management) Regulations 2007 and a copy of form F10 can be found on the Health and Safety Executive website: **www.hse.gov.uk/construction/cdm.htm**.

1.7 BATS

1.7.1 Bats and their roosts are fully protected by
the Wildlife and Countryside Act 1981 and
the Conservation (Natural Habitats etc.)
Regulations 1994. If there are bats living in a
roof (the usual evidence of roosting is their
droppings), they may not by law be disturbed
or removed. One of the Statutory Nature
Conservation Organisations (SNCOs) should
be notified in the relevant area of the UK for
advice on the bats' protection before any work is
commenced.

Note:
The local SNCO should always be contacted before
an attempt is made to catch bats, as they may be
carrying a rare form of bat rabies for which there is, at
present, no cure

2. EXISTING STRUCTURE

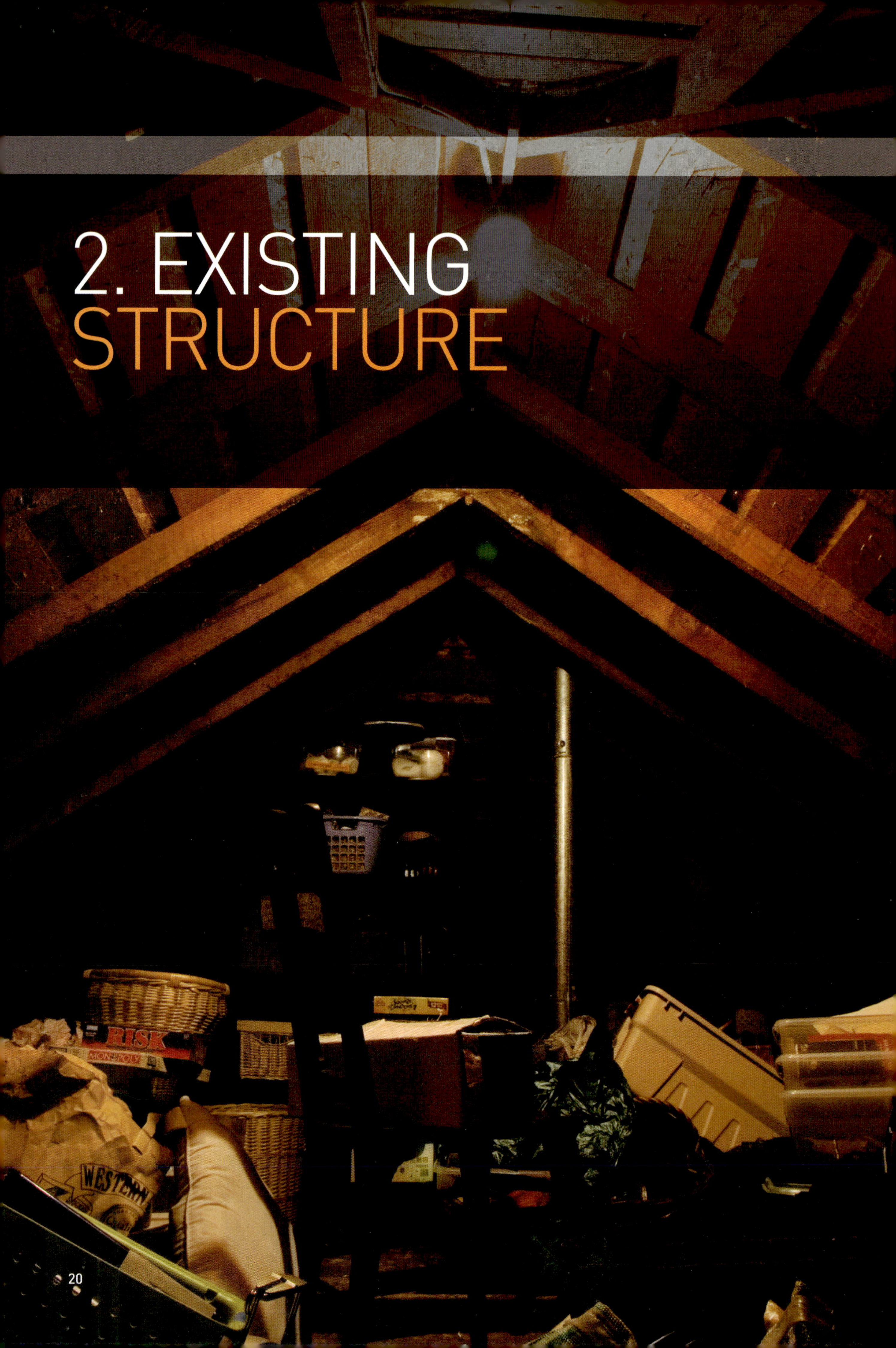

2.0 INTRODUCTION

2.0.1 This chapter provides information on the feasibility of converting a loft area into a habitable space. It takes into account applicable parts of the Building Regulations and how they relate to establishing a design for a loft conversion. It also details fundamental areas inspected when surveys are undertaken to ensure that satisfactory in-service performance for the design life of the building is likely to be achieved. An experienced structural engineer should be employed to carry out this assessment and advise on how to accommodate the proposed new structure.

2.1 The feasibility of the building for conversion:

- Assessment of the building's available space should be made including floor plan and means of escape, to enable feasibility of design to be established. The design may have implications that should be taken into account when assessing structure.

2.2 The existing structure:

- Where the loading on an existing building is increased by the addition of a new structure, the existing building must be assessed to make sure it can support the additional load.

- Stability of the structure should be checked. This is particularly important where walls, chimneys or existing structural members are removed or modified.

- Surveys will normally be required to establish the current condition of the existing building and ensure that satisfactory in-service performance for the design life of the building is likely to be achieved. Where doubt exists that performance may not be achieved the appropriate remedial work should be specified.

- Competent and qualified persons with relevant knowledge and experience should carry out the survey(s).

2.3 A loft conversion may be the best and in some cases the only way to extend or increase the habitable area of a building. However, there are considerations that should be taken into account that may complicate what at first looks like the most straightforward proposal.

This section advises on how to assess the feasibility of a building in terms of existing space and change of use.

2.4 Where it is intended to change the internal structure of an existing building, accurate measurements are essential. Changing the design of an existing space restrains any new design to existing dimensions. Limited space will make it more difficult to work to accurate dimensions. Small on-site design tolerances may be unavoidable.

2.5 LOFT SPACE AND ROOF

2.5.1 The loft as a three-dimensional space and the type of existing roof determines the feasibility of a loft conversion. The floor area, pitch of the roof and existing roof structure may restrict any design to unworkable tolerances. Where this is evident the entire roof structure should be replaced. Types of roofs include those shown in Figure 2.1.

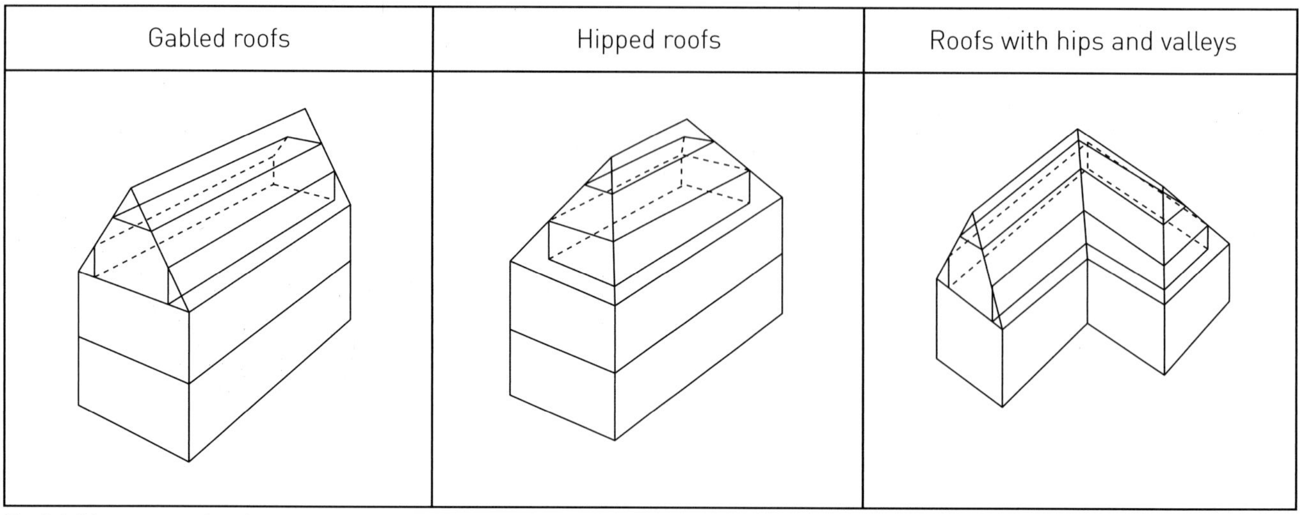

Gabled roofs	Hipped roofs	Roofs with hips and valleys

Fig 2.1: Main types of roofs

2.5.2 Roofs could be asymmetrical with offset pitches such as the north light and mono pitch. As shown in Figure 2.2.

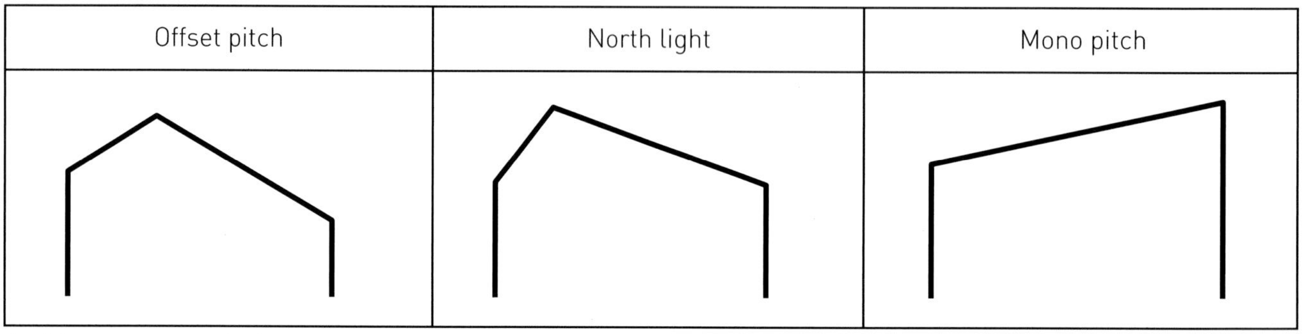

Offset pitch	North light	Mono pitch

Fig 2.2: Asymmetric pitched roofs

2.5.3 Roofs could also have more than one pitch each side of the ridge, as shown in Figure 2.3.

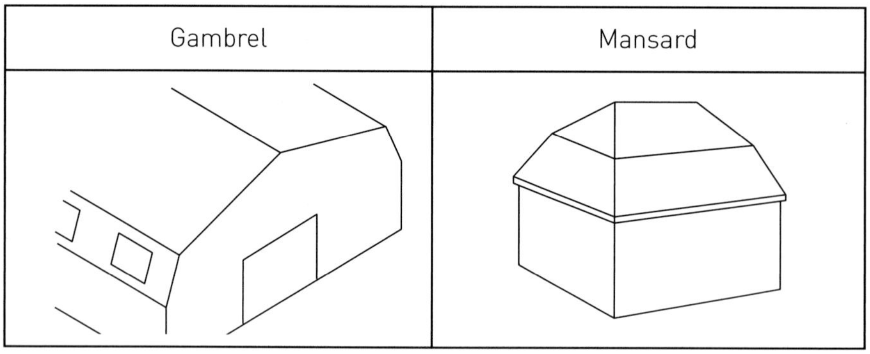

Gambrel	Mansard

Fig 2.3: Roofs with more than one pitch

2.6 EXISTING FOUNDATION

2.6.1 Foundations shall be capable of transmitting proposed loads to the ground without excessive movement. Therefore the condition of the existing foundation and supporting ground should be assessed for suitability. Items to be taken into account include:

- Subsidence and settlement.
- Heave.
- Chemical attack.
- Frost damage.
- Adjacent works.
- Underground erosion.
- Trees (mature height and root growth).
- Level and type of foundations.
- Level of water table (may have altered since construction).
- Existing water courses.
- Condition of foundations where drains/services pass through or beneath.

2.7 PROPOSED ALTERATIONS TO FOUNDATION

2.7.1 Where alterations are proposed to foundations to accommodate extra loading or to remediate damage, competent and qualified engineers with relevant knowledge and experience should be responsible for:

- Design of foundations.
- Supervision of the foundation work.
- Ensuring that specialist works are carried out by approved contractors.
- Ensuring that the design of the foundation takes into account any potential for differential settlement between existing and new foundations.

2.8 LOAD-BEARING WALLS

2.8.1 Existing walls shall be able to support and transfer the proposed loading to the foundation without undue movement:

- Structural elements where performance is shown to be insufficient for the proposed design should be replaced.
- Bricks and blocks require adequate density for purpose.
- Existing lintels must be able to sustain proposed load.
- Lintels should be shown to have adequate bearing. Inadequate bearings need to be repaired or replaced. Lintels will be replaced where length is not sufficient to allow minimum bearing.

2.9 CRACKING AND ASSOCIATED DAMAGE

2.9.1 Where cracking or damage has occurred in brickwork or joints, professional advice should be sought to identify the cause and where appropriate a suitable remedial scheme. The likelihood of non-progressive cracks becoming progressive will increase with additional loading. Where cracking occurs it may be acceptable to:

- Remove and replace cracked bricks.
- Re-point cracked joints.
- A competent and qualified person with relevant knowledge and experience should assess damage over larger areas of brickwork. Remedial work should progress safely and without undue stress to the structure.

Damaged structural elements such as lintels must be safely replaced.

2.10 CHIMNEYS AND FLUES

2.10.1 Chimneys and flues should be structurally stable, resistant to the effect of gases and heat, and resistant to the passage of moisture into the building. The following should be taken into account when assessing an existing chimney:

- Structural stability: where chimneys or flues are to be removed, they should be either totally removed or have any part that remains adequately supported. Where existing mortar has eroded or is cracked or crumbling it should be raked back to sound mortar and re-pointed.

- Where extensive breakdown of mortar has occurred the chimney may need to be rebuilt.

- The flue lining should achieve satisfactory in-service performance. Existing chimneys may not be suitable for the installation of linings. Specialist advice should be sought.

- Weatherproofing: the necessary DPC and flashings must be provided to ensure that no moisture will penetrate the flue or masonry. Where existing chimneys are to be retained but no longer used they should be fitted with a suitable capping and ventilated.

- Existing chimneys should not be used to support structural members. Where the chimney is not redundant, timbers must be kept away from the flue.

2.11 HISTORICAL ALTERATIONS TO THE BUILDING

2.11.1 It is not uncommon that alterations to the building may have occurred previously. Historical work on the building should be assessed in isolation and in relation to the building. Assessment of works should be carried out by a competent person and should include:

- Standard of work.

- Influence of work on the original structure.

- How the proposed changes to the building and loading will be transmitted safely through the original structure and any historical changes to the foundation and to the ground.

2.12 FLOORS

2.12.1 Upper floors shall be designed to support and transmit loads safely to the supporting structure without undue deflection. When assessing floors for suitability the following should be taken into account:

- Timber that shows signs of rot should be dealt with in an appropriate manner.

- Remedial work may include additional strutting, reduction in span or having additional timber added as appropriate.

- Guidance for the structural design of timber is given in appropriate load/span tables published by TRADA Technology Ltd. in support of the Building Regulations.

- Alternatively the structural design could also be carried out in accordance with one of the following:
  - BS 5268 or BS EN 1995
  - I-joists and metal web joists should be specified in accordance with the manufacturer's recommendations, but not used in situations where any part of the joist is exposed to external conditions.

Dead and imposed loads

2.12.2 Dead loads to be taken into account when surveying the structure include the following:

- Floor structure, decking and finishes.

- Ceilings and applied finishes.

- Walls and partitions supported by the floor.

- Point loads from structural members.

- Permanent fixtures such as boilers, water tanks, etc.

2.12.3 Imposed loads are the variable loads imposed when the building is in use. They include the weight of furniture and people. These loads will need to be taken into account when assessing the suitability of a loft floor used only for storage that will become a habitable area.

- BS 6399-1 and BS EN 1991 recommend a minimum imposed loading allowance of $1.5kN/m^2$ for self-contained dwellings.

Proposed loading

2.12.4 Proposed loading that will be transmitted through an existing floor must be assessed. Where the existing floor is unsatisfactory it may be necessary to remove the existing structure. An engineer should design floor joists where loads are concentrated. A change of loading on floor structures may be caused by:

- Structures for access such as stairs.

- Changes in room layout to accommodate stairs or compliance with Building Regulations.

- Redeployment of permanent fixtures such as water tanks or boilers.

- Support to proposed en-suite rooms.

Solid timber joist sizes are given in the span tables in BS 8103-3.

Supporting structure

2.12.5 The floor structure should have an adequate bearing on the supporting structure. This can be achieved through various forms:

- Joist hangers are acceptable if they have an adequate bearing onto the structure. The correct type and size of hanger should be used for the joist, and the joist should bear fully on the hanger to comply with BS EN 845.

- Unless designed otherwise, restraint-type joist hangers or separate restraint straps should be provided at no more than 2 m centres along the walls that run parallel to the joists.

- Bearing can be achieved by means of an independent wall plate fixed to the structure.

BS 8103-1 gives details of the connections between structural elements.

Flooring/decking

2.12.6 Unsound or contaminated flooring/decking should be removed. Loose boards should be refixed or replaced as appropriate. Use moisture-resistant board in places where water-using appliances are installed.

Other floor types

2.12.7 Structural alterations should only be carried out on the advice of a structural engineer.

Change of use

2.12.8 Changes in use and loading should be taken account of in design. Where a change of use of a floor area is proposed its performance must be shown to be satisfactory in service. Where the existing floor is unsatisfactory it may be necessary to remove the existing structure.

2.13 PITCHED ROOFS

2.13.1 Pitched roof structures shall support and transfer loads to the supporting structure without excessive deflection, and resist the passage of rain and snow to the inside of the building. When assessing roofs for suitability items shall include:

- Roof members: structural members should be assessed for suitability for the design lifetime of the building. Where a change of loading is proposed roof members may need to be removed, replaced or strengthened. All new structural timber should be treated (in older buildings) or if there are signs of woodworm attack, even if not active.

- Coverings: existing roof coverings should be removed and replaced unless it can be demonstrated that they will perform to a satisfactory standard for the design life of the building and be adequately joined to any new covering.

- Underlay: where roof coverings are removed, underlays should also be replaced.

- Guidance for the structural design of timber is given in appropriate load/span tables published by TRADA in support of Building Regulations.

- Alternatively the structural design could also be carried out in accordance with one of the following:

  - BS 5268 or BS EN 1995.

  - I-joists and metal web joists should be specified in accordance with the manufacturer's recommendations, but not used in situations where any part of the joist is exposed to external conditions.

Dead and imposed loads

2.13.2 A change in the design/use of the roof structure may affect dead/imposed loading. Dead loads to be taken into account when surveying the structure include the weight of the following:

- Coverings, battens and underlay.
- Ceilings and applied finishes.
- Insulation.
- Structural members.

2.13.3 Imposed loads are the variable loads imposed when the building is in use. Dead and imposed loads should be calculated in accordance with BS 6399 or BS EN 1991.

Wind loads

2.13.4 The existing roof and any new design including the fixing of roof weathering materials should resist uplift from wind forces. Where the weight of the main structure is not sufficient to prevent lifting, the structure should be anchored.

- Wind loads appropriate to the site should be calculated in accordance with BS 6399 or BS EN 1991 and the pitched roof covering should be fixed in accordance with BS 5534.

Holding-down straps

2.13.5 Holding-down straps should be provided to meet with current requirements as and where necessary and should be used where a roof requires anchoring.

Lateral restraint straps

2.13.6 For dwellings of masonry construction, restraint should be provided to gables at rafter and floor level and may be required at ceiling level. This can be seen in Figure 3.10 (Chapter 3).

2.13.7 Where purlins are used, restraint of gables can be achieved when timber abuts the gable construction. The spacing of the purlins to achieve restraint of the gable must be calculated and shown in the design.

2.13.8 For dwellings of timber frame construction, the designer should ensure stability in accordance with BS 5268 or BS EN 1995.

2.14 FLAT ROOFS AND BALCONIES

2.14.1 Flat roof and balcony structures shall support and transfer loads to the supporting structure without excessive deflection, and resist the passage of rain and snow to the inside of the building. When assessing roofs for suitability items shall include:

- Roof members: structural members should be assessed for suitability for the design lifetime of the building. Where a change of loading is proposed roof members may need to be removed, replaced or strengthened. All new structural timber should be treated (in older buildings) or if there are signs of woodworm attack, even if not active.

- Coverings: existing roof coverings should be removed and replaced, unless it can be demonstrated that they will perform to a satisfactory standard for the design life of the building, and adequately joined to any new roof covering.

- Underlay: where roof coverings are removed, underlays should also be replaced. Consider using profiled board/insulation to improve the fall.

- Guidance for the structural design sizing of timber is given in appropriate load/span tables published by TRADA Technology Ltd in support of Building Regulations.

- Alternatively the structural design could be carried out in accordance with one of the following:
  - BS 5268 or BS EN 1995.
  - I-joists and metal web joists should be specified in accordance with the manufacturer's recommendations, but not used in situations where any part of the joist is exposed to external conditions.

Dead and imposed loads

2.14.2 A change in the design/use of the roof structure may affect dead/imposed loading. Dead loads to be taken into account when surveying the structure include the weight of the following:

- Coverings, battens and underlay.
- Ceilings and applied finishes.
- Insulation.
- Structural members.

Dead and imposed loads should be calculated in accordance with BS 6399 or BS EN 1991.

Wind loads

2.14.3 The existing roof and any new design including roof weathering materials should resist uplift from wind forces. Where the weight of the main structure is not sufficient to prevent lifting, the structure should be anchored.

- Wind loads appropriate to the site should be calculated in accordance with BS 6399 or BS EN 1991.

Weatherproofing

2.14.4 Existing roof coverings should be removed and replaced unless it can be demonstrated that they will perform to a satisfactory standard for the design life of the building. Where a balcony is provided, correct detailing of interfaces between the building and the balcony are essential to prevent ingress of water to the building.

- Fall: the minimum post-construction fall of balconies and flat roofs is 1:80 unless an approved tanking membrane independently assessed for use with zero falls is used strictly in accordance with the manufacturer's recommendations.

- Fixings and penetrations: care must be taken not to penetrate waterproofing details with fixings and penetrations. Areas of risk include drainage outlets through parapets and fixings for balustrading.

- For details on balcony guarding, see Chapter 5.

2.15 ROOF DRAINAGE

2.15.1 Gutters and downpipes should be provided to roofs. It is likely that existing drainage systems will be interfaced with new systems when designing a loft conversion. Existing drainage shall be assessed for suitability and should be replaced where deemed inadequate.

2.15.2 Items to be taken into account include:

- Gutters and downpipes should be of sufficient size to accommodate normal rainfall. Where a dormer type construction is proposed care is needed in sizing gutters to accommodate the localised effect of the extra roof area and concentrated flow.

- Where the roof or balcony has an upstand on all sides, an overflow outlet should be provided through parapet walls or perimeter upstands to prevent a build-up of water in the event of other outlets becoming blocked. The position and height of the overflow should be such that any build-up of water will not enter the building. The capacity of the overflow should not be less than the size of the outlet (or the aggregated capacity of two outlets, if there are several outlets).

2.16 ROOF INSULATION

2.16.1 Recent increases in Building Regulations requirements for thermal insulation values and airtightness make it unlikely that the existing insulation within a loft will be sufficient or relevant when designing a loft conversion. For further detailed information, see Chapter 8.

2.17 VENTILATION OF MAIN ROOF SPACES (COLD ROOF)

2.17.1 To avoid condensation, roof voids must be ventilated above insulation. There are various acceptable details for achieving the ventilation performance required. The design must take into account the construction parameters and materials when calculating ventilation values. Elements that might affect ventilation design include:

- Tiles, underlay, vapour check, breather membrane, airtightness, sealing of penetrations. The individual performance of materials may have an effect on one another and on the overall performance of the roof. Different tile types, for example, and their ability to ventilate in weather will affect the performance of a breather membrane. This in turn will affect the amount of ventilation required to the roof. Material performance should be taken account of in design. For further information, see Chapter 8 on insulation and Chapter 10 on ventilation.

2.18 THERMAL COLD BRIDGING

2.18.1 The thermal resistance of a structure should remain constant across its surface to avoid cold spots, condensation and other related problems. In some circumstances a condensation risk analysis may be required.

Areas of risk include:

- Openings: the design should take account of thermal details around proposed windows and dormers.

- Thermal interfaces: cavity, roof, stud wall and ceiling thermal insulation should lap at interfaces.

- Structural steel: structural steel used to support the roof structure should be sufficiently insulated.

2.19 VENTILATION

2.19.1 Where existing extract ducts are relocated or new ducts proposed in the design, the following measures should be taken:

- Joints should be appropriately sealed.

- Insulate to an equivalent of 25mm of material having a thermal conductivity of ≤0.04 W/mK in unheated voids.

- Provide for dispersal of condensate within the duct. Ducts can be laid to a fall or require a condensation trap and drain.

- See Chapter 10 for full guidance.

2.20 SERVICES

2.20.1 Adding habitable rooms to an existing building may have implications for the existing services. Interfaces between existing and new services may also be unavoidable. Work should be undertaken by a competent person where new services are installed or changes/upgrades to existing services are proposed. It must be established that the existing services or the proposed services will provide a satisfactory in-service performance. Services include the following.

Hot and cold water services

2.20.2 Existing hot and cold water systems may need to be removed, replaced or upgraded. The water demand of the building may change with the introduction of more habitable rooms, particularly bathrooms, wet areas, WC and kitchens.

Electrical services

2.20.3 Electrical installations should comply with BS 7671 and be carried out by a person competent to do so. See Chapter 11 for further guidance.

Gas services

2.20.4 Where provided, gas services shall be adequate and in accordance with relevant standards and codes:

- All gas services must comply with the Gas Safety (Installation and Use) Regulations.

- British Standards relevant to the design of gas installations include BS 6891 and, for butane and propane gas, BS 5482. Other authoritative publications such as those prepared by the Institution of Gas Engineers and Managers and the Gas Safe Register can be used.

- Installation of gas services must be undertaken by a Gas Safe registered installer.

Space heating

2.20.5 It may be necessary to upgrade or replace existing heating systems. Where space heating is provided it shall be in accordance with relevant standards:

- British Standards relevant to heating systems include BS EN 12828, BS EN 12831, BS EN 14336, BS 5410 and BS 8303, and underfloor heating systems should be designed in accordance with BSRIA guides AG12 and AG13.

2.20.6 When a loft conversion includes the main living room of a dwelling, the heat output as part of whole home heating should be capable of maintaining a temperature of at least 21ºC in the room when the outside temperature is −3ºC.

2.20.7 The provision of whole home or central heating is discretionary. Where it is provided, it should be designed to recognised standards and based generally on the following: external temperature −3ºC and the design temperatures and ventilation rates given in Table 2.1.

Room	Room temperature (°C)	Ventilation rate (air changes per hour)
Living room	21	1.5
Dining room	21	1.5
Bedroom	18	1
Hall and landing	18	1.5
Kitchen	18	2
Bathroom	22	2
Toilet	18	2

Table 2.1: Design temperatures and ventilation rates
Source: NHBC

Soil and waste systems

2.20.8 It is likely that existing above-ground drainage systems will be incorporated into the design of a loft conversion. Existing systems to be retained, new systems and integrated systems should be assessed for suitability of design. Items to be taken into account include the following:

- Guidance and recommendations for building drainage and sanitation are given in BS EN 752 and BS EN 12056.

- Most post-war suburban housing will have separate foul and surface water drains. New connections should be checked to prevent cross-connections that could lead to pollution or sewer overflow.

- Waste systems should be arranged so that foul air is kept from entering the building.

- The system is adequately ventilated at the head of underground drains. This may be by a soil pipe or separate ventilation pipe.

- Precautions should be taken to limit noise transmission from soil pipes. Existing soil pipes in areas that will become habitable and new soil pipes should be encased and insulated.

3. PROPOSED
STRUCTURE

3.0 INTRODUCTION

3.0.1   This chapter provides information on how a loft conversion will alter and affect the existing structure. It discusses the four main types of roof design that are found within existing dwellings and how converting this space can have an effect on the wall construction below. Guidance has been included on how to notch and drill roof members when installing wiring and pipework. An experienced structural engineer should be employed to carry out this assessment and advise on how to accommodate the proposed new structure.

3.1   A loft conversion will alter the existing structure in a variety of ways depending on the type of conversion being undertaken. It will affect the wall construction, roof construction and the internal layout in respect of means of escape in case of fire. (The internal layout in respect of means of escape in case of fire is covered in Chapter 7.)

3.2   This chapter continues on from discussing the existing structure and highlights what to expect from different roof designs and how converting this space can have an effect on the wall construction below. Care should be taken to maintain structural integrity throughout the construction process.

3.3   For a loft conversion to be feasible you need to ascertain that the usable floor area will be such that it improves the size of the home. It must be remembered that to gain access to this space you may lose a sizable portion of living space below. The usable floor area in the loft is dictated by the type of roof construction that is in place. In general, there are three types of roof construction to be found in existing homes and these are discussed briefly over the following pages. A fourth type is the attic/room in roof (RIR) truss. If you are lucky enough to have this in your home, a conversion will be very simple indeed. In most cases this truss is used in new build properties that are designed as a home with a room in the roof space; however, they can be used as an option when the existing roof is unconvertible, in which case the existing roof can be stripped and replaced. Again, this is covered below.

3.4   The usable floor area in a loft and the preferred minimum ceiling height is detailed in Figure 3.1. It should be noted that this preferred minimum ceiling height is not required throughout the entire loft conversion, and lower levels are acceptable.

3.5   When measuring this ceiling height in the existing roof, you should deduct on average between 250mm and 300mm from the 'measured' height. The reason for this is that the overall height will be reduced once a new floor is installed and the ceiling has been insulated. This dimension may be greater if a level ceiling is preferred as shown in Figure 3.1.

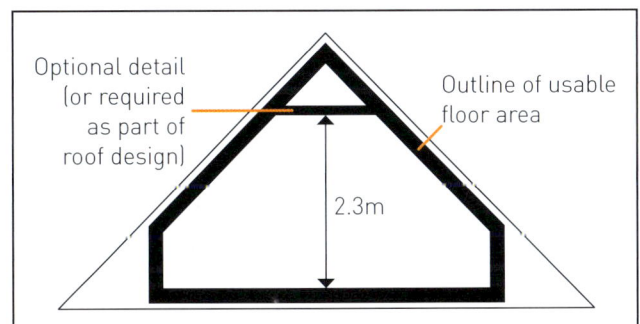

Optional detail (or required as part of roof design)

Outline of usable floor area

2.3m

Fig 3.1: 2.3m preferred minimum ceiling height

3.6 TRADITIONAL ROOFS

3.6.1 These roofs are generally made up from a series of rafters and purlins spanning between load-bearing walls. Such roofs are less complicated to convert than trussed rafter roofs and normally offer generous headroom. When converting, to provide support to the new floor structure or the existing purlins, new structural members, pad stones, lintels and upgrading of existing foundations are often required and a **structural engineer's design should be obtained**.

3.6.2 When considering a loft conversion don't be tempted to simply board over your existing ceiling joists and rafters, as the existing ceiling joists are probably too small to carry floor loadings. Doing this can adversely affect the value of the property, and in the majority of circumstances can cause overloading and endanger the structural stability of the building.

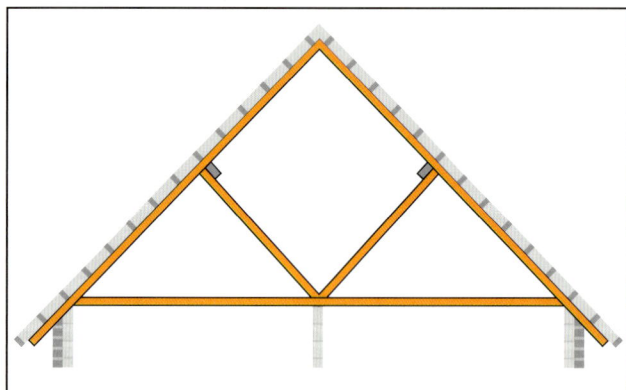

Fig 3.2: Traditional Roof

3.7 TDA ROOF

3.7.1 This roof was developed by the Timber Development Association (now TRADA) after the Second World War, as materials were in short supply. It uses significantly less timber than traditional roofs, say 30 per cent, but still maintains its strength without the need for internal walls. This is achieved through a series of 'A' framed hangers that are bolted to the ridge with struts bolted from purlins to their feet which in turn make a distinct 'W' shape.

These 'A' frames are spaced at set centres, so you may only find two or three within the loft space. Such roofs are considered more difficult to convert than the traditional roofs and again **require advice from a structural engineer** as structural members, pad stones, lintels and upgrading of existing foundations are often required.

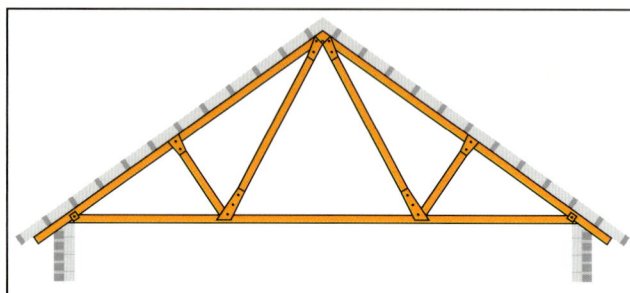

Fig 3.3: TDA Truss

3.8 TRUSSED RAFTER ROOFS

3.8.1 These roofs have been common since the 1970s, and roofs of this type are difficult to convert: roof trusses are complex pieces of engineering and they should not be altered without **the advice of a structural engineer**. When converting this type of roof it is common for a series of structural members (steel beams bearing on pad stones) to be installed to provide support to the new floor and to strengthen the rafters. This allows the bracing sections of the trusses to be cut out to create a clear floor area. Care should be taken with this type of roof as they were designed to span great lengths, and thus negate the need for load-bearing walls. Another problem is that they were brought into production when shallow-pitched roofs were the craze, and therefore the early properties may not be suitable to convert without the addition of dormers etc. or completely removing the existing roof and starting all-new construction above eaves level.

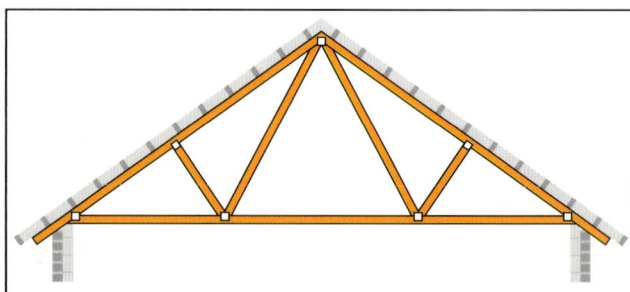

Fig 3.4: Trussed Rafter

3.9 ATTIC/ROOM IN ROOF (RIR) TRUSSES

3.9.1 It is possible, if planning permission permits, to strip the existing roof and replace with attic/RIR trusses. These are a complete unit, and will provide the new structural floor and avoid the need for additional structural elements to be included. By placing the new trusses alongside the existing ceiling joists, the existing ceiling can be retained and not disturbed.

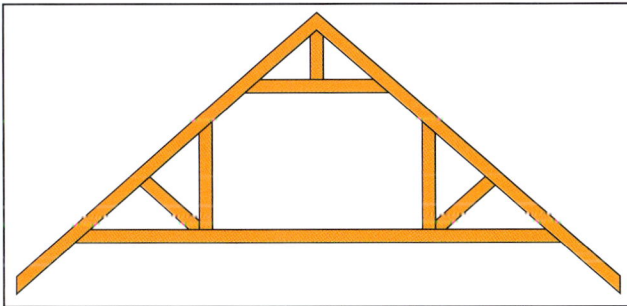

Fig 3.5: Attic/Room in Roof Truss

3.10 NOTCHING AND DRILLING

3.10.1 While discussing the overall roof structure it is appropriate to highlight another issue at this early stage. When installing wiring and pipework for the heating, electrical and lighting many individuals cause serious damage to structural timber without realising. (Guidance on heating, electrical and lighting can be found in Chapter 11.)

3.10.2 Following the simple guidance below will assist towards compliance:

- This guidance only applies to solid timber joists.

- Timber engineered joists should not be notched or drilled. Services should pass through the pre-formed holes in the web.

- The safe zones apply to both ends of the joist.

- Where notching and drilling is carried out that does not conform to this guidance the timber joist will be rejected unless its structural stability can be substantiated by structural calculations.

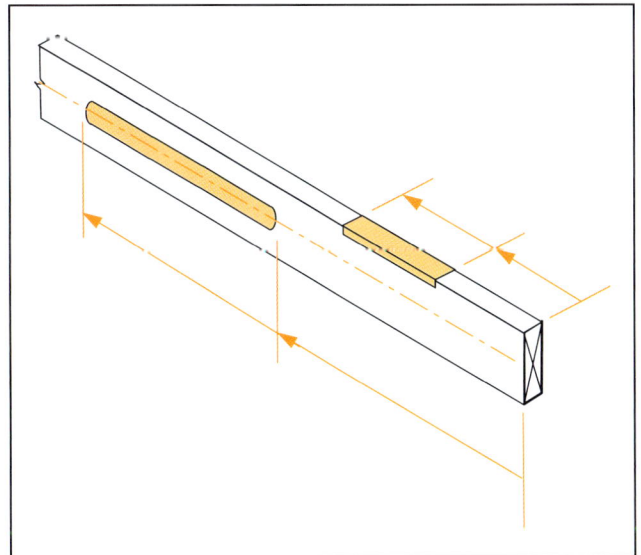

Fig 3.6: Permitted areas for notching and drilling

Notes for notching and drilling (Figure 3.6):

- Maximum diameter of holes should be 0.25 x joist depth.

- Maximum depth of notch should be 0.15 x joist depth.

- Notches on top in a zone between 0.1 and 0.2 x clear span.

- Holes on centre line in a zone between 0.25 and 0.4 x clear span.

- Holes to be kept apart by at least three times hole diameter.

- Notches and drilling in the same joist at least 100mm apart horizontally.

Notes for drilling only (Figure 3.7):

- Holes on centre line in a zone between 0.25 and 0.4 x clear span.

Limitations:

- Joist must be at least 150mm deep.

- Holes to be no greater than 30mm diameter.

- Holes to be drilled along centre line of joist.

- Holes to be at least three times the diameter of the largest hole apart.

- Maximum of 8 x 30mm holes can be accommodated in each zone.

- No notching permitted.

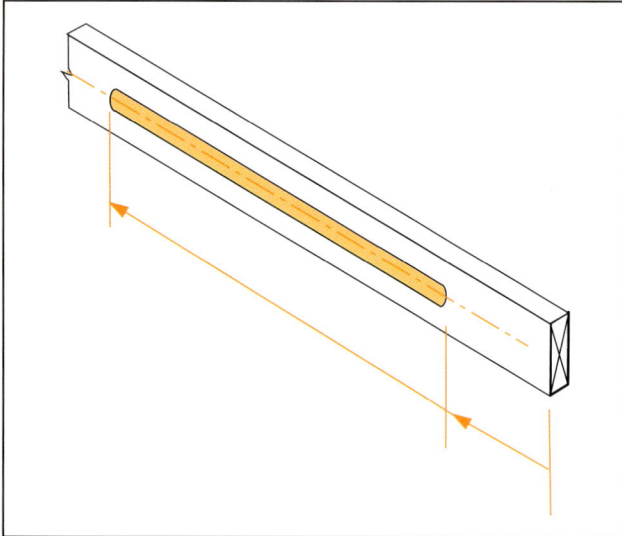

Fig 3.7: Permitted areas for drilling only

3.10.3 Notches or holes should not be cut in rafters, purlins or binders unless approved by the manufacturer. However, there are occasions when holes can be provided to truss rafters. You should always check the manufacturer's recommendations and design details in this situation. The information below has been provided as guidance only.

- Holes may be drilled only within areas shown in Figure 3.8 and if they are more than 500mm from a load bearing support or more than 250mm from a plated splice joint.

- Holes must be drilled on the centre line of the member.

- There must be at least 100mm between holes.

- Maximum size of drilled holes is shown in Figure 3.8.

- No other cutting, drilling or other alteration should be made to the trussed rafter.

3.11 WALL CONSTRUCTION

3.11.1 When adding an additional storey it is essential that you ensure that effective anchorage of walls to floors and roofs has been provided. This is very important and especially so for gable walls where negative pressure from the wind can 'suck out' the gable, as shown in Figure 3.9.

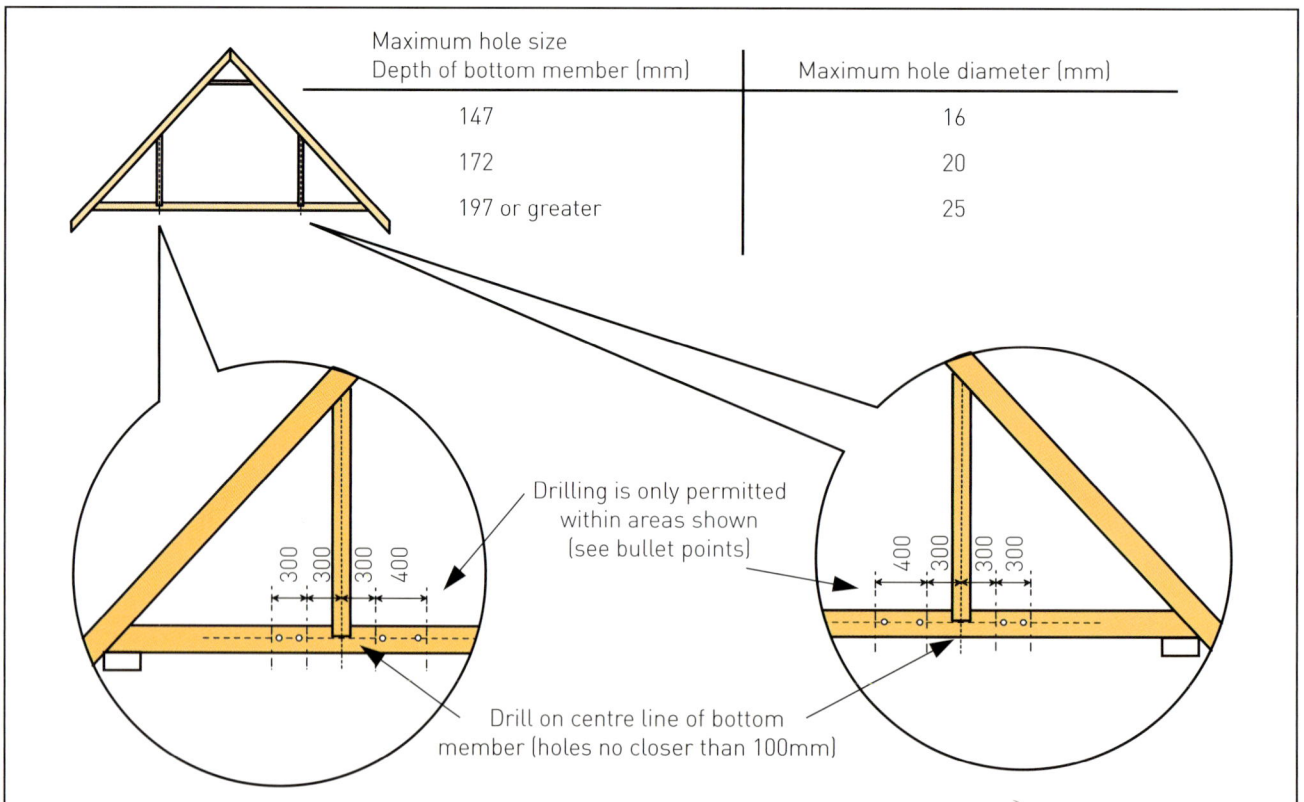

Maximum hole size Depth of bottom member (mm)	Maximum hole diameter (mm)
147	16
172	20
197 or greater	25

Drilling is only permitted within areas shown (see bullet points)

Drill on centre line of bottom member (holes no closer than 100mm)

Fig 3.8: Permitted drilling locations in bottom member

Fig 3.9: Gable wall failure

3.11.2 The common practice since the 1970s of using truss rafters leads to a situation where none of the roof weight (traditionally from purlins and binders) passes into the gable wall. With this form of construction the lateral restraint to the gable has to be provided by adequate strapping at the verge (or gable ladder) and at ceiling level if required.

3.11.3 As well as providing lateral restraint to gable walls, strapping also contributes to the robustness of the building and reduces the sensitivity of the building to disproportionate collapse in the event of an accident. Restraint straps therefore provide a critical function.

3.11.4 Figure 3.10 shows an acceptable method of satisfying Building Regulations for residential dwellings not exceeding three storeys. Where dwellings exceed three storeys and have been designed in accordance with BS 5628-1:2005 *Code of practice for the use of masonry* and Approved Document A : Structure, the connections to gable walls should be provided at intervals of not more than 1.25m centres for all storeys or as specifically required by the design engineer.

3.11.5 When following this method you should ensure that:

- The straps are installed and fixed fully in accordance with the Building Regulations guidance and in accordance with manufacturer's and designer's requirements.

- Rafters are not notched to make the straps flush with the rafter.

- The strap goes under the rafter and over ceiling joists.

- At the verge the strap turndown should be on a substantial piece of blockwork, preferably the centre of an uncut block.

- The strap should turn down vertically a minimum of 100mm and be tight against the face of the inner leaf wall.

- Packing should be provided, at the strap position, between the inner leaf and the first truss.

- Noggings are provided and set horizontal unless the strap has pre-formed twist to line it up with the roof slope.

- A high level of workmanship is maintained throughout the construction.

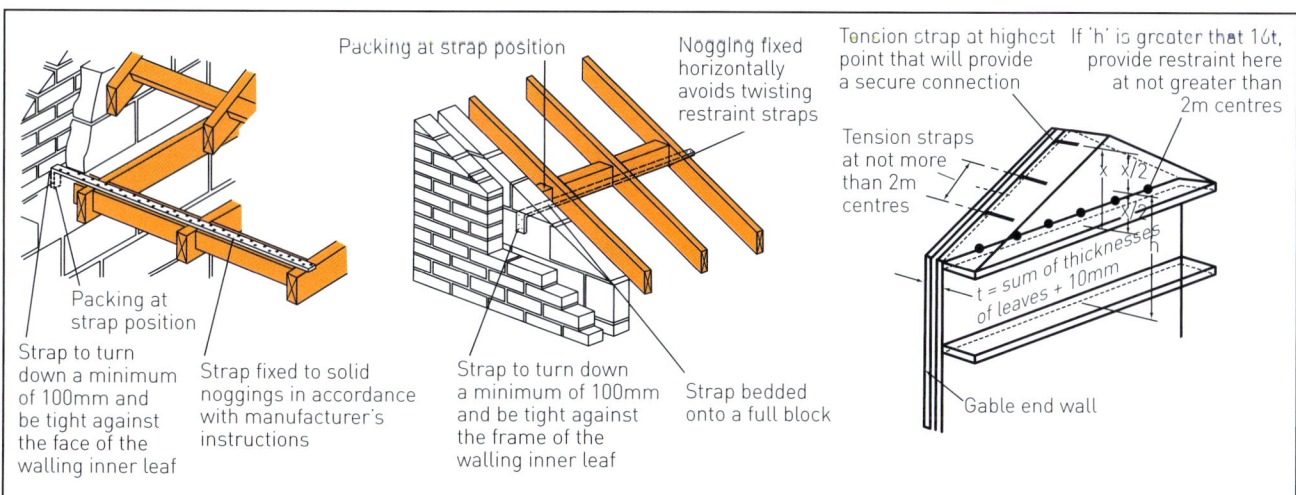

Packing at strap position

Nogging fixed horizontally avoids twisting restraint straps

Tension strap at highest point that will provide a secure connection

If 'h' is greater that 16t, provide restraint here at not greater than 2m centres

Tension straps at not more than 2m centres

t = sum of thicknesses of leaves + 10mm

Packing at strap position

Strap to turn down a minimum of 100mm and be tight against the face of the walling inner leaf

Strap fixed to solid noggings in accordance with manufacturer's instructions

Strap to turn down a minimum of 100mm and be tight against the frame of the walling inner leaf

Strap bedded onto a full block

Gable end wall

Fig 3.10: Effective strapping

4. STAIRS

4.0 INTRODUCTION

4.0.1 This chapter provides information on the importance of the new stairs location when carrying out a loft conversion. It highlights the four types of stairs available for use, the stair construction, minimum headroom requirements and guidance for creating the stairwell opening.

4.1 When considering a loft conversion, the position and type of permanent stair provided for access is extremely important. The position of the stair will depend on the existing layout of the property. In an ideal world the new stair would continue in the existing stairwell as this saves space and provides continuity. If this is not possible, part or all of an existing room will be required to accommodate the new stair. (All aspects regarding the protected staircase, where required, are covered in Chapter 7.)

4.2 Another factor to consider that is sometimes overlooked is the position of the new stair in the converted loft. The stair will generally need to terminate at or near to where the roof pitch is at its highest, as the Building Regulations stipulate a minimum headroom to a staircase. Overall the stair position will have a great impact on the size and possibly the number of rooms that can be created, if any at all.

4.3 There are four basic types of stair that are available when constructing a loft conversion. These are detailed here with a brief description.

1. Conventional stairs

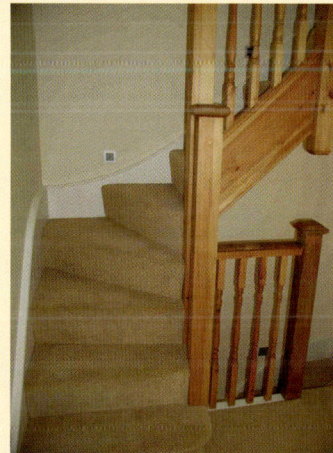

Fig 4.1

Ideally a conventional/traditional stair should be provided similar to that which provides access from ground to first floor. The stair must be designed and installed as per the Building Regulations, meeting certain criteria in areas such as pitch, rise and going, headroom, etc. You will need to install a stair of this type if you intend to provide more than one habitable room in the converted loft space.

2. Spiral and helical stairs

Fig 4.2

Spiral stairs wind around a central pole: they typically have a handrail on the outer side only, and on the inner side just the central pole. A squared spiral stair assumes a square stairwell and expands the steps and railing to a square, resulting in unequal steps (larger where they extend into a corner of the square). A pure spiral assumes a circular stairwell, and the steps and handrail are equal and positioned screw-symmetrically. A tight spiral stair with a central pole is very space efficient in the use of floor area. One should always take care to continuously use the handrail so that additional support is available in the event that a step is missed. Using the handrail will also direct the user to the safer outer portion of the treads. Helical stairs do not have a central pole and there is a handrail on both sides when over 1m wide. These have the advantage of a more uniform tread width compared to the spiral staircase. Where the stair diameter is less than the recommendations in BS 5395-2:1984 this type of stair is only allowed in loft conversions to access one habitable room.

3. Alternating tread stairs

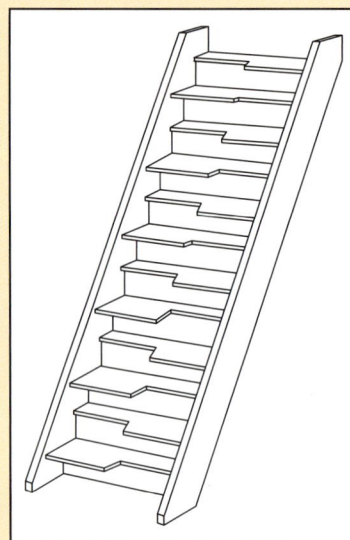

Fig 4.3

Where there is insufficient space for the full run length of normal stairs, alternating tread stairs can be used. Alternating tread stairs allow for safe forward-facing descent of very steep stairs. The treads are designed such that they alternate between treads for each foot: one step is wide on the left side; the next step is wide on the right side. There is insufficient space on the narrow portion of the step for the other foot to stand, hence the person must always use the correct foot on the correct step. The advantage of alternating tread stairs is that people can descend face forward. Alternating tread stairs may not be safe for small children or the elderly. The user relies on familiarity and regular use for reasonable safety. This type of stair is only allowed in loft conversions to access one habitable room, together if desired with a bathroom and/or a WC. This WC must not be the only WC in the dwelling.

4. Fixed ladders

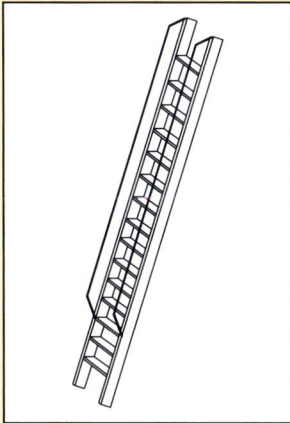

Fig 4.4

Where there is insufficient space for a full run length of normal stairs, a fixed ladder can be used as a last resort. The fixed ladder will have fixed handrails on both sides and allows for a safe descent of very steep stairs. Where a fixed ladder is to be used, a number of health and safety issues should be considered and may prevent this. Care should be taken to limit the height that a person can fall from when ascending or descending the stair, i.e. given the likely location of a fixed ladder within an existing stair enclosure, designers should consider whether some form of guarding is required to reduce the likelihood of a person falling down more than one flight. Designers should also consider how likely it is that people will be regularly using a fixed ladder while carrying objects in their hands. Carrying objects while utilising a fixed ladder increases the likelihood of a fall, and a more traditional solution would be preferable. This type of stair is only allowed in loft conversions to access one habitable room. Note that retractable ladders are not acceptable, as constant access and egress is required for means of escape.

4.4 Another type of stair that may be acceptable is the cottage stair. This stair is a compact staircase which can be installed at a steeper pitch than a conventional stair. As far as the Building Regulations are concerned the cottage stair is a non-standard staircase and may not be accepted to all Building Control Bodies. If you wish to install this type of stair you should discuss your individual needs with your chosen inspecting body.

4.5 For a new staircase to comply with the Building Regulations it is relatively straightforward. The following guidance highlights the key issues.

4.6 STAIRWELL OPENING

4.6.1 The existing roof construction will dictate how the stairwell opening is formed. Generally there are three options to providing this:

1. In most cases a new floor will be required to support the increased loads. This will have been designed and calculated by a structural engineer. Within the package will be information on the stairwell opening.

2. In exceptional circumstances the entire roof will be stripped and removed and replaced by attic trusses. Again, these trusses will have been designed and calculated by the truss manufacturer taking into account the position and 'make-up' of the stairwell opening.

3. It cannot be ruled out that the existing ceiling joists may be suitable for the increased loads as floor joists. With this in mind, these joists may be apt, when altered, to provide the support for the stairwell opening.

4.6.2 Options 1 and 3 above use traditional joists. For detailed information on calculating the size of the joists for the formation of a stairwell opening, see the recommendations in: *Span tables for solid timber members in floors, ceilings and roofs for dwellings*, second edition (TRADA Technology Ltd, 2009).

4.7 HEADROOM

4.7.1 When considering the construction of a new stair it is important to understand that an adequate headroom height of 2m is required on the access between levels. This is shown in Figure 4.5. Where this measurement is restrictive, in exceptional circumstances the dimension can be reduced and deemed satisfactory where the height measured from the centre of the stair is no less than 1.9m, reducing to no less than 1.8m at the side of the stair, as detailed in Figure 4.6.

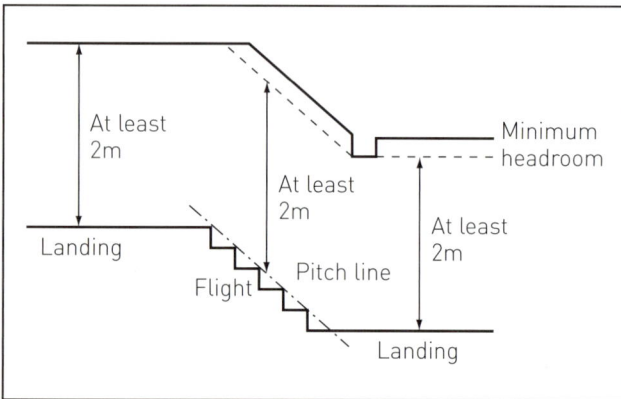

Fig 4.5: Normal headroom requirements

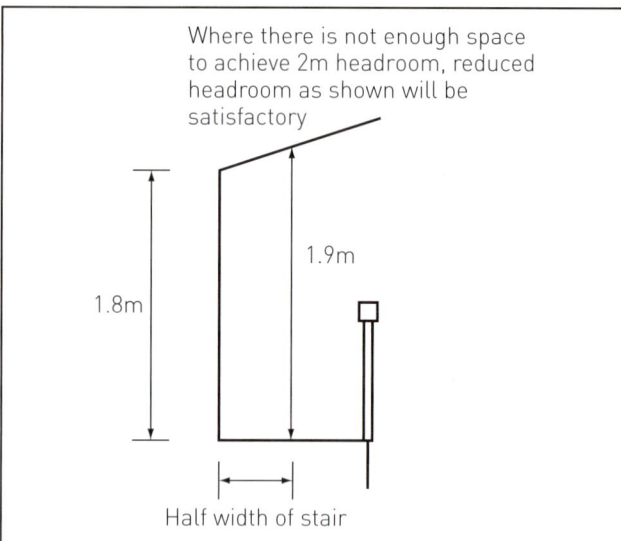

Fig 4.6: Reduced headroom

4.8 STAIR CONSTRUCTION

Rise and going

4.8.1 To comply with the regulations it is a necessity to have any rise between 155mm and 220mm used with any going between 245mm and 260mm **or** any rise between 165mm and 200mm used with any going between 223mm and 300mm.

4.8.2 There are seven key points to remember:

1. The maximum pitch of a stair is 42°.
2. The maximum individual rise is 220mm.
3. The minimum individual going is 220mm.
4. The normal relationship between the rise and the going is that twice the rise plus the going (2R + G) should be between 550mm and 700mm.
5. The rise and going of a stair must be consistent throughout its flight.
6. Treads must be level and slip-resistant.
7. Open risers can be provided but must be constructed in such a way that a 100mm sphere will not pass through the opening.
8. Where open risers are used the treads must overlap each other by a minimum 16mm.

Change of direction

4.8.3 When constructing the stair you must provide a level landing at the top and bottom of every flight. The landing length and width must be at least as great as the smallest width of the flight.

4.8.4 You must allow safe passage of landings; therefore they should be clear of permanent obstruction. In some instances, however, existing or new doors may be such that they open onto the landing. In this instance the following will apply:

- A door to a habitable room may only open over a landing at the bottom of a stair, and only if a clear space of 400mm is maintained.
- Only cupboard doors are allowed to open over a landing at the top or bottom of a stair; again, a 400mm clear space is required.

Both of these scenarios are detailed in the Figures 4.7 and 4.8.

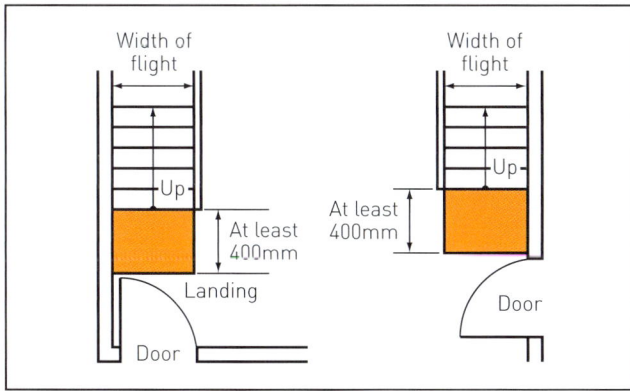
Fig 4.7: Doors and stairs

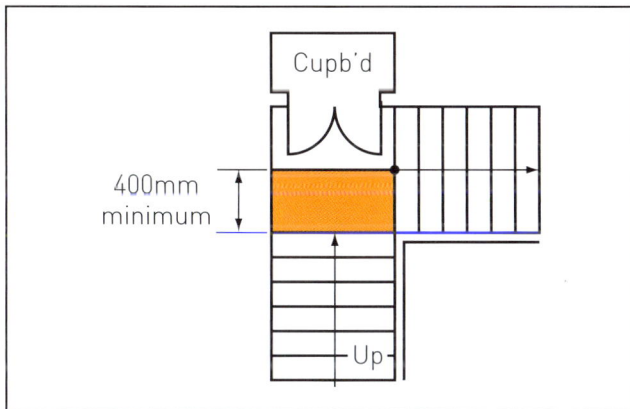
Fig 4.8: Cupboard doors and stairs

4.8.5 As well as landings at the top and bottom of the stair, you may have a level landing within the flight to change direction. It is not just level landings that can be used to change direction; you can turn the stairs using winders positioned at the top, bottom or within the stair flight. Where winders are provided you must ensure that the going of the tapered treads meet set requirements. These are outlined below:

- Where consecutive tapered treads are used the going should be consistent.

- If tapered treads are combined with straight flights the going should be consistent.

- Depending on the stair width, you will generally need three or four winders per change of direction.

- When measuring the going of a tapered tread to a stair less than 1m wide, the measurement should be taken from the middle.

- When measuring the going of a tapered tread to a stair greater than 1m wide, the going should be measured 270mm in from either side.

- The going to the tapered tread should be a minimum 50mm at the narrowest point.

4.8.6 The drawings in Figure 4.9 illustrate a selection of landings and stair turns. Figures 4.10 and 4.11 demonstrate how to measure the going of tapered treads. This only applies to conventional stairs, because fixed ladders and alternating tread staircases are required to be in uninterrupted straight flights.

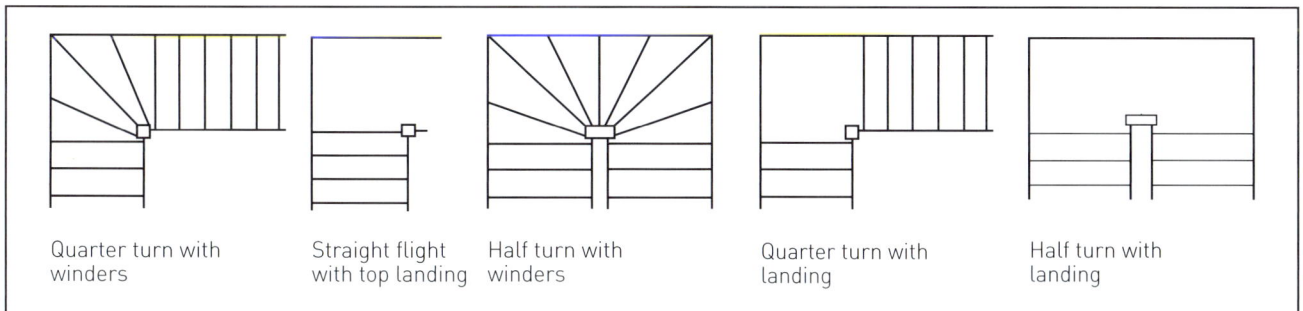

Quarter turn with winders

Straight flight with top landing

Half turn with winders

Quarter turn with landing

Half turn with landing

Fig 4.9: Landings and stair turns

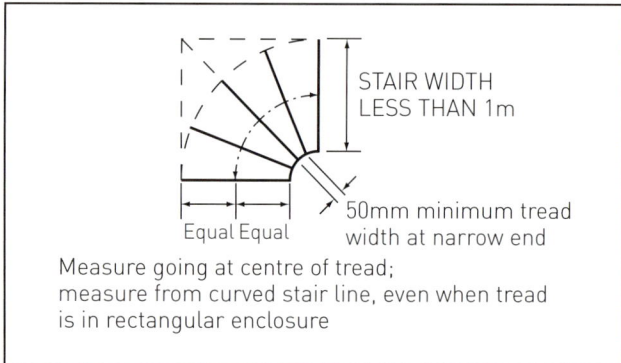

Fig 4.10: How to measure the going of tapered treads 1

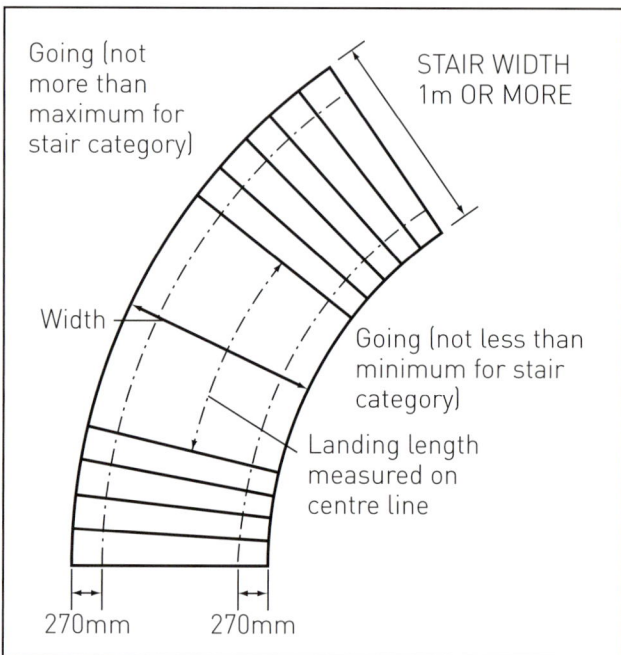

Fig 4.11: How to measure the going of tapered treads 2

Stair width and balustrading

4.8.7 The Building Regulations do not stipulate a minimum dimension for a staircase width; however, it is good practice to consider the user of the stair and practicalities, e.g. moving furniture up and down. There are seven key points to balustrading:

1. One handrail is sufficient where the stair width is less than 1m. Where greater than 1m or using either an alternating tread or a fixed ladder, a handrail should be provided to both sides.

2. The handrail height should be between 900mm and 1000mm measured vertically to the top of the handrail from the pitch line or floor.

3. Handrails to stairs incorporating winders or tapered treads should be sited to the side with the greatest going.

4. Flights and landings require guarding if the drop exceeds 600mm.

5. The guarding should be a minimum height of 900mm.

6. Where the guarding is 'open' it must be constructed in such a way that a 100mm sphere will not pass through the opening.

7. Children must not be able to effortlessly climb the guarding.

4.9 ADDITIONAL ALTERNATIVE STAIR CONSTRUCTION

4.9.1 As previously stated, there are three alternative staircase designs other than a conventional stair. Of these three, only the spiral and helical stair can be used when serving more than one habitable room; however, this is restricted to one room where the stair diameter is less than the recommendations in BS 5395-2:1984 *Stairs, ladders and walkways. Code of practice for the design of helical and spiral stairs*.
Table 4.1 stipulates the minimum rise, going and clear width of two different diameter spiral and helical staircases.

Stair category	Rise (r)	Going (g)			$2r + g$		Clear width
		Minimum inner going	Minimum centre going	Maximum outer going	Min.	Max.	Min.
A. Small private stair intended to be used by a limited number of people who are generally familiar with the stair. Typical outside diameter 1300mm to 1800mm, e.g. internal stair in a dwelling serving one room not being a living room or kitchen, access stair to a small room or plant in an office, shop or factory, not used by the public, or fire escape for small number of people.	mm 170 to 220	mm 120	mm 145	mm 350	mm 480	mm 800	mm 800
B. Private stair similar to category A but also providing the main access to the upper floor of a private dwelling. Typical outside diameter 1800mm to 2250mm.	170 to 220	120	190	350	480	800	800

Table 4.1: Minimum dimensions for spiral and helical staircases

5. WINDOWS AND DOORS

5.0 INTRODUCTION

5.0.1 This chapter provides information on minimum, good and best U-values and energy ratings for windows and external doors. Protection from falling through new windows and external doors is covered, including the need for safety glazing in critical locations and cleanability. Guidance is included on how to install a roof window within the roof structure, as well as the use of sun pipes where borrowed light is needed.

5.1 The provision of fire doors is covered in Chapter 7 and will not be discussed here.

5.2 Table 5.1 highlights the generic types of windows and doors that could be used within a loft conversion together with the minimum, good and best U-values and window energy ratings that can be achieved.

5.3 The 'minimum standard' is that currently set by the Building Regulations and is the bare minimum that Building Control will accept. The other two values are when you would prefer to insulate above the 'minimum standard' set out in the Building Regulations and wish to achieve a 'good standard' or 'best standard'. These improved standards offer the likelihood of reduced energy bills and an enhanced rating of the home's Energy Performance Certificate (EPC). (Further information on EPCs can be found in Chapters 12 and 14.)

5.4 The regulations state that the area of windows, roof windows and doors in the proposed works should be limited so that it does not exceed 25% of the floor area of the extension plus the area of any windows or doors which, as a result of the works, either no longer exist or are no longer exposed.

5.5 The new window and door locations within a conversion need careful consideration. There are three main areas where they will be provided:

a. New openings within the existing gable walls.

b. New dormers.

c. Roof windows.

5.6 Key points to consider for the above include:

- Sill height, openable window size and boundary conditions (unprotected areas) – this is covered in Chapters 7 and 10.

- Safety glazing, protection from falling, cleanability and provision of roof windows – this is covered on the following pages.

Standard / Element	Window, roof window and roof light	Doors with more than 50% of their internal face glazed	Other doors
	Window energy rating	U-Value (W/m²K)	U-Value (W/m²K)
Minimum (B. Regs)	C or U-value 1.6	1.8	1.8
Good	B	1.8	1.8
Best	A	1.6	1.6

Table 5.1: Window and door performance levels

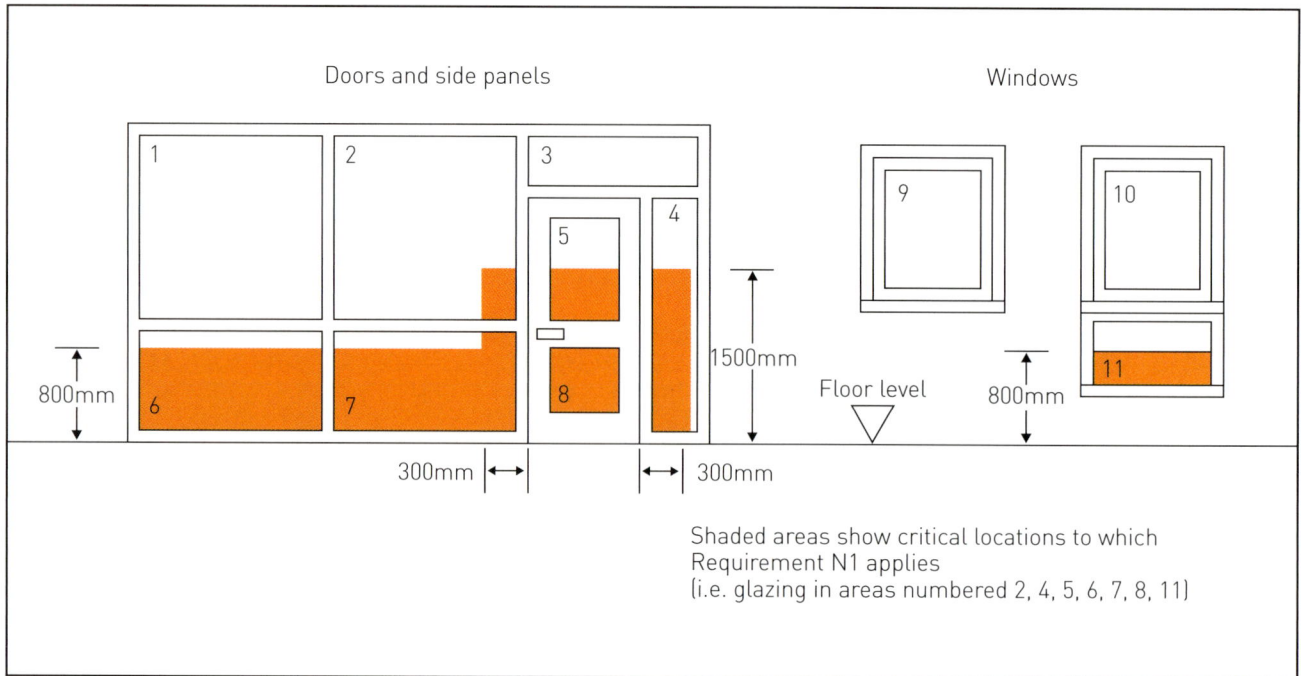

Fig 5.1: Critical locations for protection

5.7 There may be critical locations to glazing that require protection, for example glazing following the line of a new stair. Figure 5.1 outlines the areas that require safety glass.

This glass should either:

a. Break safely – safety glass should conform to BS EN 572-3, BS EN 572-6, BS EN 12150-1, BS EN ISO 12543-2 or BS EN 13024-1 and should have a performance classification in accordance with BS EN 12600. The requirement will be met if the glazing material has a Class 3 rating, or a Class 2 rating if located in a door or door side panel with a pane width exceeding 900mm;

b. Be robust – some glazing materials, for example polycarbonates and glass blocks, are inherently strong; or

c. Be permanently protected – if, as part of a design solution, glazing in a critical location is installed behind permanent screen protection, the screen should:

- Prevent a 75mm sphere from coming into contact with the glazing.

- Be robust.

- If it is intended to protect glazing that forms part of a protection from falling, be difficult to climb.

The glazing when protected in this way does not require safety glazing. For further guidance, see Figure 5.2.

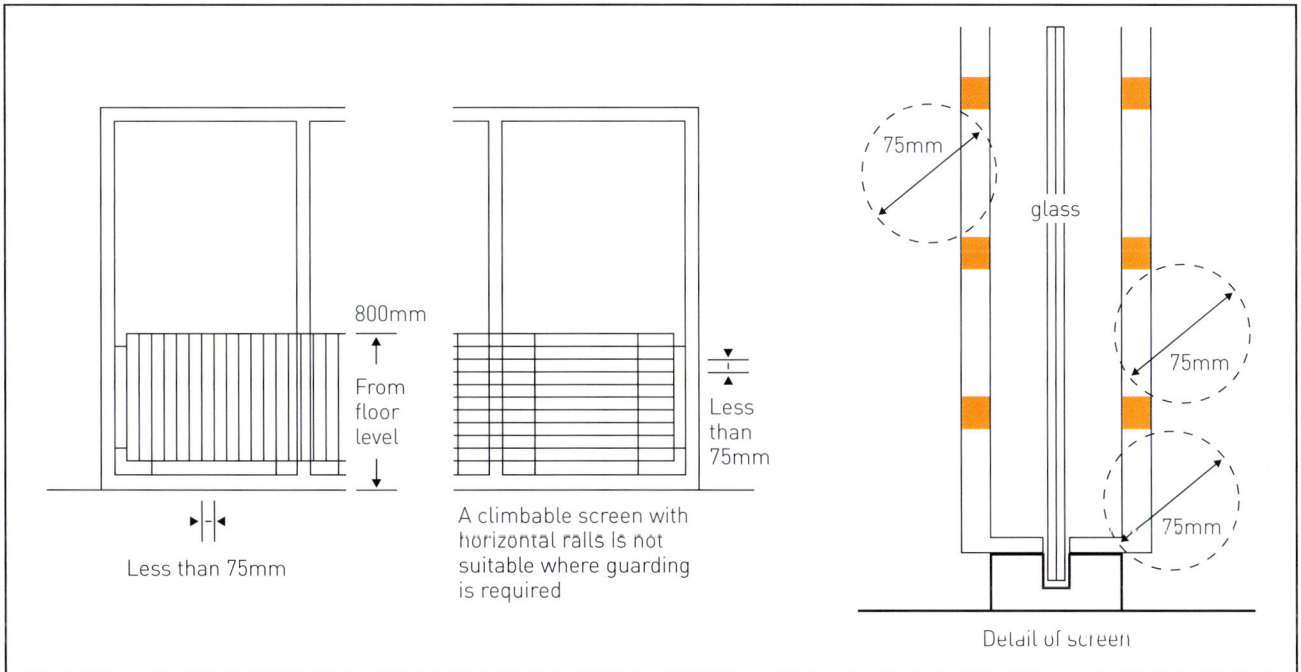

Fig 5.2: Using screens as protection

5.8 Another area of consideration is doors with small panes. These should have a dimension not exceeding 250mm and an area not exceeding 0.5m^2, each measured between glazing beads or similar fixings. Annealed glass in a small pane should not be less than 6mm nominal thickness, except in traditional leaded or copper lights in which 4mm would be acceptable. Figure 5.3 illustrates this further.

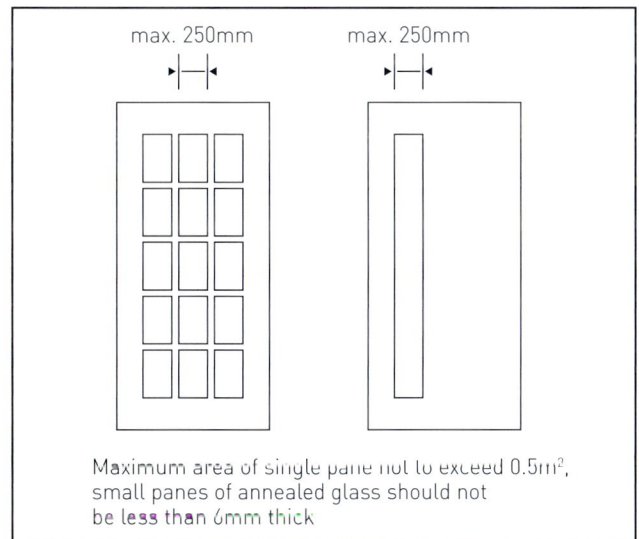

Maximum area of single pane not to exceed 0.5m^2, small panes of annealed glass should not be less than 6mm thick

Fig 5.3: Requirements for small pane areas

5.9 The safety glass in critical locations should be indelibly marked in such a position that the marking is visible after installation and includes the following information:

- The name or trademark of the manufacturer, merchant or installer.

- The identifier of the product standard that the safety glass conforms to, e.g. BS EN 12150; BS EN 14179; BS EN 14449.

- The classification according to BS EN 12600.

5.10 In the instance where doors are provided in the gable wall, for example, measures need to be taken in the form of guarding against the risk of injury. This type of detailing is normally called a Juliet balcony and should meet the following criteria:

- Have a minimum height of 1100mm – measurement is taken from floor to handrail height.

- Where an upstand (up to 300mm high) is formed to the base of the opening, a minimum 800mm guarding height should be maintained above the upstand.

- The guarding should be constructed in such a way that a 100mm sphere will not pass through any openings.

- Children must not be able to effortlessly climb the guarding.

- The guarding should be capable of resisting at least a horizontal uniformly distributed line load of 0.74 kN/m and fixed with corrosion-resistant fixings. BCBs may require justification for fixings.

An example of a Juliet balcony and a diagram detailing the above are provided in Figures 5.4 and 5.5 respectively.

Fig 5.4: Juliet balcony

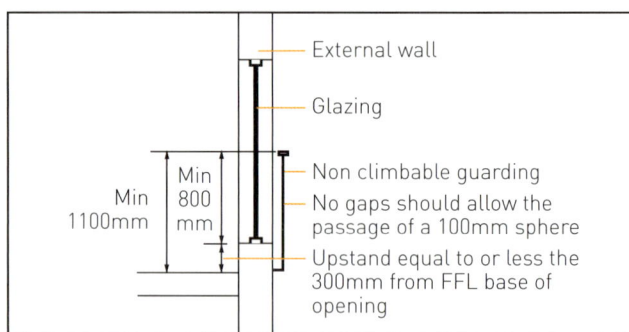

Fig 5.5: Guarding to French doors

5.11 Where windows are provided with sill heights less than 800mm, protection should be provided and the following guidance should be followed. It should be noted that roof windows can be installed to 600mm minimum without guarding.

- Windows with sill heights between 300mm and 600mm above finished floor level require guarding of minimum 700mm above the upstand. Figure 5.6 shows an acceptable arrangement with guarding internal or external, dependent on whether the glazing is safety glass.

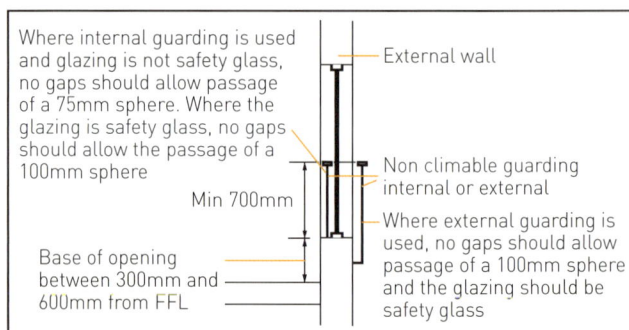

Fig 5.6: Guarding for sill heights 300 – 600mm

- Windows with sill heights between 600mm and 800mm above finished floor level should include guarding above the sill to a minimum 800mm above finished floor level. Figure 5.7 shows an acceptable arrangement with guarding internal or external, dependent on whether the glazing is safety glass.

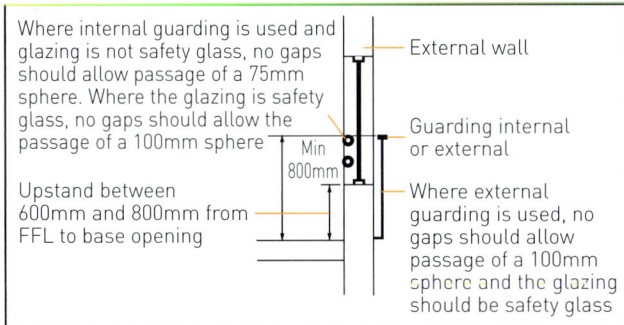

Where internal guarding is used and glazing is not safety glass, no gaps should allow passage of a 75mm sphere. Where the glazing is safety glass, no gaps should allow the passage of a 100mm sphere

External wall

Guarding internal or external

Min 800mm

Upstand between 600mm and 800mm from FFL to base opening

Where external guarding is used, no gaps should allow passage of a 100mm sphere and the glazing should be safety glass

Fig 5.7: Guarding for sill heights 600 – 800mm

5.12 Although not a requirement the Building Regulations, consideration should be given to the ability to access windows and doors safely for cleaning. The information in Figure 5.8 is for guidance only and details the provision for windows of a size and design that allows cleaning to take place from inside the property.

5.13 Roof windows should comply with the recommendations given in BS 5516-2 *Patent glazing and sloping glazing for buildings. Code of Practice for sloping glazing.*

5.14 Where new roof windows are installed, the roof structure may be required to accommodate and support the roof window. Two scenarios are provided:

- If the roof window is of a size that fits between the existing rafter spacings you should provide timber trimmers to the top and bottom of the opening.

- If the roof window is larger than the rafter spacing, the rafters should be cut and trimmed at the top and bottom of the opening. One additional full-length rafter for each rafter cut should be distributed evenly each side of the opening. This will prevent the rafters becoming over stressed, leading in time to local sagging of the roof.

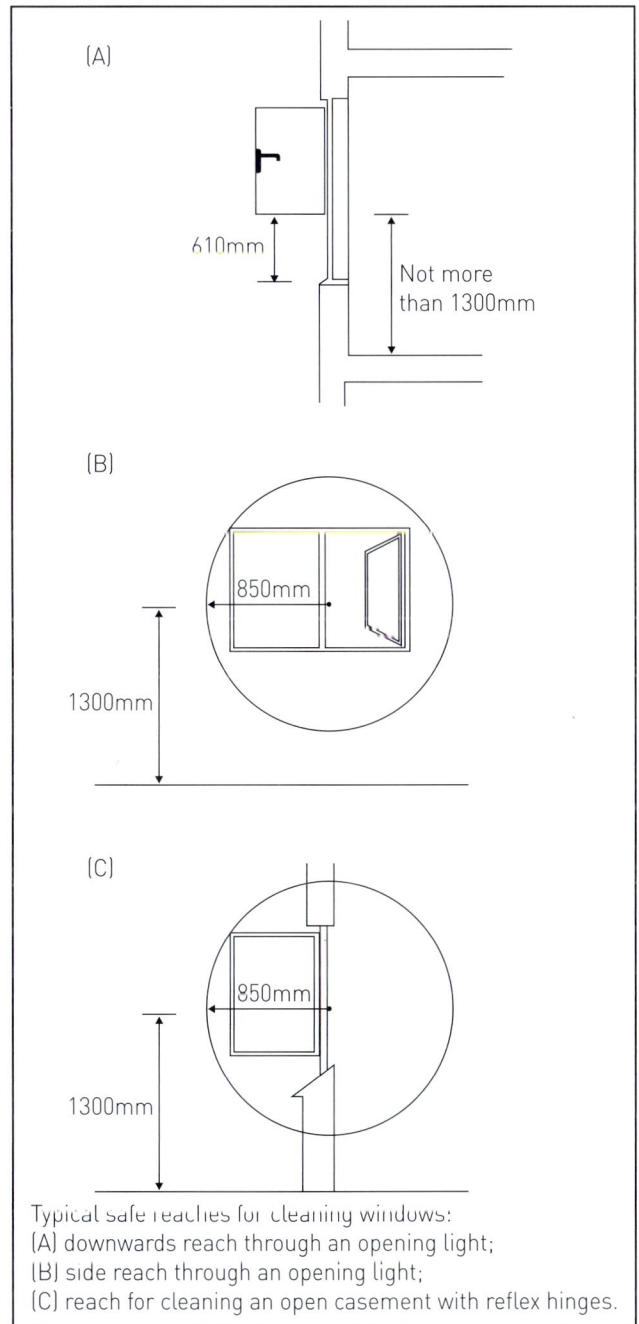

(A)

610mm

Not more than 1300mm

(B)

850mm

1300mm

(C)

850mm

1300mm

Typical safe reaches for cleaning windows:
(A) downwards reach through an opening light;
(B) side reach through an opening light;
(C) reach for cleaning an open casement with reflex hinges.

Fig 5.8: Considerations for cleaning access

Fig 5.9: Inserting the support frame

Fig 5.11: Installation of weatherproofing arrangement

Fig 5.10: Securing the frame

Fig 5.12: The fully installed window

Figs 5.9 - 5.12: Stages in installing a roof window

5.15 When installing a roof window, it is important to consider air leakage. The following detail for a roof window with a ventilated rafter void shows a typical installation with insulation around the window. Figure 5.13 also shows the internal vapour barrier and the use of felt around the construction, areas which are often missed during installation.

5.16 When installing roof windows, consideration should be given to the risk of overheating during the summer months. Solar control glass or film can be used in hot conditions to minimise solar heat gain by rejecting solar radiation and to help control glare. In temperate conditions, it can be used to balance solar control with high levels of natural light.

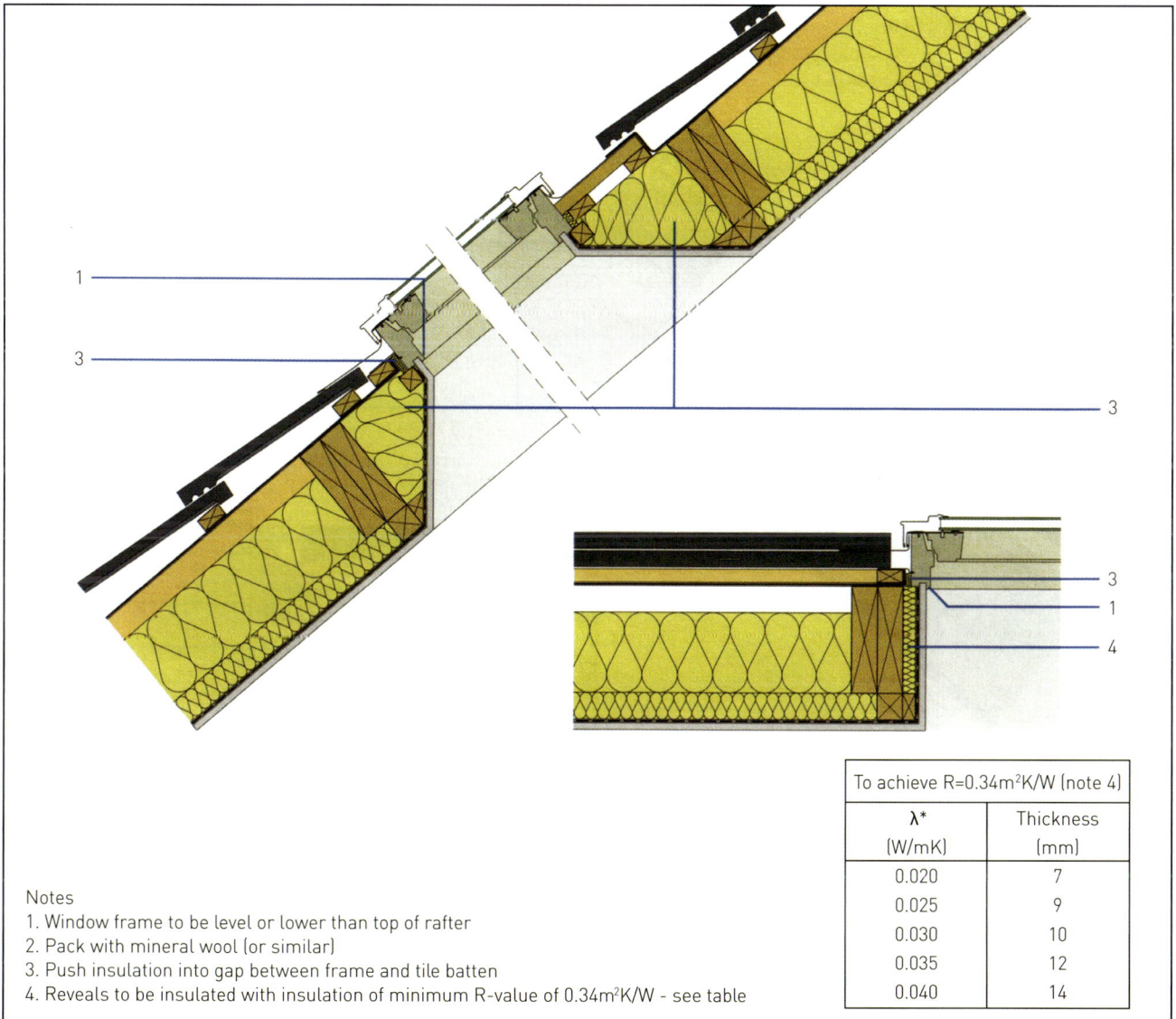

Notes
1. Window frame to be level or lower than top of rafter
2. Pack with mineral wool (or similar)
3. Push insulation into gap between frame and tile batten
4. Reveals to be insulated with insulation of minimum R-value of 0.34m²K/W - see table

To achieve R=0.34m²K/W (note 4)	
λ* (W/mK)	Thickness (mm)
0.020	7
0.025	9
0.030	10
0.035	12
0.040	14

Fig 5.13: Best practice detail to minimise air leakage around roof windows

5.17 SUN PIPES

5.17.1 On occasions the addition of a roof window to provide sunlight to a bathroom, for example, is not achievable. A solution that is available is to provide a sun pipe. This in simple terms is a hollow reflective tube that allows daylight to reach areas that would otherwise be left in darkness. These tubes are available in rigid pipe form or flexible ducting which makes them easy to install and can easily blend into the external roof finish. They are available in a number of different diameters and are a complete sealed unit; therefore they do not require cleaning to maintain the quality of borrowed light.

5.17.2 When installing the sun pipe care and attention should be taken at the intersection with the roof construction to maintain adequate weather protection.

5.17.3 Figures 5.14 to 5.16 are examples of sun pipes that are available.

Fig 5.14: Top dome of sun pipe

300mm (12") Sun Pipe System to suit Pitched Plain Tiled Roof Arrangements, Timber Construction c/w 30" Adjustable Elbow

UV protected Diamond polycarbonate top dome

Brushed Nylon Condensation trap positioned between dome and collar

ABS flashing complete with integrated collar

Code 4 lead skirt

Adjustable elbow

3-piece ceiling diffuser arrangement

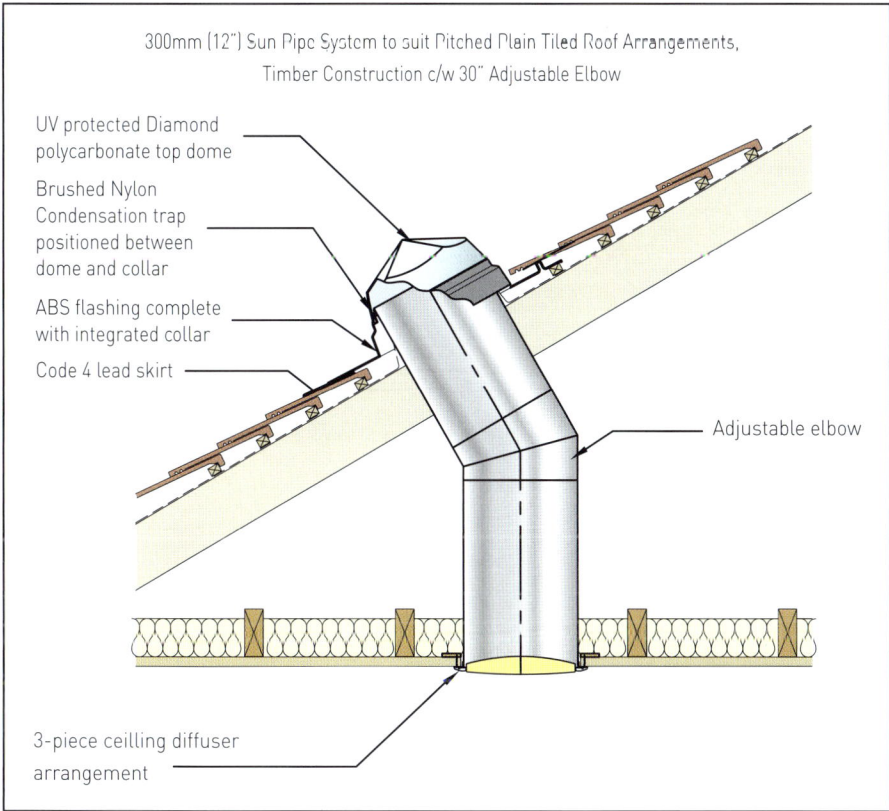

Fig 5.15: Rigid sun pipe

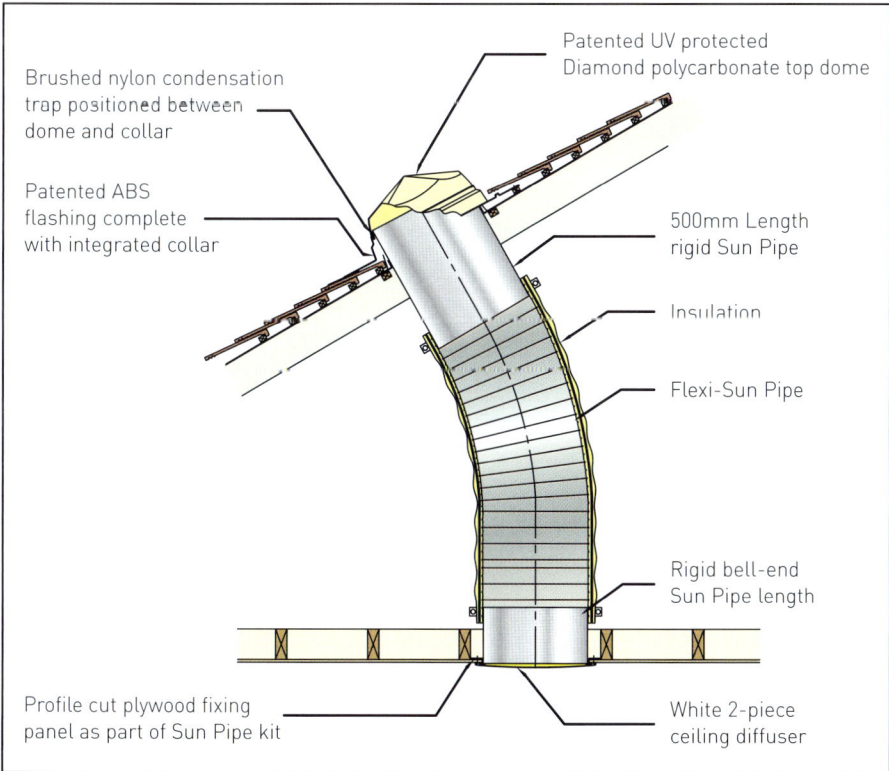

Brushed nylon condensation trap positioned between dome and collar

Patented ABS flashing complete with integrated collar

Patented UV protected Diamond polycarbonate top dome

500mm Length rigid Sun Pipe

Insulation

Flexi-Sun Pipe

Rigid bell-end Sun Pipe length

Profile cut plywood fixing panel as part of Sun Pipe kit

White 2-piece ceiling diffuser

Fig 5.16: Flexible sun pipe

6. DRAINAGE

6.0 INTRODUCTION

6.0.1 This chapter discusses above-ground drainage work only. It has been assumed that the addition or relocation of a bathroom or room containing a WC will connect directly into the existing system without the need to carry out any work below ground. If you intend to carry out work to the drainage system below ground either through upgrading existing or installing new, refer to Approved Document H of the Building Regulations.

6.1 FOUL DRAINAGE

6.1.1 If the intention is to provide a bath/shower or WC within the conversion it is best to plan its location in advance. For ease and to keep costs to a minimum it is advisable to install the wet room directly above or as close as possible to the existing bathroom, so that you can utilise the existing foul drainage system and extend accordingly.

6.1.2 The information below assumes that this is the case and provides information relating to the sanitary pipework which includes pipe lengths, diameters, gradients, etc. and common issues that are encountered.

6.1.3 All points of discharge into a system should be fitted with a trap. Table 6.1 provides trap sizes and seal depths for appliances that are most used.

Appliance	Diameter of trap (mm)	Depth of seal (mm of water or equivalent)	Appliance	Diameter of trap (mm)	Depth of seal (mm of water or equivalent)
Washbasin[1]	32	75	WC pan – outlet <80mm	75	50
Basin[2] Shower[2]	40	50	WC pan – outlet >80mm	100	50
Food waste disposal unit Urinal bowl Sink Washing machine[2] Dishwashing machine[2]	40	75	[1] The depth of seal may be reduced to 50mm only with flush grated wastes without plugs on spray tap basin. [2] Where these appliances discharge directly to a gully the depth of seal may be reduced to not less than 38mm. [3] Traps used on appliances with flat bottom (trailing waste discharge) and discharging to a gully with a grating may have a reduced water seal of not less than 38mm.		

Table 6.1: Minimum trap sizes and seal depths
Source: Approved Document H

6.1.4   Pressure fluctuations will be present in the sanitary pipework. To prevent the seals from being broken by these pressures the following guidance should be followed:

- Branch pipes should discharge into another branch pipe or discharge stack. If the pipe discharges into a stack it must do so without causing crossflow.

- Where a branch pipe serves a single appliance the pipe diameter should be at least the same as the trap diameter on the appliance. Where the pipe serves more than one appliance, the pipe diameter should be in accordance with Table 6.2.

Appliance	Max. no to be connected	Max. length of branch pipe (m)	Min. size of pipe (mm)	Gradient limits (mm fall per metre)
WC outlet >80mm	8	15	100	18[2] to 90
WC outlet <80mm	1	15	75[3]	18 to 90
Urinal – bowl		3[1]	50	
Urinal – trough		3[1]	65	18 to 90
Urinal – slab[4]		3[1]		
Washbasin or bidet	3	1.7	30	18 to 22
		1.1	30	18 to 44
		0.7	30	18 to 87
		3.0	40	18 to 44
	4	4.0	50	18 to 44

[1] Should be as short as possible to prevent deposition.
[2] May be reduced to 9mm on long drain runs where space is restricted, but only if more than one WC is connected.
[3] Not recommended where disposal of sanitary towels may take place via the WC, as there is an increased risk of blockages.
[4] Slab urinals longer than seven persons should have more than one outlet.

Table 6.2: Minimum diameters for branch pipes
Source: Approved Document H

6.1.5   If a new discharge stack is provided the minimum diameter should be in accordance with Table 6.3.

Stack size (mm)	Max. capacity (litres/sec)
50*	1.2
65*	2.1
75†	3.4
90	5.3
100	7.2

Notes:
* No WCs.
† Not more than one WC with outlet size <80mm.

Table 6.3: Minimum diameters for discharge stacks
Source: Approved Document H

6.1.6 To prevent water seals in the traps in the system from being lost, discharge stacks should be ventilated. If the pipe is open to outside air it should finish at least 900mm above an opening where they are within 3m of one another and have a wire or perforated cover fixed to the end of the pipe. This can be seen in Figure 6.1. This design may be inappropriate; in such cases the use of ventilated roof tiles should be considered.

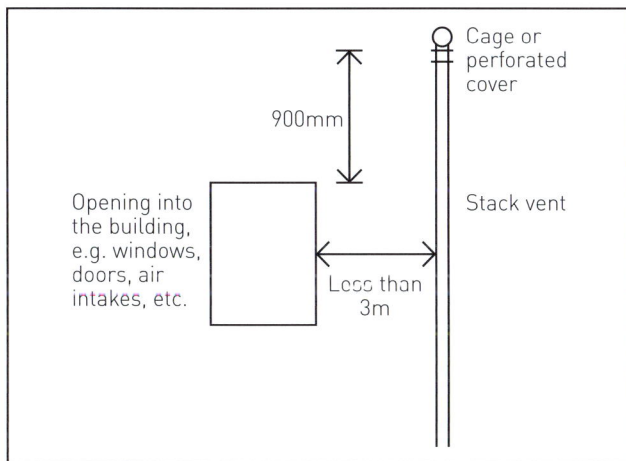

Fig 6.1: Discharge stacks and openings

6.1.7 Ventilated discharge stacks may terminate within a building when fitted with an air admittance valve. It should be noted that these should only be installed if the following recommendations are met:

- Located in areas with adequate ventilation, free from dust.

- Care taken to ensure that the air admittance valve is not positioned in a location that will give risk of freezing.

- Accessible for maintenance.

- Removable to give access for clearance of blockages.

- Air admittance valves not be used outside of buildings.

Note 1:
If you are connecting into an existing drainage run it is advisable to ascertain the type of drainage system your property is connected to. If you use a separate system, i.e. the foul drainage and surface water drainage have their own drainage pipes, you need to ensure that you connect your new drains to the correct system.

Note 2:
The property may not connect to a main sewer. In this instance it may have a waste water treatment system, septic tank or cess pool. When increasing the number of bedrooms/bathrooms in a property this also increases the required capacity of your treatment system, even though the number of users will not have increased. You should make provisions for future occupation of the home and ensure that the capacity is still adequate.

Note 3:
The Building Control Body holds the right to request an above and/or below ground drain test. Therefore the pipes, fittings and joints should be capable of withstanding an air test of positive pressure of at least 38mm water gauge for at least three minutes.

6.2 RAINWATER DRAINAGE

6.2.1 Where minimal work is carried out to the roof structure, for example the addition of dormers, the existing system under normal circumstances would be deemed satisfactory although consideration should be given to the localised effect that may cause a concentrated flow of rainwater.

6.2.2 Where the existing roof has been dramatically changed, i.e. the roof has been replaced in its entirety, the provision of rainwater drainage must be considered.

- Gutter and outlet sizes need to be calculated. The location of the property and the area to be drained will affect the flow capacity, which will dictate the sizes required.

- Gutters should be laid with any fall towards the nearest outlet.

- If the rainwater discharges into a combined system, it should do so through a trap.

6.2.3 There are alternative methods of rainwater drainage which include:

- Siphonic roof drainage systems.

- Eaves drop systems.

- Rainwater recovery systems.

For further details and information on these types of systems, see Chapter 12 and Approved Document H of the Building Regulations.

7. FIRE SAFETY

7.0 INTRODUCTION

7.0.1 This chapter covers the fire safety information relevant to three dwelling types. Areas within this chapter include: fire detection and fire alarm systems, means of escape, compartmentation, the building fabric and load-bearing elements. Building Control providers have varying views as to which of the technical solutions for Fire Safety described in this chapter they are willing to approve. It is therefore very important to check fire safety issues with the particular building control provider at the earliest opportunity for any given project.

7.1 The protection of life in the event of fire is extremely important and should not be taken lightly. The requirements needed to achieve an acceptable standard vary considerably depending on the form of construction and type of property being converted (detached bungalow, two-storey terraced house, etc.). Different forms of construction can present different problems and opportunities for the provision of structural fire protection. Further information on timber frame construction can be found in BRE 454 *Multi-storey Timber Frame Buildings: A Design Guide* and TRADA's *Timber Frame Construction*.

7.2 FIRE DETECTION AND FIRE ALARM SYSTEMS

7.2.1 Where new habitable rooms are provided above ground-floor level, a fire detection and fire alarm system should be installed as their installation can significantly increase the level of safety by automatically giving an early warning of fire.

7.2.2 It is essential that fire detection and fire alarm systems are properly designed, installed and maintained. Where a fire alarm system is installed, an installation and commissioning certificate should be provided. Third-party certification schemes for fire protection products and related services are an effective means of providing the fullest possible assurances, offering a level of quality, reliability and safety. BS 5839-1 and BS 5839-6 recommend that occupiers should receive the manufacturer's instructions concerning the operation and maintenance of the alarm system.

7.2.3 The type of fire detection and fire alarm system to be installed is dictated by the storey height and size of the dwelling. It should be designed and installed in accordance with the relevant recommendations of BS 5839-6:2004, and for the majority of dwellings this is to at least a Grade D Category LD3 standard.

7.2.4 Where a two-storey dwelling (excluding basement storeys) is large (large being any storey exceeding 200m^2) the fire detection and fire alarm system should be upgraded to a Grade B Category LD3 system as described in BS 5839-6:2004.

7.2.5 Where a three-storey dwelling (excluding basement storeys) is large (large being any storey exceeding 200m^2) the fire detection and fire alarm system should be upgraded to a Grade A Category LD2 system as described in BS 5839-6:2004, with detectors sited in accordance with the recommendations of BS 5839-1:2002 for a Category L2 system.

7.2.6 Where a four-storey dwelling (excluding basement storeys) is large (large being any storey exceeding 200m^2) the fire detection and fire alarm system should be upgraded to a Grade A Category LD2 system as described in BS 5839-6:2004, with detectors sited in accordance with the recommendations of BS 5839-1:2002 for a Category L2 system.

7.2.7 The following guidance is provided with regard to the positioning of fire detection and fire alarm systems and is appropriate to most common situations. It should be noted, however, that to avoid false alarms the type of detector used should be considered. BS EN 14604:2005 covers smoke alarms based on ionization chamber smoke detectors and optical (photoelectric) smoke detectors. Optical detectors tend to be affected less by low levels of 'invisible' particles, such as fumes from kitchens that often cause false alarms. Accordingly they are generally more suitable than ionization chamber detectors for installation in circulation spaces adjacent to kitchens.

- Smoke alarms should be positioned in the circulation spaces within 7.5m of every habitable room.

- No bedroom door should be further than approximately 3m from the nearest smoke alarm.

- There should be at least one smoke alarm on every storey of a dwelling, interlinked so that the detection of smoke or heat by one unit operates the alarm signal in them all. (The manufacturer's instructions regarding the maximum number of units that can be interlinked should be observed.)

- Where the kitchen area is not separated from the stairway or circulation space by a door, there should be a compatible interlinked heat detector or heat alarm in the kitchen, in addition to whatever smoke alarms are needed in the circulation space(s). An open plan arrangement on the ground floor to conversions is only acceptable if constructed as per paragraph 7.3.9.

- If units are designed for wall mounting, they should be above the level of doorways opening into the space and fixed in accordance with manufacturers' instructions.

- If ceiling-mounted, they should be at least 300mm from walls and light fittings (unless, in the case of light fittings, there is test evidence to prove that the proximity of the light fitting will not adversely affect the efficiency of the detector).

- The sensor in ceiling-mounted devices must be between 25mm and 600mm below the ceiling (25mm and 150mm in the case of heat detectors or heat alarms).

Note 1:
This guidance applies to ceilings that are predominantly flat and horizontal.

Note 2:
It should be possible to reach the smoke alarms to carry out routine maintenance, such as testing and cleaning, easily and safely. For this reason smoke alarms should not be fixed over a stair or any other opening between floors.

Note 3:
Smoke alarms should not be fixed next to or directly above heaters or air conditioning outlets.

Note 4:
Smoke alarms should not be fixed in bathrooms, showers, cooking areas or garages, or any other place where steam, condensation or fumes could give false alarms.

Note 5:
Smoke alarms should not be fitted in places that get very hot (boiler rooms) or very cold (unheated porches).

Note 6:
They should not be fixed to surfaces that are normally warmer or colder than the rest of the space, because the temperature difference might create air currents that move smoke away from the unit.

7.2.8 The smoke and heat alarms should be mains operated and conform to BS EN 14604:2005 or BS 5446-2:2003. They should have a standby power supply, such as a battery (either rechargeable or non-rechargeable) or capacitor.

7.2.9 The power supply for a smoke alarm system should be derived from the dwelling's mains electricity supply. The mains supply to the smoke alarm(s) should comprise a single independent circuit at the dwelling's main distribution board (consumer unit) or a single regularly used lighting circuit. The latter has the advantage that the circuit is unlikely to be disconnected for any prolonged period. There should be a means of isolating power to the smoke alarms without isolating the lighting. The electrical installation should comply with Approved Document P and is covered in Chapter 11.

7.2.10 Any cable suitable for domestic wiring may be used for the power supply and interconnection to smoke alarm systems. It does not need any particular fire survival properties except in large houses (BS 5839-6:2004 specifies fire-resisting cables for Grade A and B systems). Any conductors used for interconnecting alarms (signalling) should be readily distinguishable from those supplying mains power (e.g. by colour coding).

Note:

Mains-powered smoke alarms may be interconnected using radio links, provided that this does not reduce the lifetime or duration of any standby power supply below 72 hours. In such a case, the smoke alarms may be connected to separate power circuits. Please see BS 5839-1:2002 and BS 5839-6:2004 for other effective options.

7.3 MEANS OF ESCAPE IN CASE OF FIRE

7.3.1 The allowable means of escape in case of fire from a converted dwelling vary depending on the dwelling's number of storeys.

Figures 7.1 - 7.3 outline how means of escape in case of fire can be achieved for the three dwelling types.

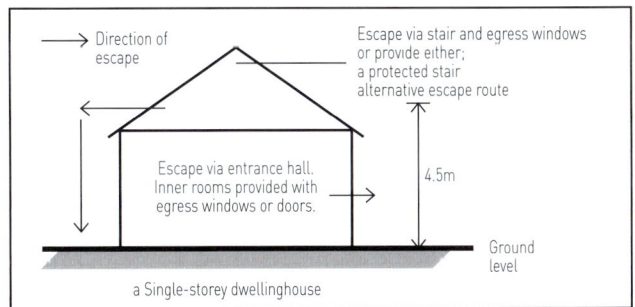

Fig 7.1 Single storey dwelling with loft conversion

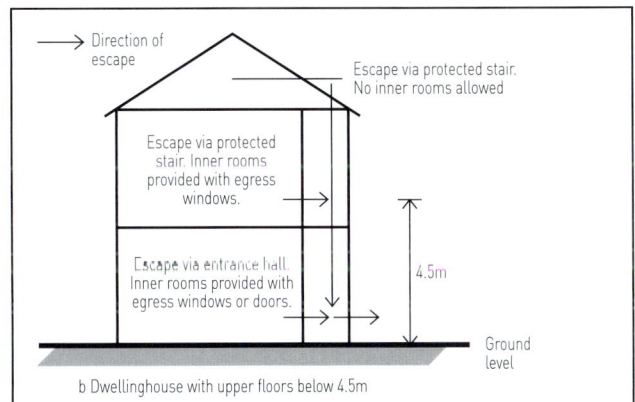

Fig 7.2 Two storey dwelling with loft conversion

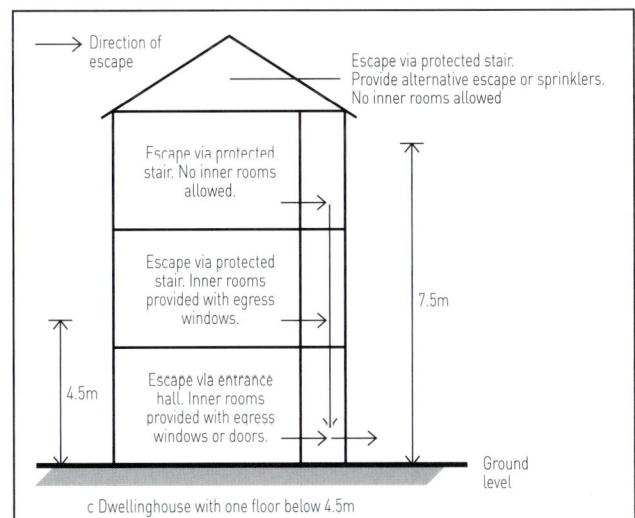

Fig 7.3 Three storey dwelling with loft conversion

7.3.2 The layout of the dwelling once converted should be considered in the event that inner rooms are created or may already exist with open plan arrangements at ground-floor level. Inner rooms are only allowed at ground- and first-floor level. For clarity, an inner room is a room the only escape route from which is through another room, and this is only acceptable where the inner room is:

- A kitchen.

- A laundry or utility room.

- A dressing room.

- A bathroom, WC or shower room.

- Any other room on a floor, not more than 4.5m above ground level, provided with an emergency egress window which complies with Option 1 below.

Option 1 – Emergency egress windows and external doors (single-storey dwelling with loft conversion only)

7.3.3 When the converted dwelling is served by only one stair, all habitable rooms in the upper storey should have an emergency egress window or external door. It is acceptable to have a single window serve two rooms as long as a communicating door is provided between these rooms and they both have separate access to the stairs.

7.3.4 The emergency egress windows or external door should comply with the following:

- The window should have an unobstructed openable area of at least 0.33m² **and** at least 450mm high and 450mm wide.

- The bottom of the openable area for standard windows should not be more than 1100mm above the floor; where it is less than 800mm, please refer to Chapter 5.

- The bottom of the openable area for roof windows may be 600mm above the floor.

- The window or door should enable the person escaping to reach a place free from danger from fire. This is a matter of judgement in each case, but in general a courtyard or back garden from which there is no exit other than through other buildings would have to be at least as deep as the dwelling is high. This is shown in Figure 7.4.

Note 1:
Locks (with or without removable keys) and stays may be fitted to egress windows, subject to the stay being fitted with a release catch, which may be child-resistant.

Note 2:
Windows should be designed in such a way that they will remain in the open position without needing to be held by a person making their escape.

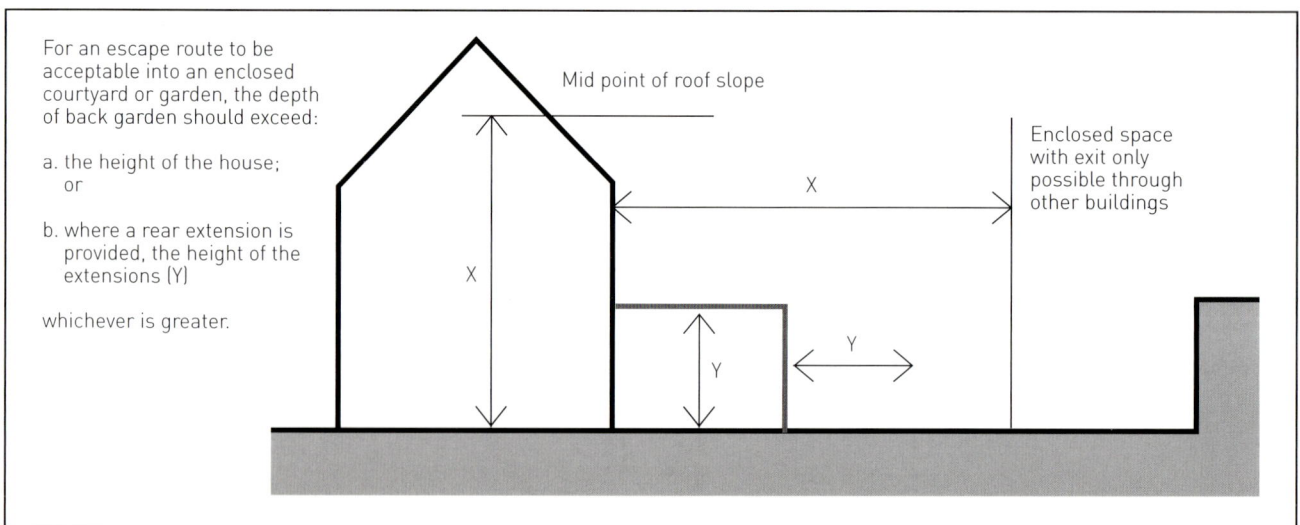

For an escape route to be acceptable into an enclosed courtyard or garden, the depth of back garden should exceed:

a. the height of the house; or

b. where a rear extension is provided, the height of the extensions (Y)

whichever is greater.

Mid point of roof slope

Enclosed space with exit only possible through other buildings

Fig 7.4: Exit into an enclosed space

Option 2 – Protected stair (all dwelling types)

7.3.5 When the converted dwelling is served by only one stair, and no egress windows or external doors are provided for emergency use, the upper storey should be served by a protected stair (at all levels) and should either:

a. Extend to a final exit; or

b. Give access to at least two escape routes at ground level, each delivering to final exits and separated from one another by fire-resisting construction and fire doors.

7.3.6 To achieve a protected stair in a loft conversion, the stair requires to be enclosed with fire-resisting partitions and fire doors as shown in Figure 7.5.

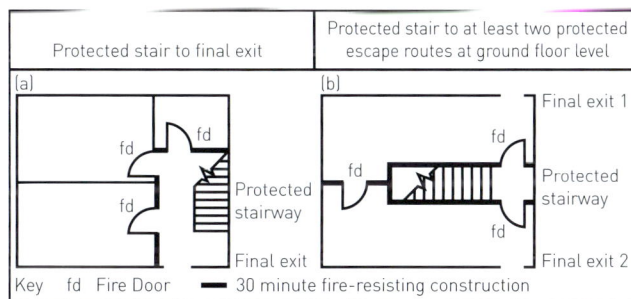

Fig 7.5: Protected stairs

7.3.9 Where an open plan arrangement exists, new partitions will be required to enclose the escape route, or a fast response sprinkler system may be installed in the open plan area in conjunction with a fire-resisting partition and fire door in order to separate the ground floor from the upper storeys. This door should allow the occupants of the loft room(s) to access an emergency egress window at first-floor level in the event of a fire in the open plan area.

7.3.10 The guidance in the following paragraphs has been provided regarding fire-resisting partitions.

7.3.11 Fire-resisting partitions must be capable of achieving 30 minutes' fire resistance. Below are two options on how this can be achieved:

- Timber stud partitions – 12.5mm plasterboard and skim on 75mm timber studs (to each side).

- Metal frame partitions – 12.5mm plasterboard and skim on 45mm metal studs (to each side).

7.3.12 Any glazing incorporated in the enclosure of a protected stair or within fire-resisting separation should achieve 30 minutes' fire resistance in terms of integrity and insulation and should be marked with the manufacturer and product name. If the glazing achieves 30 minutes' fire resistance in terms of integrity, only then should its use be limited to that shown in Table 7.1.

7.3.13 Further guidance can be found in *A guide to best practice in the specification and use of fire resistant glazed systems*, published by the Glass and Glazing Federation and available at: **www.ggf.co.uk**.

Position of glazed element	Maximum total glazed area	
	Walls	**Door leaf**
1. Within the enclosures of a protected stairway, or within fire-resisting separation	Unlimited above 1100mm from floor or pitch of the stair	Unlimited
2. Within fire-resisting separation	Unlimited above 100mm from floor	Unlimited above 100mm from floor
3. Existing window between an attached/ integral garage and the dwellinghouse	Unlimited	Not applicable
4. Adjacent to an external escape stair	Unlimited	Unlimited

Notes:
1. The 100mm limit is intended to reduce the risk of fire spread from a floor covering.

Table 7.1: Limitations on use of uninsulated glazed elements on escape routes
Source: Approved Document B Vol 1

7.3.14 The following guidance has been provided regarding fire doors.

7.3.15 All doors (including those to cupboards) leading onto the protected stair are required to be fire doors designed to achieve a minimum 20 minutes' fire resistance. Where a door serving an attached or integral garage opens onto the protected stair it should achieve a minimum 30 minutes' fire resistance, be fitted with a positive self-closing device and incorporate smoke seals. It is generally accepted that a bathroom poses a low fire risk and therefore the door need not be a fire door unless access can be gained directly into a bedroom from the bathroom.

7.3.16 A fire door's resistance to fire is rated by its performance under test to either:

- BS 476-22:1987, in terms of integrity for a period of minutes, e.g. FD30. A suffix (s) is added for doors where restricted smoke leakage at ambient temperatures is needed; or

- BS EN 1634, in terms of integrity for a period of minutes, e.g. E30. A suffix (s_a) is added for doors where restricted smoke leakage at ambient temperatures is needed.

Note:
From this point forward, for ease of reference, fire doors will be referred to as FD.

7.3.17 Over 75% of fire doors manufactured for use in the UK are certified under the BWF-CERTIFIRE Fire Door and Doorset Scheme, which covers fire door ratings of FD30, FD60, FD90 and FD120 tested to BS 476-22 or BS EN 1634. The scheme does not certify and supply FD20 doors as for them to work effectively they have to be installed with intumescent seals. The result is that the performance of this door specification (FD20) becomes the same as an FD30.

7.3.18 There are three ways to purchase a fire door. They are split into types and are defined below:

1. Fire doorset – a fire door leaf supplied pre-hung, in its compatible fire door frame, hinges, glazing, intumescent fire (and smoke) seals and latch, supplied complete.

2. Fire door kits – all the required compatible components supplied in kit form, factory prepared for on-site assembly.

3. Fire door assembly – all the correct, compatible and certified elements of a fire doorset, but collated together from different sources. BWF-CERTIFIRE scheme manufacturers identify suitable components in their installation instructions.

7.3.19 A test certificate will be provided for all door make-ups and should be adhered to at installation, i.e. door/frame/hinges/seals/hardware. When replacing existing doors, the frame should also be upgraded.

7.3.20 As this will be a labour-intensive task, at least one manufacturer has produced and received certification for a fire door that negates the need for the frame and surround to be replaced. Thus it is ideal for the loft conversion market.

Note 1:
Fire doors are labelled with identification marks so that it is possible to inspect them to determine their fire rating and to ensure that they have been certified. Two types of identification marks are provided in Figures 7.6 and 7.7.

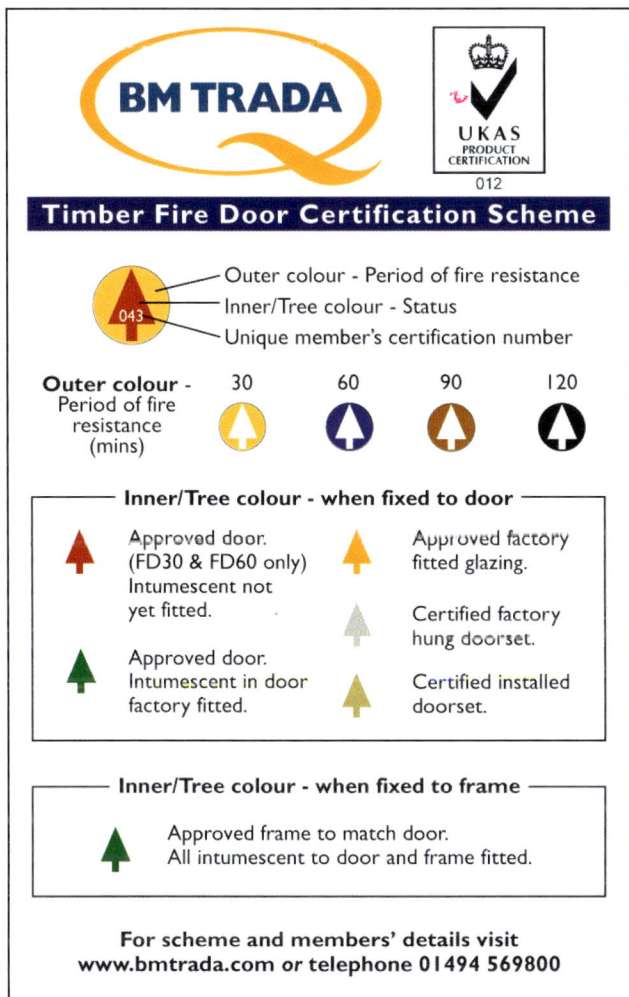

Fig 7.6: Timber Fire Door Certification Scheme label

Note 2:
Where a loft conversion is being carried out in a dwelling that has doors of historical or architectural merit, it may be possible to retain the doors or upgrade them to an acceptable standard. Upgrading is achieved through the use of intumescent paper and paint; however, each door in the conversion would have to be inspected and approved on its individual merits. Factors affecting this include:

- How the door fits in the frame.

- The actual door make-up – quality of the joints/glue and wood itself.

- Type of hinges and door hardware present.

Because of this it is advisable to replace existing doors with actual fire doors rather than attempt an upgrade.

Option 3 – Alternative escape route (single-storey and two-storey dwellings with loft conversion):

7.3.21 When the converted dwelling is served by only one stair, the top storey should be separated from the lower storeys by fire-resisting construction and be provided with an alternative escape route leading to its own final exit.

An alternative escape is defined as a route sufficiently separated by either direction and space, or by fire-resisting construction, to ensure that one is still available should the other be affected by fire.

Note:
A second stair, balcony or flat roof which enables a person to reach a place free from danger from fire is considered an alternative escape route for the purposes of a dwellinghouse.

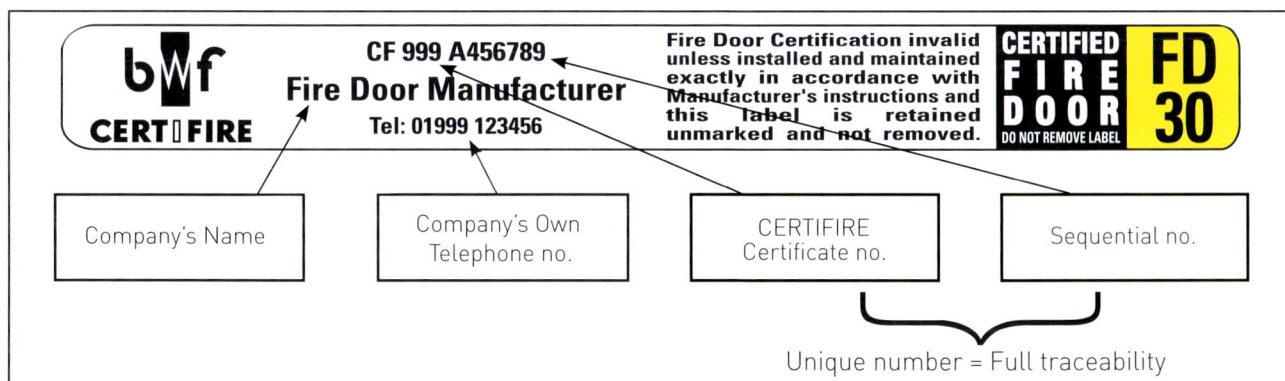

Fig 7.7: BWF-CERTIFIRE label

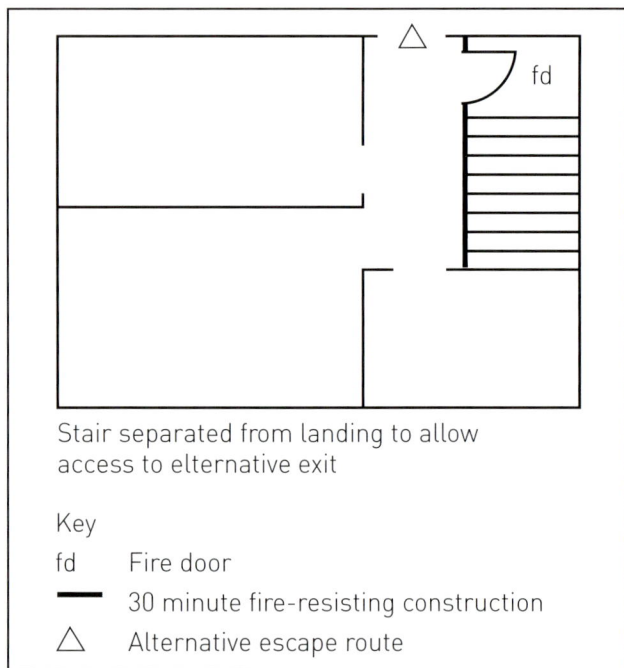

Stair separated from landing to allow access to elternative exit

Key

fd	Fire door
▬	30 minute fire-resisting construction
△	Alternative escape route

Fig 7.8: Example of an alternative exit

7.3.22   When an external escape stair is provided from the alternative escape (Figures 7.8 and 7.9), the provisions outlined in Option 2 should be met where a fire door and fire-resisting construction is required as well as the following:

- Any part of the external envelope of the building within 1800mm of the flight and landing of an external escape stair should be of fire-resisting construction. The 1800mm can be reduced to 1100mm above the top level of the stair.

- There is protection by fire-resisting construction for any part of the building (including any doors) within 1800mm of the escape route from the stair to a place of safety, unless there is a choice of routes from the foot of the stair that would enable the people escaping to avoid exposure to the effects of the fire in the adjoining building.

- Glazing in areas of fire-resisting construction mentioned above should achieve 30 minutes' fire resistance in terms of integrity, and fixed shut.

- All doors giving access to the stair should be fire-resisting except for the door at the head of the stair.

- Any stair more than 6m in vertical extent should be protected from the effects of adverse weather conditions.

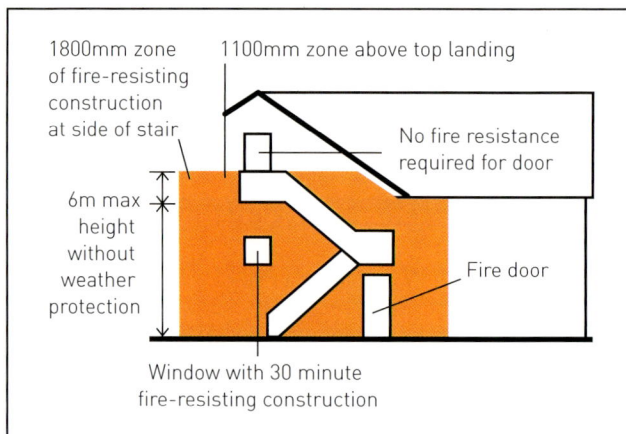

Fig 7.9: Fire resistance of areas adjacent to external stairs

Option 4 – Extended fire alarm and detection system (all dwelling types)

7.3.23   Within *Approved Document B: Fire Safety Volume 1 – Dwellinghouses*, clause 2.2 states: 'In providing any kind of fire protection in dwellings it should be recognised that measures which significantly interfere with the day-to-day convenience of the occupants may be less reliable in the long term'.

7.3.24   With this in mind, it may be possible to provide a more comprehensive fire alarm and detection system rather than providing a protected stair as defined in Option 2 or an alternative escape route as defined in Option 3 above. If the proposal is to use this option, it is advisable to consult the Building Control Body to discuss the proposals at the design stage.

7.3.25   For this to be satisfactory it is essential that the design of the system, particularly in respect of factors such as the number and siting of detectors and the form of power supply, takes into account the following probabilities:

a. The probability of fire occurring.

b. The probability of injury or death of occupants if fire occurs.

c. The probability of the system operating correctly at the time of a fire.

d. The probability of early detection and warning of occupants in the event of fire.

7.3.26 As the system is the only means of protection from fire, it is advisable to have the circuits monitored to provide greater reliability to perform correctly in the event of a fire. This can be achieved through the installation of Grade A or B systems of a type described in BS 5839-6, BS 5839-1 where appropriate. These systems comprise dedicated fire alarm control and indicating equipment, fire detectors and fire alarm sounders. Where wiring is used to connect the fire detectors and fire alarm sounders to the control and indicating equipment, the wiring is monitored so that a fault indication is given at the control and indicating equipment in the event of a fault in the wiring.

7.3.27 The power supply to each Grade of system varies, and the following recommendations have been provided for guidance.

7.3.28 Grade A system:

- Power supplies should comply with the recommendations of Clause 25 of BS 5839-1.

- The circuit serving the fire detection and fire alarm system should be such that it is not isolated within the dwelling, except in the event of deliberate isolation of the supply or in the event of fault conditions. It is not, for example, acceptable for the mains supply to be connected via a card-operated meter or similar.

- The standby supply should be capable of automatically maintaining the system in normal operation (while giving an audible and visual indication of mains failure) for a period of 72 hours, after which sufficient capacity should remain to supply the maximum alarm load for at least 15 minutes.

7.3.29 Grade B system:

- The normal supply should be derived from the public electricity supply, transformed or modified as necessary. The mains power should be supplied from an independent circuit at the dwelling's main distribution board. No other electrical equipment should be connected to this circuit.

- The mains supply to the fire detection and alarm system should be supplied, via an isolating protective device (such as a circuit breaker), from the load ('dead') side of the main isolating device for the dwelling. The isolating protective device should be labelled 'FIRE ALARM DO NOT ISOLATE'.

- The circuit serving the fire detection and fire alarm system should be such that it is not isolated within the dwelling, except in the event of deliberate isolation of the supply or in the event of fault conditions. It is not, for example, acceptable for the mains supply to be connected via a card-operated meter or similar.

- The circuit serving the fire detection and fire alarm system should preferably not be protected by any residual current device (RCD). If RCD protection is required for reasons of electrical safety (e.g. in an installation forming part of a TT system), either of the following conditions should be satisfied:
  - The RCD should serve only the circuit supplying the fire detection and fire alarm system.
  - The RCD protection of the fire detection and fire alarm system circuit should operate independently of any RCD protection for circuits supplying socket outlets or portable equipment.

- The mains supply should be backed up by a standby supply, comprising a secondary battery with an automatic charger, that is capable of automatically maintaining the system in normal operation (while giving an audible and visual indication of mains failure) for a period of 72 hours, after which sufficient capacity should remain to support the maximum alarm load for 15 minutes.

- The normal and standby supplies should each be capable of supplying the maximum alarm load irrespective of the condition of the other supply.

- Batteries used should be of a type that has an expected life of at least four years under the conditions of use likely to be experienced in the system. Automotive lead–acid batteries (i.e. the type normally used for starting service in cars) are not suitable for fire alarm service and should not be used.

- The battery charger for the standby supply should be compatible with the batteries used, and should be capable of recharging a battery from its final voltage to a capacity sufficient to comply with the recommendations within a charging period of 24 hours.

7.3.30 The category of system installed is related to the fire risk of occupants. The greatest benefit to life safety is given by a full coverage system (Category LD1 – installed throughout the dwelling, incorporating detectors in all circulation spaces, rooms and areas in which a fire may start, other than toilets, bathrooms and shower rooms) as such a system will give the earliest practicable warning of fire to occupants, wherever ignition occurs. However, a good level of protection can normally be obtained from a Category LD2 system, in which detection is only provided at points where the fire risk is high. A Category LD2 system should have detectors in circulation areas of the dwelling and all rooms in which detection is deemed necessary.

7.3.31 Detectors within rooms should be sited in such a way that no point is further than 7.5m from the nearest smoke detector or, in rooms protected by heat detectors, no further than 5.3m.

Important information for a three-storey dwelling with loft conversion

7.3.32 In addition to meeting Option 2 or Option 4 above, the four-storey dwelling once converted should either:

a. Have an alternative escape route from the storey situated 7.5m or more above ground level, separated from the lower storeys by fire-resisting construction; or

b. Be fitted throughout with a sprinkler system designed and installed in accordance with BS 9251:2005.

Further information on alternative escape routes can be found in Option 3 above.

7.4 COMPARTMENTATION

7.4.1 The separating/party wall in semi-detached and terraced dwellings should be constructed as a compartment wall and as such should:

- Form a complete barrier to fire between the compartments it separates.

- Achieve a minimum 60-minute fire resistance.

- Run in a continuous vertical plane.

- Be taken up to meet the underside of the roof covering or deck, with fire stopping at the wall/roof junction to maintain the continuity of fire resistance. This is shown in Figure 7.10.

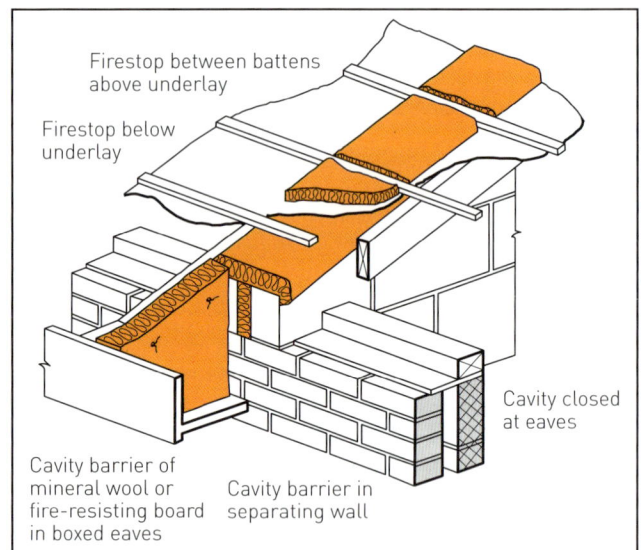

Firestop between battens above underlay

Firestop below underlay

Cavity closed at eaves

Cavity barrier of mineral wool or fire-resisting board in boxed eaves

Cavity barrier in separating wall

Fig 7.10: Separating wall as a compartment wall

Note:
Further information for owners of homes where separating walls currently do not exist in the loft space is provided in Chapter 9.

7.5 BUILDING FABRIC (UNPROTECTED AREAS)

7.5.1 The building fabric can be split into two key areas: the external walls and the roof. These will be dealt with separately as different measures will apply.

External walls

7.5.2 The definition of an external wall includes a roof with habitable space pitched at an angle of more than 70° to the horizontal. Similarly, vertical parts of a pitched roof such as dormer windows, where taken in isolation might be regarded as a wall. It is a matter of judgement, whether a continuous run of dormer windows occupying most of a steeply pitched roof should be treated as a wall rather than a roof.

7.5.3 The external walls of dwellings should achieve a minimum 30 minutes' fire resistance to prevent fire spread across the relevant boundary unless they form an unprotected area such as openings and areas with a combustible surface.

7.5.4 When calculating the allowable proportion of unprotected areas in relation to separation distance, it is possible to use the distance to a boundary, rather than a building.

Note 1:
A relevant boundary is a boundary which a wall faces, whether it is the actual boundary of the site or a notional boundary.

Note 2:
A notional boundary is an assumed boundary between two buildings.

Figures 7.11 and 7.12 set out the rules that apply in respect to this.

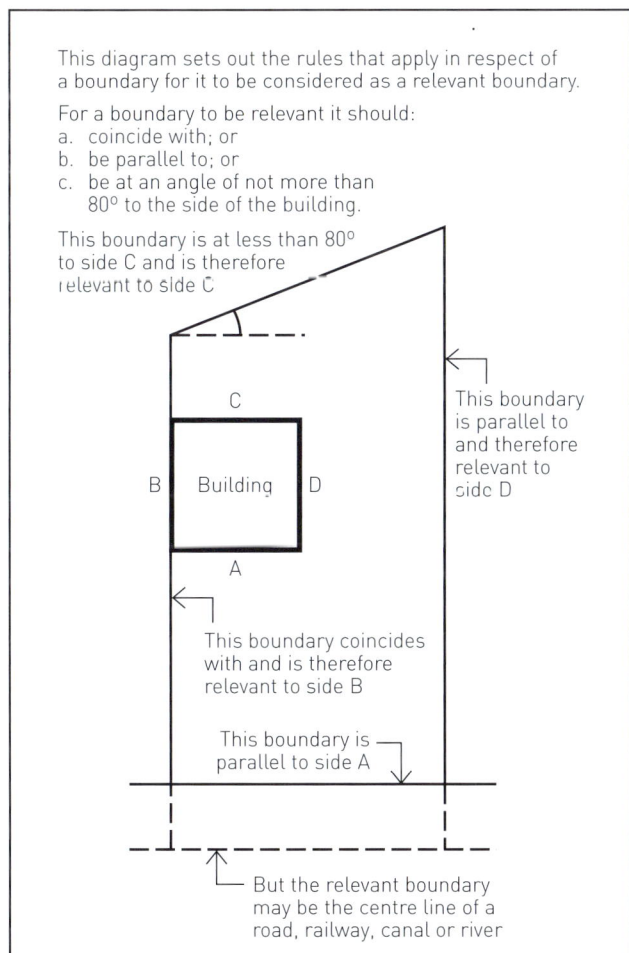

This diagram sets out the rules that apply in respect of a boundary for it to be considered as a relevant boundary.

For a boundary to be relevant it should:
a. coincide with; or
b. be parallel to; or
c. be at an angle of not more than 80° to the side of the building.

This boundary is at less than 80° to side C and is therefore relevant to side C

C

B   Building   D

A

This boundary is parallel to and therefore relevant to side D

This boundary coincides with and is therefore relevant to side B

This boundary is parallel to side A

But the relevant boundary may be the centre line of a road, railway, canal or river

Fig 7.11: Relevant boundary

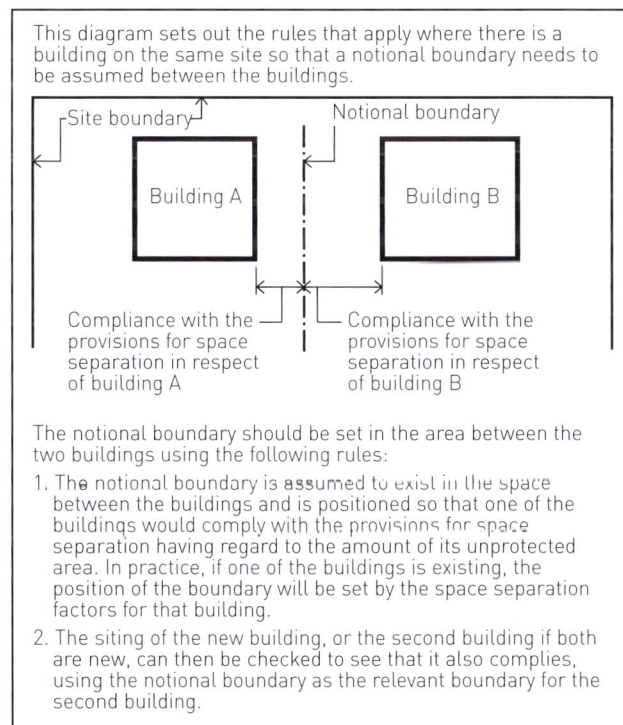

This diagram sets out the rules that apply where there is a building on the same site so that a notional boundary needs to be assumed between the buildings.

Site boundary   Notional boundary

Building A   Building B

Compliance with the provisions for space separation in respect of building A

Compliance with the provisions for space separation in respect of building B

The notional boundary should be set in the area between the two buildings using the following rules:
1. The notional boundary is assumed to exist in the space between the buildings and is positioned so that one of the buildings would comply with the provisions for space separation having regard to the amount of its unprotected area. In practice, if one of the buildings is existing, the position of the boundary will be set by the space separation factors for that building.
2. The siting of the new building, or the second building if both are new, can then be checked to see that it also complies, using the notional boundary as the relevant boundary for the second building.

Fig 7.12: Notional boundary

7.5.5 Where the external walls of the dwelling are less than 1m from the relevant boundary provisions are made to restrict their combustibility by ensuring the external surfaces meet Class 0 (National Class) or Class B-s3,d2 or better (European Class). It should be noted, however, that it is allowable to have unprotected areas in the external wall of no more than $1m^2$ each as long as they are a minimum 4m apart.

7.5.6 If an external wall has the appropriate fire resistance, but has a combustible material more than 1mm thick as its external surface, then that wall is counted as an unprotected area amounting to half the actual area of the combustible material. If the material has a Class 0 (National Class) or Class B-s3, d2 (European Class) rating it need not be counted as unprotected area.

7.5.7 Figure 7.13 has been provided for clarity and Table 7.1 gives examples of a selection of materials and products that meet these classifications.

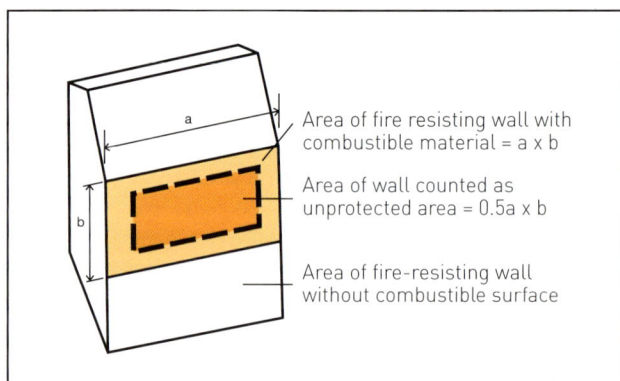

Fig 7.13: Combustible surface material as unprotected area

Rating	Material or product
Class 0 (National)	1. Any non-combustible material or material of limited combustibility. 2. Brickwork, blockwork, concrete and ceramic tiles. 3. Plasterboard (painted or not with a PVC facing not more than 0.5mm thick) with or without an air gap or fibrous or cellular insulating material behind. 4. Woodwool cement slabs. 5. Mineral fibre tiles or sheets with cement resin binding.
Class 3 (National)	6. Timber or plywood with density more than 400kg/m^3. 7. Wood particle board or hardboard, either untreated or painted. 8. Standard glass reinforced polysters.
Class A1 (European)	9. Any material that achieves this class or is defined as 'classified without further test' in a published Commission Decision.
Class A2-s3, d2 (European)	10. Any material that achieves this class or is defined as 'classified without further test' in a published Commission Decision.
Class B-s3, d2 (European)	11. Any material that achieves this class or is defined as 'classified without further test' in a published Commission Decision.
Class C-s3, d2 (European)	12. Any material that achieves this class or is defined as 'classified without further test' in a published Commission Decision.
Class D-s3, d2 (European)	13. Any material that achieves this class or is defined as 'classified without further test' in a published Commission Decision.

Notes (National):

1. Materials and products listed under Class 0 meet Class 1.
2. Timber products listed under Class 3 can be brought up to Class 1 with appropriate proprietary treatments.
3. The following materials and products may achieve the ratings listed below. However, as the properties of different products with the same generic decription vary, the ratings of these materials/products should be substantiated by test evidence.

   Class 0 – aluminium faced fibre insulating board, flame-retardant decorative laminates on a calcium silicate board, thick polycarbonate sheet, phenolic sheet and UPVC.

   Class 1 – phenolic or melamine laminates on a calcium silicate substrate and flame-retardant decorative laminates on a combustible substrate.

Notes (European):

For the purposes of Building Regulations
1. Materials and products listed under Class A1 also meet Classes A2-s3, d2, B-s3, d2, C-s3, d2 and D-s3, d2.
2. Materials and products listed under Class A2-s3, d2 also meet Classes B-s3, d2, C-s3, d2 and D-s3, d2.
3. Materials and products listed under Class B-s3, d2 also meet Classes C-s3, d2 and D-s3, d2.
4. Materials and products listed under Class C-s3, d2 also meet Classes D-s3, d2.
5. The performance of timber products listed under Class D-s3, d2 can be improved with appropriate treatments.
6. Materials covered by the CWFT process (classification without further testing) can be found by accessing the European Commission's website.
7. The national classifications do not automatically equate with the equivalent classifications in the European column, therefore products cannot typically assume a European class unless they have been tested.
8. When a classification includes 's3, d2', this means that there is no limit set for smoke production and/or flaming droplets/particles.

Table 7.2: Typical performance rating of some generic materials and products
Source: Approved Document B Vol 1

7.5.8 There are two methods available to calculate the acceptable amount of unprotected area in an external wall at least 1m from any point on the relevant boundary. The method used will depend on the property being converted. Alternatively, if a building is fitted throughout with a sprinkler system, it is reasonable to assume that the intensity and extent of a fire will be reduced. The sprinkler system should meet the recommendations of BS 9251 *Sprinkler systems for residential and domestic occupancies. Code of practice.* In these circumstances the boundary distance may be reduced by half, subject to there being a minimum distance of 1m from the boundary, or if the boundary distance is maintained the amount of unprotected area may be doubled.

7.5.9   Method 1 applies only to a dwelling that is 1m or more from any point on the relevant boundary and meets the following rules:

a. The dwelling should not exceed three storeys in height (basements are not counted) or be more than 24m in length; and

b. Each side of the dwelling will meet the provisions for space separation:

i. The distance of the side of the dwelling from the relevant boundary, and

ii. The extent of the unprotected area

are within the limits given in Figure 7.14; and

c. Any parts of the side of the dwelling in excess of the maximum unprotected area should be fire-resisting.

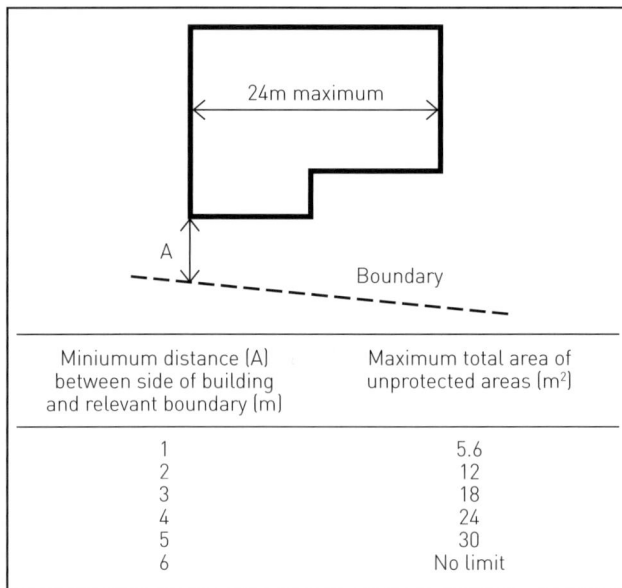

Miniumum distance (A) between side of building and relevant boundary (m)	Maximum total area of unprotected areas (m²)
1	5.6
2	12
3	18
4	24
5	30
6	No limit

Fig 7.14: Permitted unprotected areas for method 1

7.5.10   Method 2 applies to a dwelling that is more than 1m from any point on the relevant boundary and meets the following rules:

a. The dwelling or compartment should not exceed 10m in height.

b. Each side of the dwelling will meet the provisions for space separation – either:

i. The distance of the side of the dwelling from the relevant boundary, or

ii. The extent of unprotected area

are within the appropriate limits given in Table 7.3; and

c. Any parts of the side of the dwelling in excess of the maximum unprotected area should be fire-resisting.

Minimum distance between side of building and relevant boundary (m)	Maximum total percentage of unprotected area %
1	8
2.5	20
5	40
7.5	60
10	80
12.5	100

Notes:
a. Intermediate values may be obtained by interpolation.
b. For buildings which are fitted throughout with an automatic sprinkler system.
c. The total percentage of unprotected area is found by dividing the total unprotected area by the area of rectangle that encloses all the unprotected areas and multiplying the result by 100.

Table 7.3: Permitted unprotected areas for method 2
Source: Approved Document B Vol 1

Roof

7.5.11 The roof should achieve a minimum performance standard when exposed to external fire. This is determined by reference to either BS 476-3:2004 *External fire exposure roof tests*, which is a National test, or to the latest Commission Decision, which is a European test.

7.5.12 Types of roof construction are classified within the National system by two letters in the range A–D, with an AA designation being the best. The first letter indicates the time to penetration and the second letter a measure of the spread of flame. The notional performance of some common roof coverings is given in Table 7.4.

Pitched roofs covered with slates or tiles		
Covering material	**Supporting structure**	**Designation**
1. Natural slates 2. Fibre-reinforced cement slates 3. Clay tiles 4. Concrete tiles	Timber rafters with or without underfelt, sarking, boarding, woodwool slabs, compressed straw slabs, plywood, wood chipboard or fibre insulating board.	AA (National class) or B$_{ROOF}$(t4) (European class)
Flat roofs covered with bitumen felt		
A flat roof comprising bitumen felt should (irrespective of the felt specification) be deemed to be of designation AA (National class) or B$_{ROOF}$(t4) (European class) if the felt is laid on a deck constructed of 6mm plywood, 12.5mm wood chipboard, 16mm (finished) plain-edged timber boarding, compressed straw slab, screeded wood wool slab, profiled fibre reinforced cement or steel deck (single or double skin) with or without fibre insulating board overlay, profiled aluminium deck (single or double skin) with or without fibre insulating board overlay, or concrete or clay pot slab (insitu or precast), and has a surface finish of: a. bitumen-bedded stone chippings covering the whole surface to a depth of at least 12.5mm; b. bitumen-bedded tiles of a non-combustible material; c. sand and cement screed; or d. macadam.		
Pitched or flat roofs covered with fully supported material		
Covering material	**Supporting structure**	**Designation**
1. Aluminium sheet 2. Copper sheet 3. Zinc sheet 4. Lead sheet 5. Mastic asphalt 6. Vitreous enamelled steel	timber joists and: tongued and grooved boarding, or plain edged boarding	AA* (National class) or B$_{ROOF}$(t4) (European class)
7. Lead/tin alloy coated steel sheet 8. Zinc/aluminium alloy coated steel sheet 9. Pre-painted (coil coated) steel sheet including liquid-applied pvc coatings	steel or timber joists with deck of: woodwool slabs, compressed straw slab, wood chipboard, fibre insulating board, or 9.5mm plywood	AA* (National class) or B$_{ROOF}$(t4) (European class)

Notes:
*Lead sheet supported by timber joists and plain-edged boarding should be regarded as having a BA designation and is deemed to be designated class C$_{ROOF}$(t4) (European class).

The National classifications do not automatically equate with the equivalent classifications in the European column, therefore products cannot typically assume a European class unless they have been tested accordingly.

Table 7.4: Notional designation of roof coverings
Source: Approved Document B Vol 1

7.6 LOAD-BEARING ELEMENTS

7.6.1 Single- and two-storey dwellings with a loft conversion will require the floor(s), both new and old, to have 30-minute fire resistance. However, if the following conditions are met the existing first-floor construction may be accepted if it has at least a modified 30-minute fire resistance where:

a. only one storey is being added

b. the new storey contains no more than two habitable rooms

c. the floor separates rooms only (not circulation space), and

d. the total area of the new storey does not amount to more than 50m^2.

Note:

The modified 30-minute standard satisfies the test criteria for the full 30 minutes in respect to load-bearing capacity, but allows reduced performances for integrity and insulation.

Four-storey dwellings, once converted, require elements of structure to achieve 60-minute fire resistance.

7.6.2 Timber floors can be upgraded in two ways. Examples have been provided below:

Option 1 – Upgrading from above

7.6.3 This is generally achieved by infilling between the joists with mineral wool, boarding or plaster. Where chicken wire is combined with plaster it is advisable to incorporate a DPM to prevent staining to the existing ceiling.

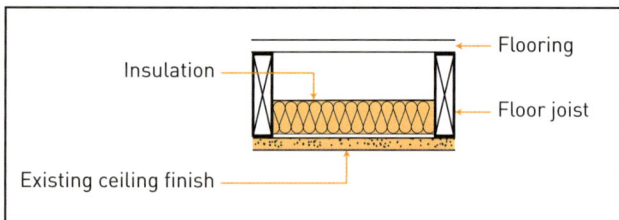

Fig 7.15: Upgrading with insulation infill

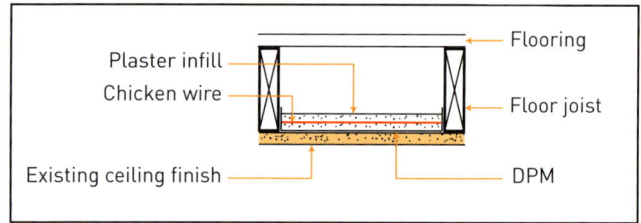

Fig 7.16: Upgrading with plaster infill

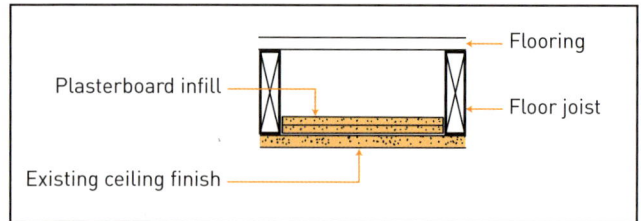

Fig 7.17: Upgrading with board infill

Option 2 – Upgrading from below

7.6.4 This can be achieved through additional boarding or a wet finish. When boarding, the ceiling should be underdrawn with chicken wire and then battened out and boarded. If providing a wet finish, the ceiling should be underdrawn with metal lathing to prevent the plaster from becoming detached.

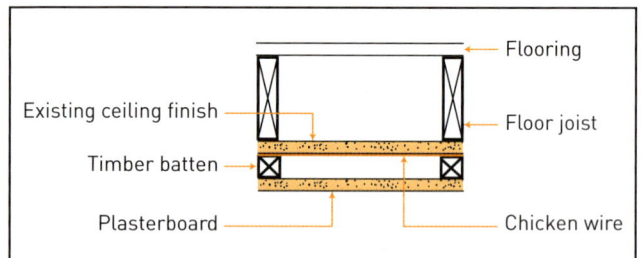

Fig 7.18: Upgrading with additional boarding

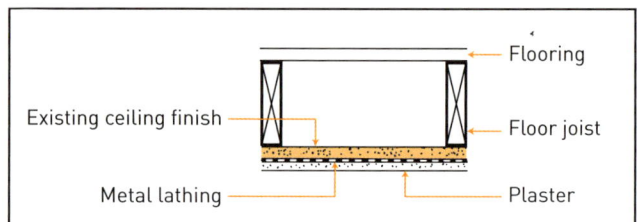

Fig 7.19: Upgrading with additional wet plaster finish

7.6.5 Care should be taken where chimneys and gas flue blocks are present in the converted loft space. A minimum separation of 40mm should be allowed between the outer surface of the chimney and structural timbers such as floor joists and roof trusses. This dimension can be reduced to 25mm for gas flue blocks.

7.6.6 Any new steelwork provided in the loft conversion should achieve 30-minute fire resistance. This can be achieved through intumescent paint or by being encased in plasterboard 'boxing'.

7.7 ADDITIONAL INFORMATION

7.7.1 Where an air circulation system is present in the dwelling the following guidance should be met to avoid the possibility of the system allowing smoke or fire to spread into the protected stairway:

- Transfer grilles should not be fitted in any wall, door or ceiling enclosed in the protected stair.

- Any duct passing through the enclosure to a protected stair or entrance hall should be of rigid steel construction and all joints between the ductwork and the enclosure should be fire-stopped.

- Ventilation ducts supplying or extracting air directly to or from the protected stair should not serve other areas as well.

- Any system of mechanical ventilation which recirculates air and which serves both the stair and other areas should be designed to shut down on the detection of smoke within the system.

- A room thermostat for a deducted warm air heating system should be mounted in the living room, at a height between 1370mm and 1830mm, and its maximum setting should not exceed 27°C.

7.7.2 For dwellings of three or more storeys, 30-minute fire-resistant loft hatches/roof void access panels may be required. Please see the following guidance:

- Loft hatches formed within the protected stair need not be fire-resisting.

- Where the stairs provide access to a single habitable room a loft hatch/roof void access panel formed within the room need not be fire-resisting.

- Where the stairs provide access to more than one habitable room, loft hatches/roof void access panels formed within the habitable rooms should achieve 30-minute fire resistance.

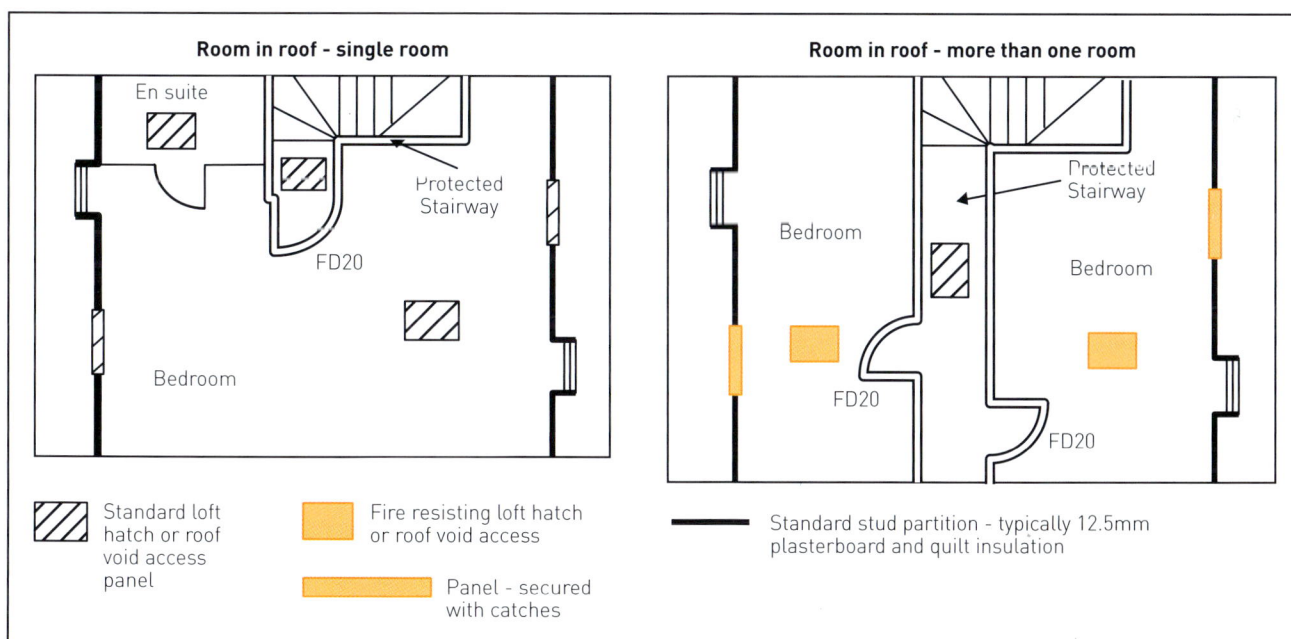

Fig 7.20: Requirements for loft hatches

8.0 INTRODUCTION

8.0.1 This chapter provides information on the seven main insulation products that are widely used when converting a loft. It also describes many other products that are readily available. It gives minimum, good and best U-values for generic construction details using the seven main insulation products. The generic construction details include an external wall, separating wall, flat roof and pitched roof.

8.1 There are a wide variety of insulation materials on the market being produced by numerous manufacturers. Below are the seven main types of insulation available, with a brief description of the generic product.

1. Rigid board (PUR/PIR)

Fig 8.1

PUR insulation products are made by reacting a liquid polyol component with a liquid polymeric isocyanate, Methylene Diphenyl di-Isocyanate (MDI), component in the presence of a blowing agent and other additives. The blowing agent evaporates during this exothermic reaction and a rigid closed-cell low-density insulation product is created.

PIR differs from PUR in that it is produced using an excess of the MDI component. The resultant PIR insulation products exhibit increased fire performance and reduced combustibility and higher working temperature limits.

2. Extruded polystyrene

Fig 8.2

Extruded polystyrene is produced from structured, closed-cell foam. It is cured for 90 days, which means that there will be no further movement of the foam, ensuring that it will retain its final structural and thermal values.

3. Mineral wool (glass/stone)

Fig 8.3

Mineral wool insulation is available in rolls or batts/slabs and is man-made from a range of materials including recycled glass and vitreous (silicate) fibres.

4. Multi-foil

Fig 8.4

Multi-foil insulation is made up of multi-layered reflective films, only a few microns thick. These layers, which are separated by wadding and foam etc., are sewn together to form a thin insulating blanket.

5. Expanded polystyrene

Fig 8.5

Expanded polystyrene is produced by expansion of beads containing pentane as a blowing agent.

The expanded beads are then re-expanded in a mould to produce large blocks from which board products are cut or shaped and mouldings manufactured; these are used in, for example, suspended beam and concrete floors.

Grey, low lambda products have a 20 per cent improved thermal performance over traditional white EPS.

6. In situ applied PUR/PIR

Fig 8.6

In-situ applied PUR/PIR insulation products are made from a similar reaction to rigid PUR/PIR board but are applied by approved installers directly to the surface to be insulated. A rigid closed-cell, low-density insulation product is created in situ.

7. Phenolic foams

Fig 8.7

Phenolic foams offer a range of thermal conductivity performance. The closed-cell type offers the lowest thermal conductivity available from any insulation material resulting from a closed-cell structure, extremely small cell diameter and low thermal conductivity gas permanently encapsulated in cells.

Phenolic foam can be up to 50 per cent more thermally efficient than other common insulation materials; this higher thermal efficiency allows reduced insulation thicknesses to be used, thereby saving valuable space.

8.2   A selection of the above products can be purchased with plasterboard laminated onto them. This is known as 'plasterboard thermal laminate'. Plasterboards can be laminated with expanded polystyrene, extruded polystyrene and phenolic foam insulants to provide thermal insulation and a plasterboard lining in one fixing operation to the underside of rafters. Certain plasterboard thermal laminates also contain a vapour check to further maximise their usage in loft conversion projects.

8.3   As well as the above insulation products, many others are available and they are listed below:

- Expanded clay aggregate.
- Cellulose loose fill or batts.
- Aerogel.
- Perlite beads.
- Cork board.
- Hemp batts.
- Extruded polyethylene.
- Vacuum insulated panel (VIP).
- Sheep's wool batts and rolls.
- Exfoliated vermiculite.
- Strawboard.
- Wood fibreboard.
- Flax batts and rolls.

8.4   MULTI-FOIL INSULATION

Introduction

8.4.1   Multi-foil insulation systems arrived in the mid 1990s when the product started to be used for insulating loft conversions. While the claims made for very high levels of insulation were almost universally greeted with scepticism within the profession, many did ultimately choose to accept multi-foil insulation systems on the basis of 'certification' provided by a reputable testing organisation. Over time, however, the testing that formed the basis of this original acceptance has been more widely scrutinised, particularly as the tests were not carried out to the existing national, European or international standards relating to insulation products.

Why is there a problem?

8.4.2   The key issue of concern relates to the way the thermal performance of multi-foil products has been tested. For many years, the appropriate method for determining insulation performance has involved the use of 'Hot Box' testing in accordance with national, European and international standards. There is no reason why multi-foil insulation systems cannot be tested using this method and some multi-foil manufacturers have both tested and marketed their products on this basis.

Several other manufacturers, however, feel that these tests do not fully reflect the special characteristics of their products and hence that a test to current BS EN standards will understate the actual insulation performance that can be achieved in real installations. They have therefore sought to develop new test methods which involve comparisons (using test rigs or actual buildings) between their own product and another insulating product (usually mineral wool).

Such tests set out to demonstrate that the actual energy consumption of buildings using multi-foil insulation will be equivalent to (or better than) an identical building using mineral wool insulation and, having done so, claim the same R-value for the multi-foil product as would be accepted for the test thickness of mineral wool.

There is currently no accepted national, European or international standard for performing tests in this way, but work is under way in Europe to examine the viability of such testing methods, and it may be that new test methodologies and standards will be developed as a result. Progress on this work has not been as quick as had been hoped, however, and we may well still be some way from knowing the official outcome.

Is there a big difference in claimed performance?

8.4.3 Tests carried out by the National Physical Laboratory (who have UKAS accreditation) using test methods in accordance with BS EN ISO 8990 have indicated an R-value for multi-foil products in a range of 1.69 to 1.71m^{2}K/W. Those manufacturers who use comparative testing are, however, claiming R-values for their products which range from 5 to 6m^{2}K/W. In other words, multi-foil manufacturers who have used the comparative testing route are claiming the insulating properties of their product to be approximately three times better than can be verified using existing national, European or international test standards.

Recommendation

8.4.4 The advice of the LABC technical working group is as follows:

1. The group acknowledges the outcome of the judicial review[1], but remains of the opinion that the thermal performance of all insulation materials should be determined by testing to national, European or international standards by organisations that have been accredited to do so. On this basis they are not aware of any multi-foil product currently on the market that can meet the normal roof U-value requirement of 0.2 when used as a single layer, without the need for additional insulation.

2. While the group supports the work currently under way to examine the viability of new test methods, their advice to members would be to wait until the outcome of the proper process is known before accepting claims of performance based on such tests. There can be no guarantee that the outcome of this work will verify the high R-values currently claimed by some manufacturers, and hence they believe if such values are accepted now, there is a significant risk that approved buildings will fail to achieve the required level of energy performance.

3. Several multi-foil manufacturers have now obtained British Board Agreement (BBA) certificates for their products, and they understand that as part of the assessment process the thermal performance of these products will be determined against existing national and European standards. They would therefore consider the use of any multi-foil product which has BBA Certificate to be acceptable, provided it is used strictly in the manner set out in the certificate.

4. They would advise all members to review their policy in the light of the judicial review, but see no reason why those who require that the thermal performance of multi-foil insulation products should be proved on the basis of current national, European or international test methods should not continue to do so.

5. This guidance note will be reviewed regularly by the Technical Working Group, and will be revised whenever the group feels that it is appropriate to do so as a result of new or updated information concerning the use of multi-foil products becoming available.

This information is taken from LABC Technical Guidance Note 06/001 Revision c.

8.5 ELEMENTS TO CONSIDER

8.5.1 Table 8.1 highlights the key elements to consider when carrying out a loft conversion along with the minimum, good and best U-values that are achievable.

Standard / Element	U-Value (W/m²K)				
	Pitched Roof (Rafter Level)	Pitched Roof (Ceiling Level)	Flat Roof	External Wall	Separating Wall
Minimum (B. Regs)	0.18	0.16	0.18	0.28	0.28
Good	0.15	0.12	0.15	0.23	0.23
Best	0.11	0.09	0.11	0.17	0.17

Table 8.1: Element performance levels

8.5.2 The 'minimum standard' is that currently set by the Building Regulations and is the bare minimum that Building Control will accept. The other two values are if you would prefer to insulate above the 'minimum standard' set out in the Building Regulations and wish to achieve a 'good standard' or 'best standard'. These improved standards offer the likelihood of reduced energy bills and an enhanced rating of the home's Energy Performance Certificate (EPC). (Further information on EPCs can be found in Chapters 12 and 14.)

8.5.3 The different types of insulating products available have been highlighted at the start of this chapter and it is not the intention of this guide to suggest one product over another. Therefore the provided U-values are there as guidance and it is for the individual user to decide which material is best suited to their particular conversion. In some cases combinations of materials such as insulated plasterboard with insulation between the rafters may be chosen as a better option than just one material.

8.5.4 It is not practicable to give all the possible combinations of insulation solutions for the different roof and wall types. Calculations for U-values will need to allow for thermal bridging, e.g. timbers and battens, and be carried out in accordance with the guidance in BR443 (**www.bre.co.uk/filelibrary/pdf/rpts/BR_443_ (2006_Edition).pdf**). Insulation manufacturers and suppliers are generally able to do this.

Note:
It is advisable to obtain the manufacturer's product specification and installation details prior to use.

8.6 EXTERNAL WALL

8.6.1 The external wall (new or existing) can take many forms, depending on the type and extent of loft conversion being carried out. Figures 8.8 and 8.9 detail all the locations that could be classed as an external wall and that will require insulating to the chosen U-value factor.

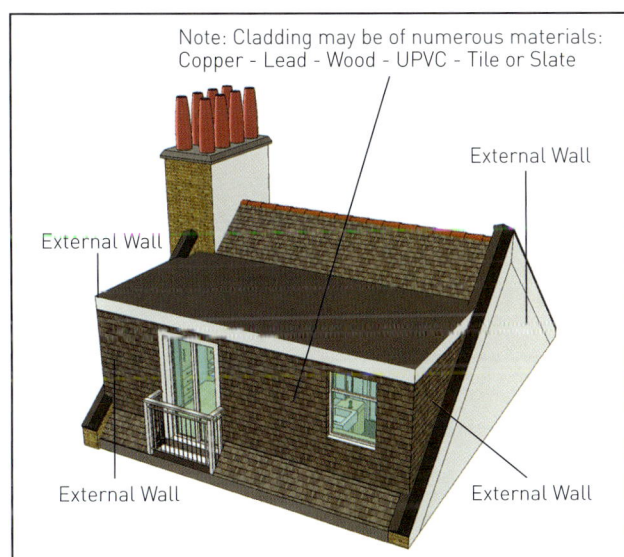

Note: Cladding may be of numerous materials: Copper - Lead - Wood - UPVC - Tile or Slate

External Wall

External Wall

External Wall

External Wall

Fig 8.8: External wall 1

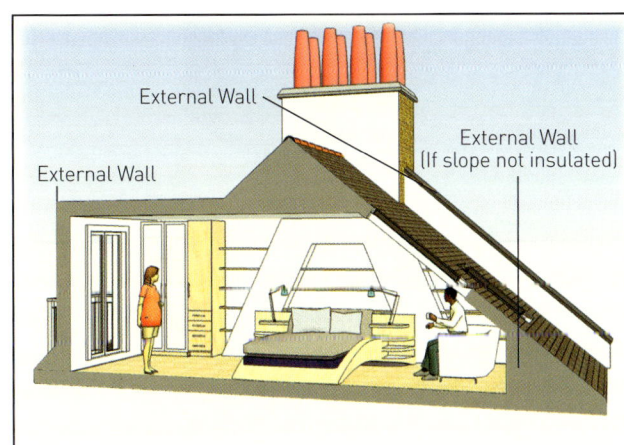

External Wall

External Wall (If slope not insulated)

External Wall

Fig 8.9: External wall 2

8.6.2 The following pages illustrate generic details for all types of external wall. The insulation thickness will depend on the brand used and the selected U-value factor.

---

1. The Judicial review was where a multifoil manufacturer took the government to court over treatment of thermal performance of multifoils.

Insulation to inside-face of brick/block wall

8.6.3 Figures 8.10 - 8.12 are generic details outlining three methods for insulating the inside face of a brick/block wall.

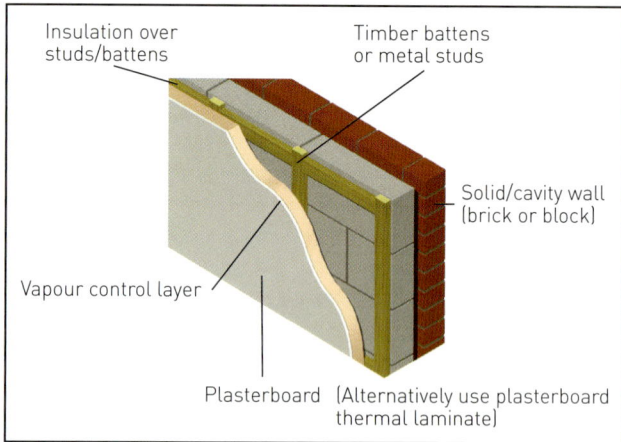

Fig 8.10

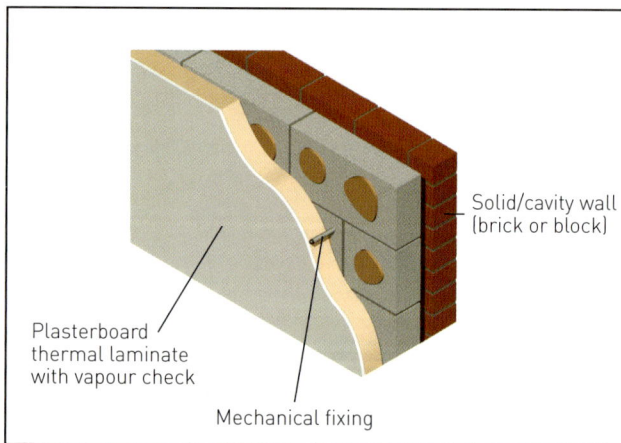

Fig 8.11

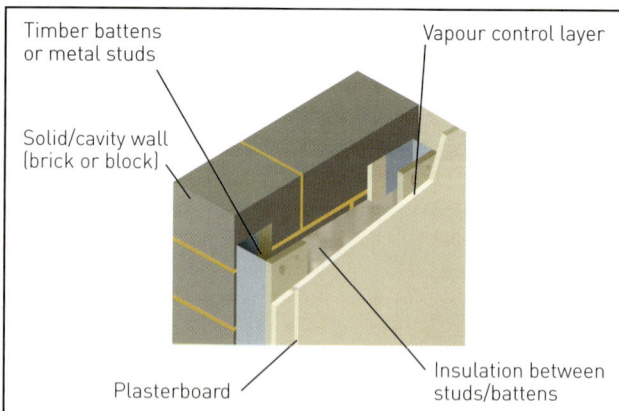

Fig 8.12

Figures 8.10 - 8.12: Insulating on inside face of brick/block wall

Note 1:
Generally 25mm x 50mm treated timber battens should be used.

Note 2:
When applying 'dot and dab' you must ensure that a continuous bead is applied along the perimeter of the wall, ceiling and skirting junction together with vertical dabs at 300mm centres applied to one board at a time. At least three mechanical fixings should be provided per board once the dabs have set. The wall should not show any sign of or be subject to water ingress if a 'dot and dab' application is used.

Note 3:
The timber battens or metal studs should be set at 600mm vertical centres and also positioned at floor and ceiling level. Timber battens should have a strip of DPC stapled to them for protection if there is any risk of water ingress.

Note 4:
When fixing to timber studs use screw or galvanised clout nails long enough to provide a 25mm fixing into the batten. When fixing to metal studs they should be screw-fixed. In both instances fixings should be provided at 150mm centres.

Insulation to cavity of brick/block wall

8.6.4 Figures 8.13 - 8.16 are generic details outlining four methods for insulating the cavity of a brick/block wall.

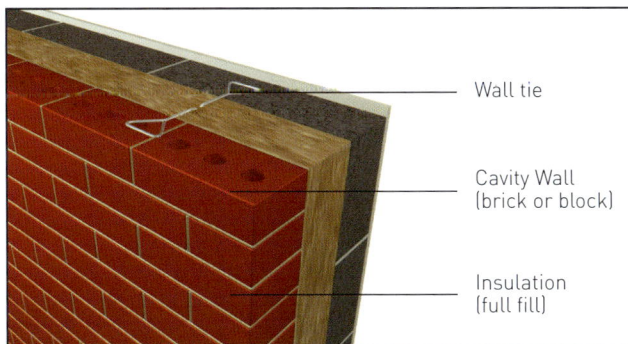

Fig 8.13

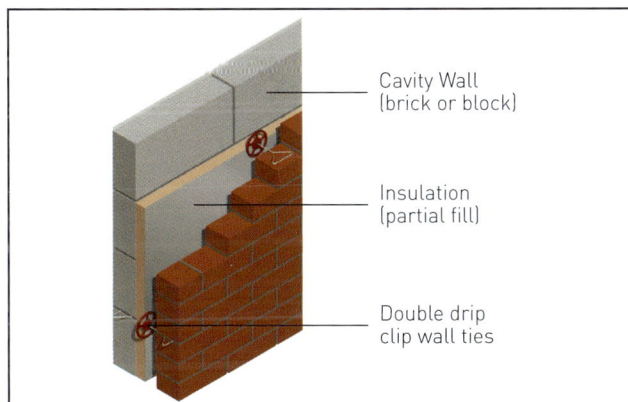

Fig 8.14

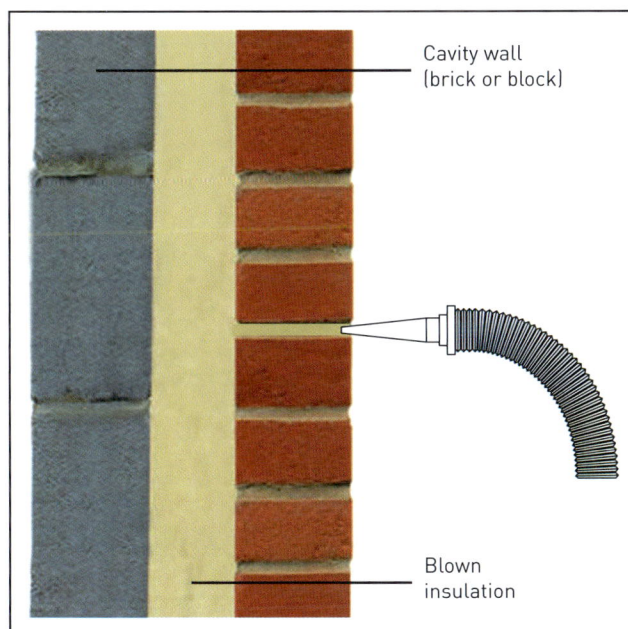

Fig 8.15

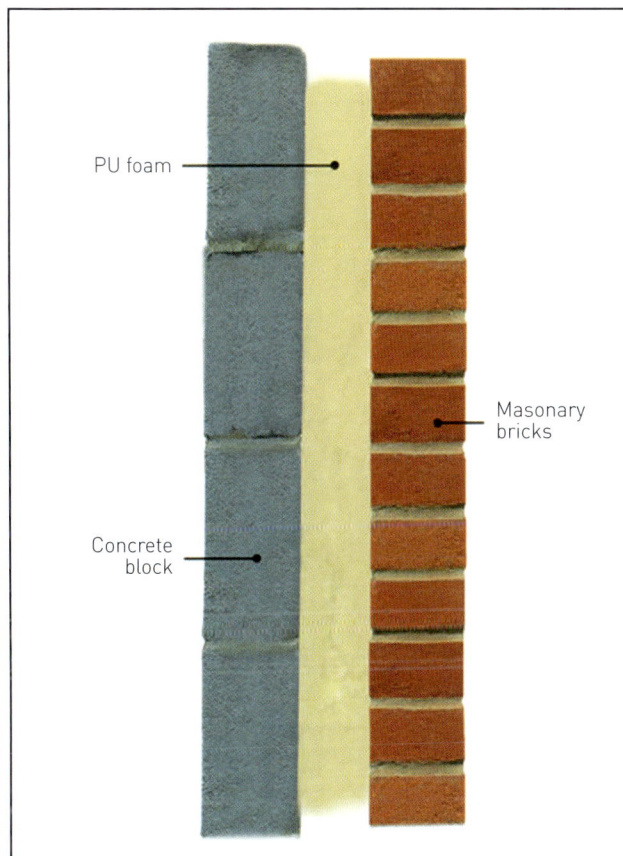

Fig 8.16

Figures 8.13 - 8.16: Insulating the cavity of a brick/block wall

Note 1:
The cavity width will be dictated by the existing dwelling's cavity wall thickness; although it is possible to corbel the brickwork this will only result in a slightly increased cavity width.

Note 2:
In all four details the cavity width is a given and thus may not be adequate to achieve the required U-value. Therefore, even with a newly constructed wall, providing insulation to the inside face of the wall may be the only option.

Note 3:
Wall ties must be stainless steel and should be spaced at 450mm x 900mm centres for a cavity width up to 75mm. For a cavity width greater than 75mm, wall ties should be spaced at 450mm x 750mm centres.

Note 4:
If using partial fill, you must maintain a clear cavity of 50mm for NHBC or Zurich warranty purposes, otherwise 25mm may be the minimum acceptable.

Insulation of timber wall with tile/ slate cladding

8.6.5 Figures 8.17 - 8.21 are generic details outlining five methods for insulating a timber wall with tile/slate cladding.

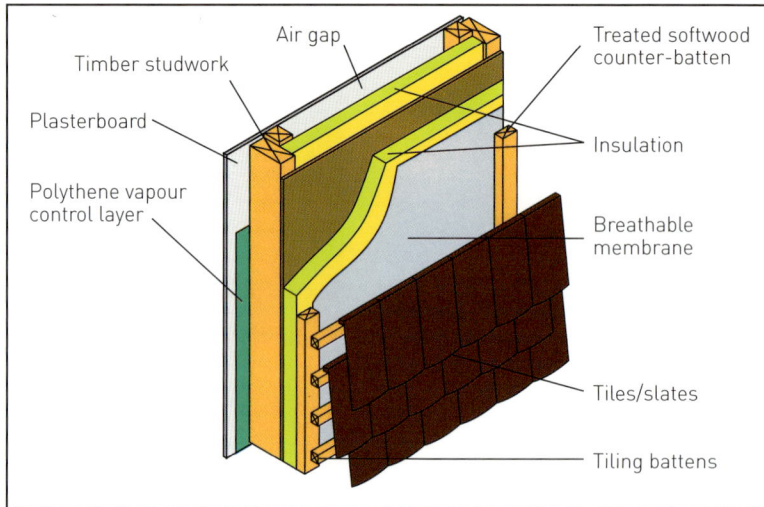

Fig 8.17: Between and over studs

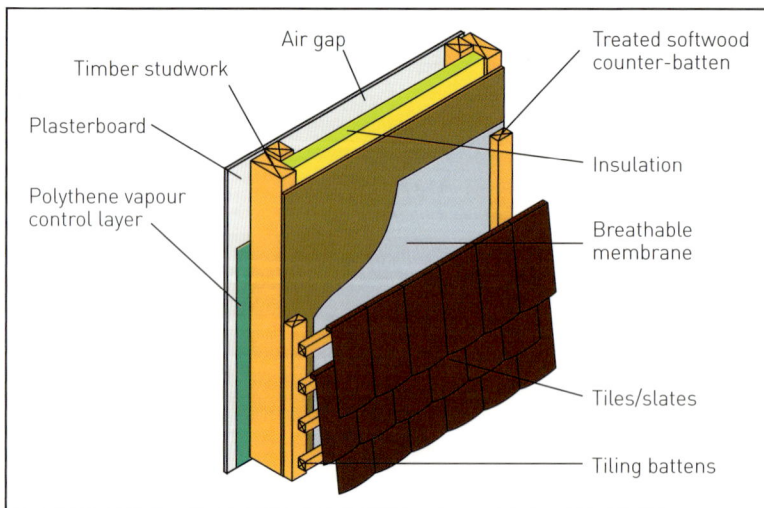

Fig 8.18: Between studs

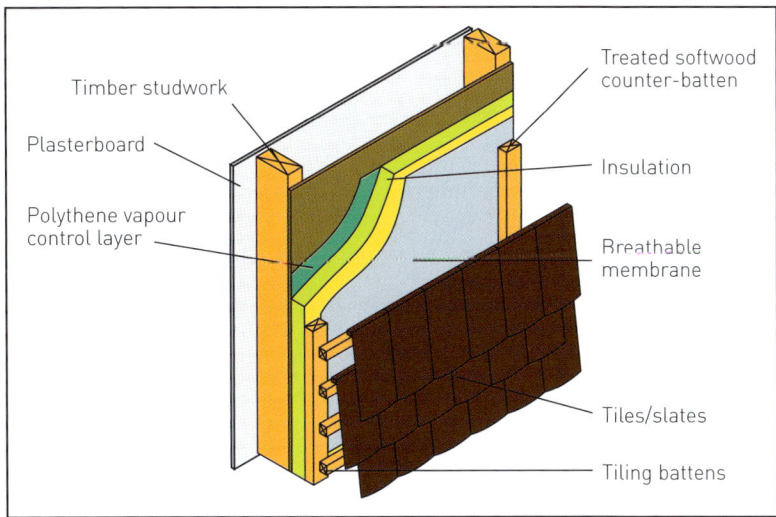

Fig 8.19: Over studs

Timber studwork
Plasterboard
Polythene vapour control layer
Treated softwood counter-batten
Insulation
Breathable membrane
Tiles/slates
Tiling battens

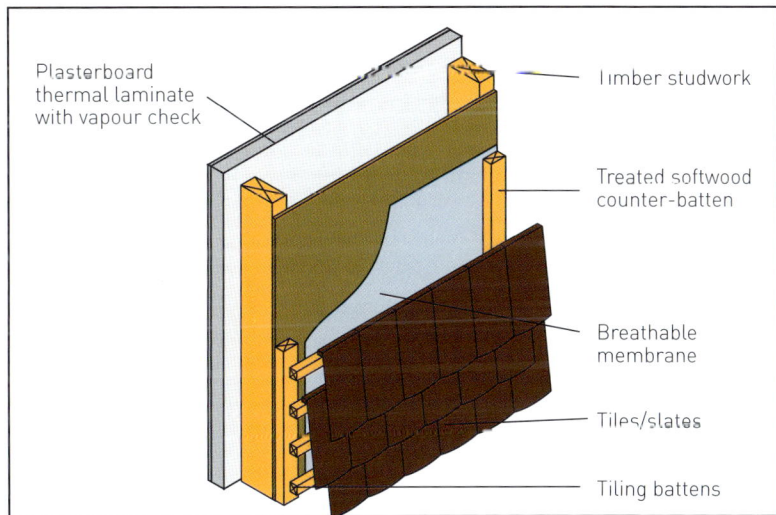

Fig 8.20: Warm side of studs

Plasterboard thermal laminate with vapour check
Timber studwork
Treated softwood counter-batten
Breathable membrane
Tiles/slates
Tiling battens

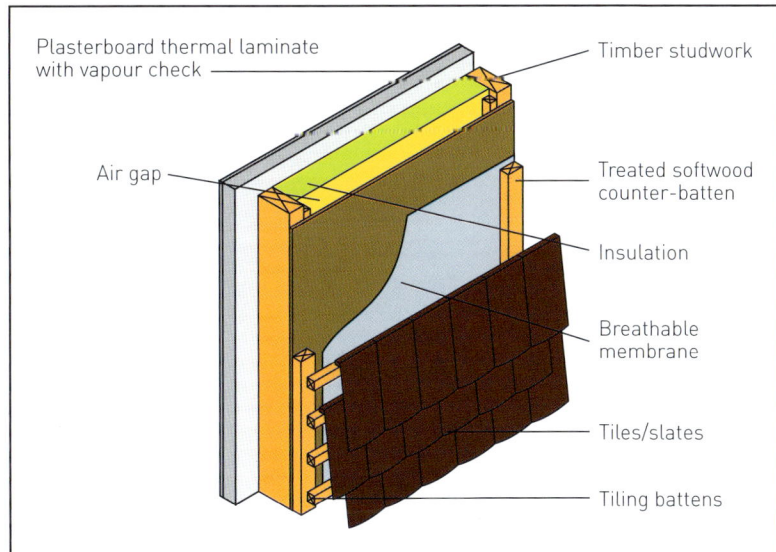

Fig 8.21: Between and to warm side of studs

Plasterboard thermal laminate with vapour check
Air gap
Timber studwork
Treated softwood counter-batten
Insulation
Breathable membrane
Tiles/slates
Tiling battens

Note 1:
Generally 38mm x 38mm treated softwood counter battens should be used.

Note 2:
The ideal plywood thickness is 9mm.

Note 3:
Generally 38mm x 25mm treated battens should be used.

Note 4:
Where two layers of insulation are provided, the layer with the greater thermal resistance should be to the cold side to prevent interstitial condensation.

Insulation of timber wall with timber cladding

8.6.6   Figures 8.22 - 8.26 are generic details outlining five methods for insulating a timber wall with timber cladding.

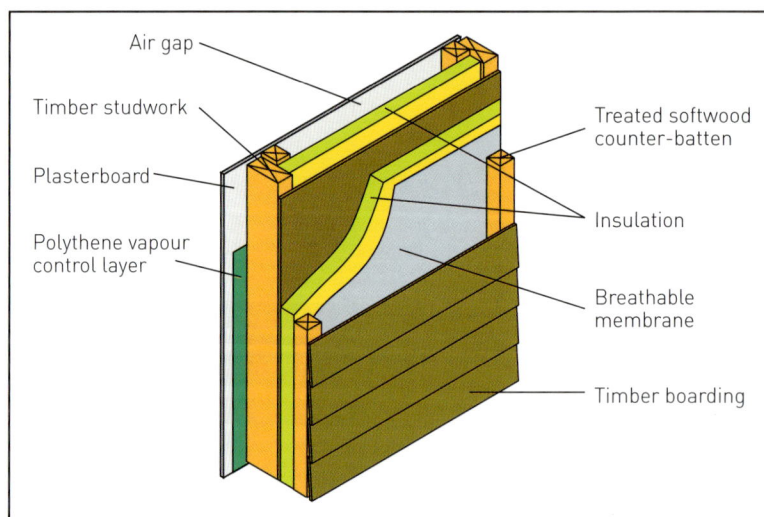

Fig 8.22: Between and over studs

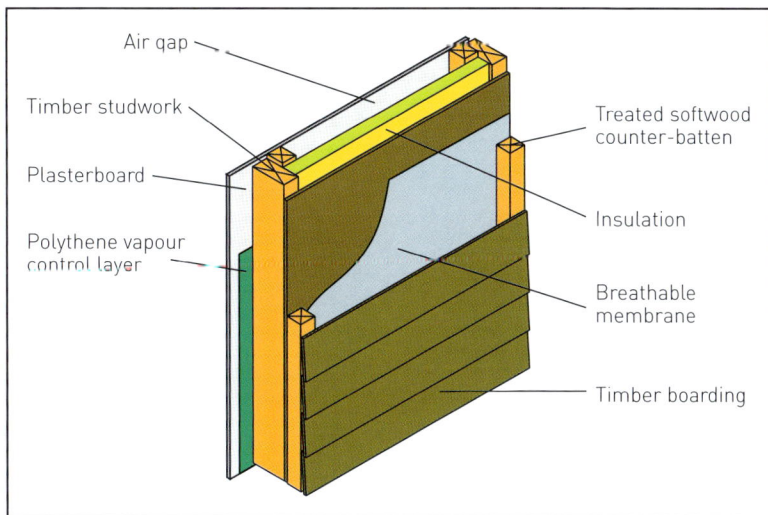

Fig 8.23: Between studs

- Air gap
- Timber studwork
- Plasterboard
- Polythene vapour control layer
- Treated softwood counter-batten
- Insulation
- Breathable membrane
- Timber boarding

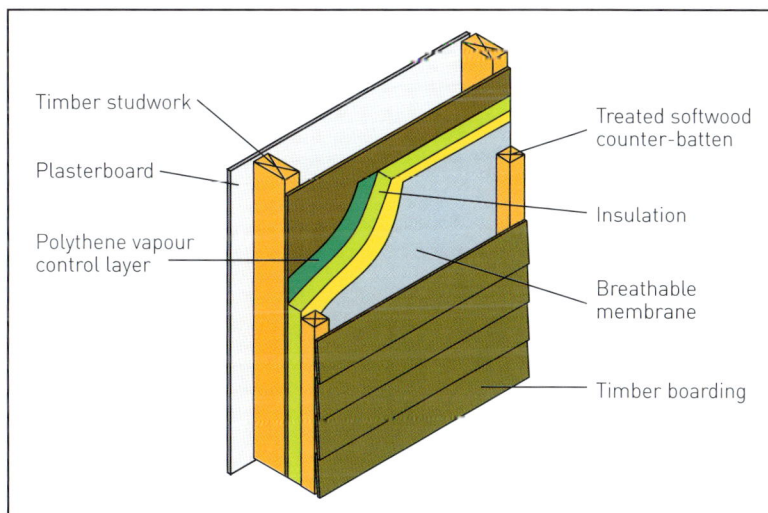

Fig 8.24: Over studs

- Timber studwork
- Plasterboard
- Polythene vapour control layer
- Treated softwood counter-batten
- Insulation
- Breathable membrane
- Timber boarding

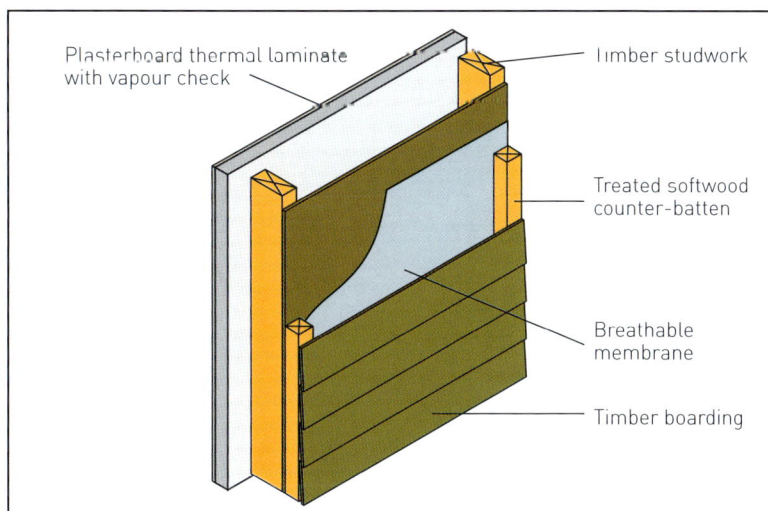

Fig 8.25: Warm side of studs

- Plasterboard thermal laminate with vapour check
- Timber studwork
- Treated softwood counter-batten
- Breathable membrane
- Timber boarding

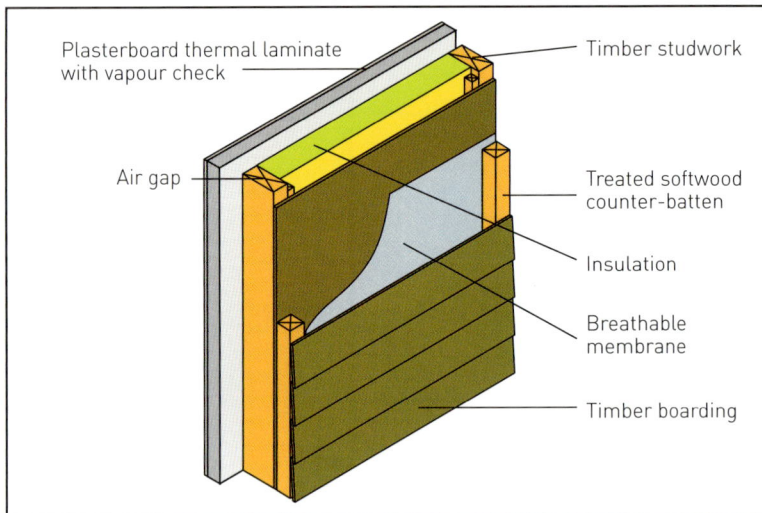

Fig 8.26: *Between and to warm side of studs*

Note 1:
Generally 50mm × 38mm treated softwood counter
battens should be used.

Note 2:
The ideal plywood thickness is 9mm.

Note 3:
Where two layers of insulation are provided, the layer
with the greater thermal resistance should be to the
cold side to prevent interstitial condensation.

Insulation to timber wall with lead cladding

8.6.7 Figures 8.27 - 8.31 are generic details outlining five methods for insulating a timber wall greater than 1 m² with lead cladding.

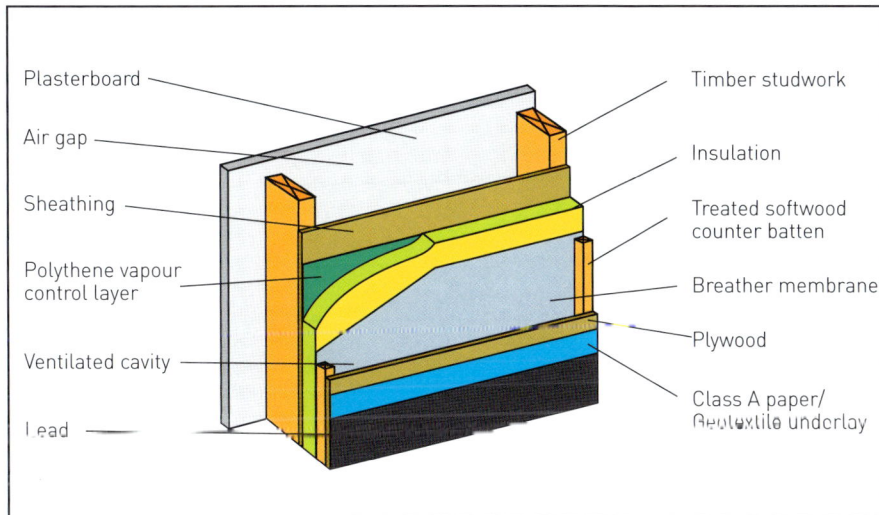

Fig 8.27: Between and over studs

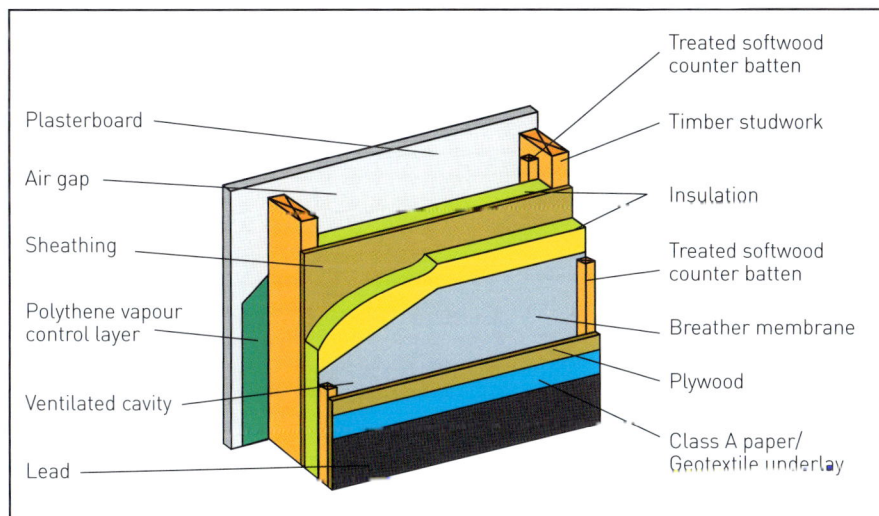

Fig 8.28: Between studs

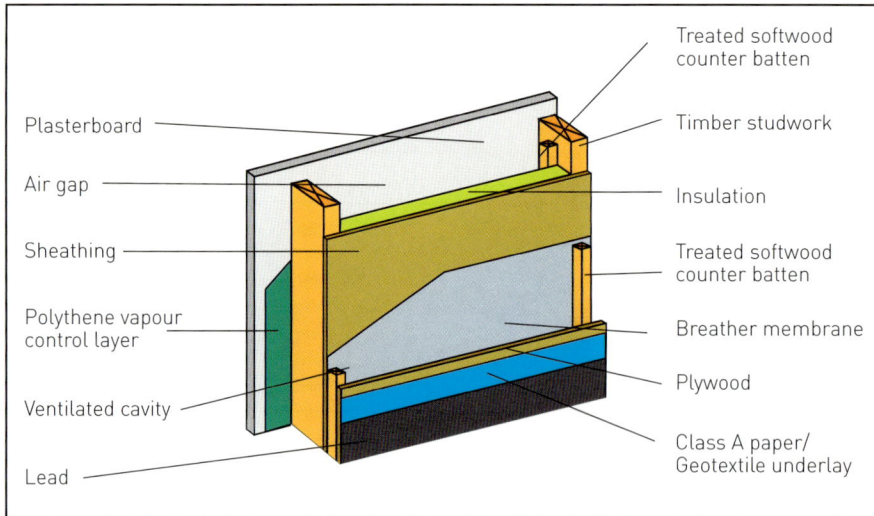

Plasterboard

Air gap

Sheathing

Polythene vapour
control layer

Ventilated cavity

Lead

Treated softwood
counter batten

Timber studwork

Insulation

Treated softwood
counter batten

Breather membrane

Plywood

Class A paper/
Geotextile underlay

Fig 8.29: Over studs

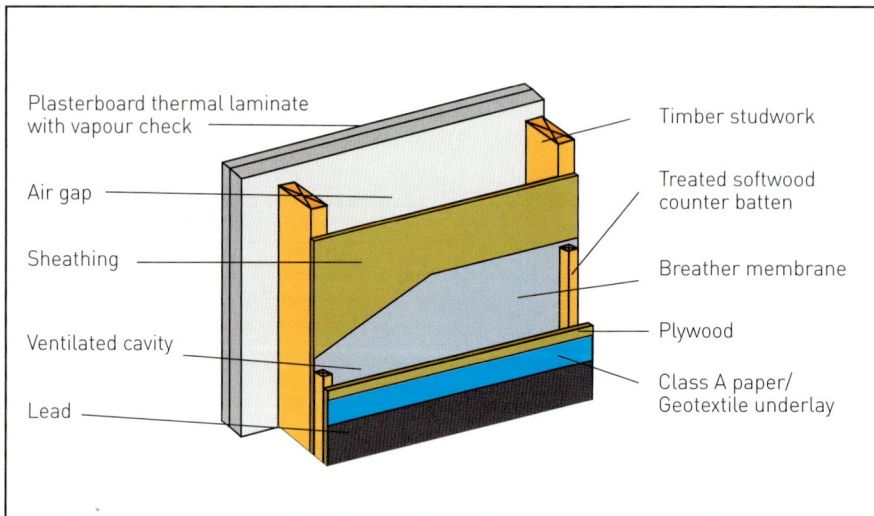

Plasterboard thermal laminate
with vapour check

Air gap

Sheathing

Ventilated cavity

Lead

Timber studwork

Treated softwood
counter batten

Breather membrane

Plywood

Class A paper/
Geotextile underlay

Fig 8.30: Warm side of studs

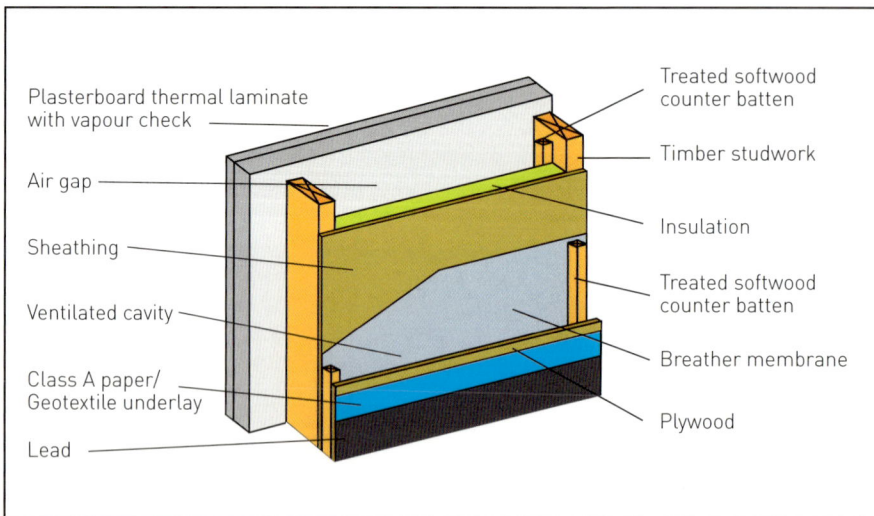

Plasterboard thermal laminate
with vapour check

Air gap

Sheathing

Ventilated cavity

Class A paper/
Geotextile underlay

Lead

Treated softwood
counter batten

Timber studwork

Insulation

Treated softwood
counter batten

Breather membrane

Plywood

Fig 8.31: Between and to warm side of studs

Note 1:

The ideal plywood thickness is 9mm.

Note 2:

For full details on the use of lead, visit the Lead Sheet Association at: **www.leadsheetassociation.org.uk**.

Note 3:

Where two layers of insulation are provided, the layer with the greater thermal resistance should be to the cold side to prevent interstitial condensation.

Insulation to timber side/knee wall

8.6.8 Figures 8.32 and 8.33 are generic details outlining two methods for insulating a timber side/knee wall:

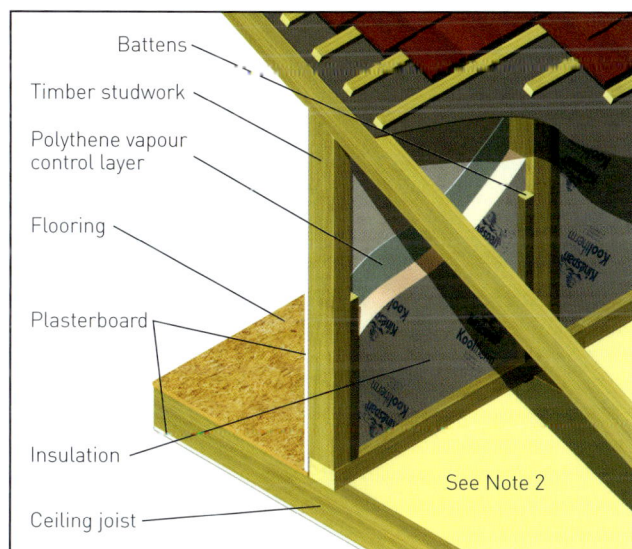

Fig 8.33: Between and to warm side of studs

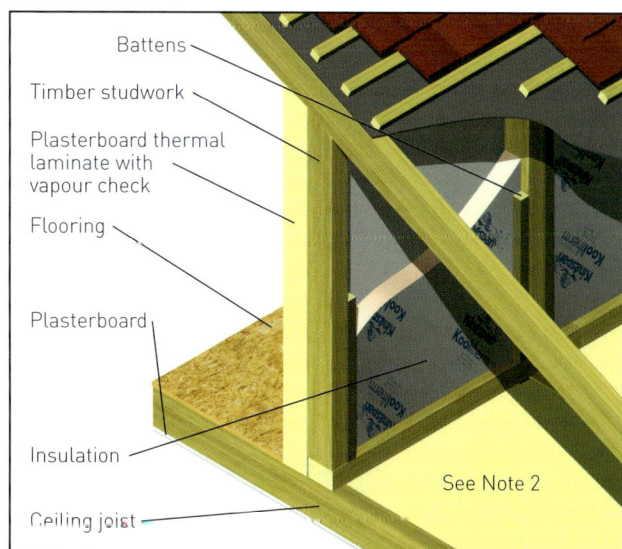

Fig 8.32: Between studs

Note 1:

If insulation does not follow the rafter line to the eaves this wall construction is classed as an external wall and therefore should be insulated accordingly.

Note 2:

The highlighted area in the diagrams should also be insulated to maintain the 'thermal envelope' of the construction. See section 8.10 for details.

Note 3:

Where two layers of insulation are provided, the layer with the greater thermal resistance should be to the cold side to prevent interstitial condensation.

8.7 SEPARATING WALL

8.7.1 If the adjacent loft has not been converted this space can be classed as semi-exposed and therefore should be insulated. The construction of the separating wall will not affect the method used to insulate, but will have an effect on the thickness of insulation required.

8.7.2 Typically there are three options available for insulating an existing solid or cavity separating wall and these are illustrated in Figures 8.34 - 8.36.

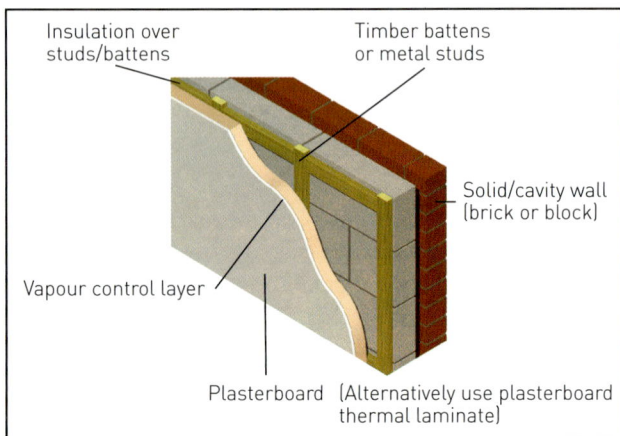

Fig 8.34: Over battens/studs

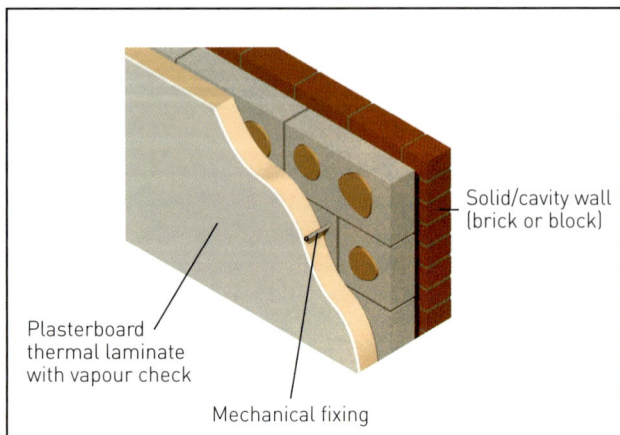

Fig 8.35: Dot and dab

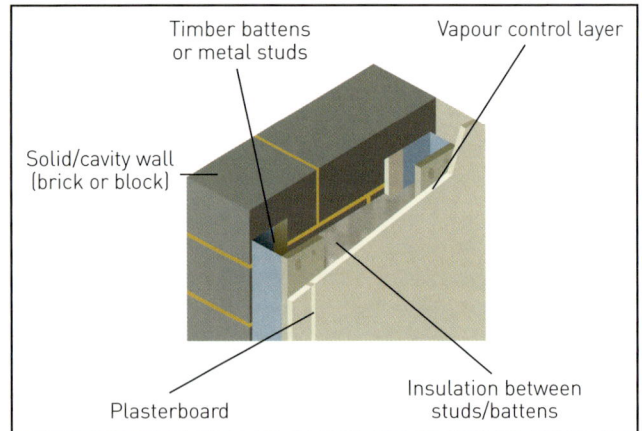

Fig 8.36: Between battens/studs

Note 1:
It is extremely important that appropriate fire precautions are carried out at the junction of the separating wall and roof structure. See Chapter 7 for further information.

Note 2:
Depending on the age of property, a separating wall may not be present in the loft space. In this instance it is advised to construct the separating wall as a continuation of the existing construction method and then insulate using one of the examples provided above.

Note 3:
The timber battens or metal studs should be set at 600mm vertical centres and also positioned at floor and ceiling level.

Note 4:
When fixing to timber studs use screw or galvanised clout nails long enough to provide a 22.5mm fixing into the batten. When fixing to metal studs they should be screw-fixed. In both instances fixings should be provided at 150mm centres.

Note 5:
Generally 25mm x 50mm treated timber battens should be used, the minimum plasterboard thickness being 12.5mm.

Note 6:
The minimum plasterboard thickness is 12.5mm, except where plasterboard thermal laminates are used, in which case the plasterboard layer is 9.5mm.

8.8 FLAT ROOF

8.8.1   Figures 8.37 - 8.41 are generic details outlining five methods for insulating a flat roof.

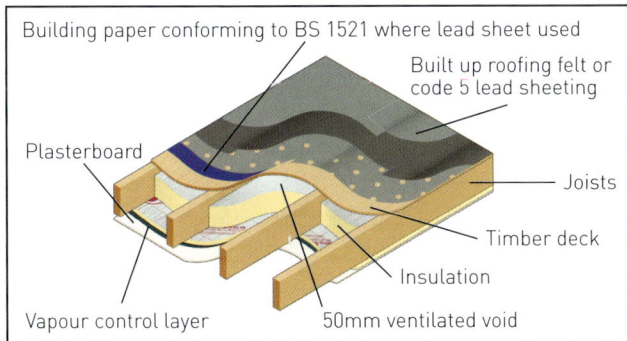

Fig 8.37: Between joists option A

Building paper conforming to BS 1521 where lead sheet used
Built up roofing felt or code 5 lead sheeting
Plasterboard
Joists
Timber deck
Insulation
Vapour control layer
50mm ventilated void

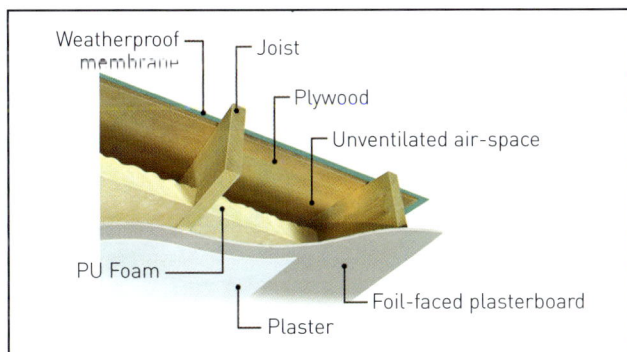

Fig 8.38: Between joists option B

Weatherproof membrane
Joist
Plywood
Unventilated air-space
PU Foam
Foil-faced plasterboard
Plaster

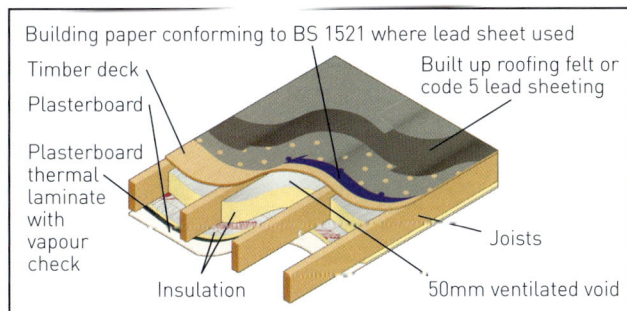

Fig 8.39: Between and under joists

Building paper conforming to BS 1521 where lead sheet used
Timber deck
Plasterboard
Built up roofing felt or code 5 lead sheeting
Plasterboard thermal laminate with vapour check
Joists
Insulation
50mm ventilated void

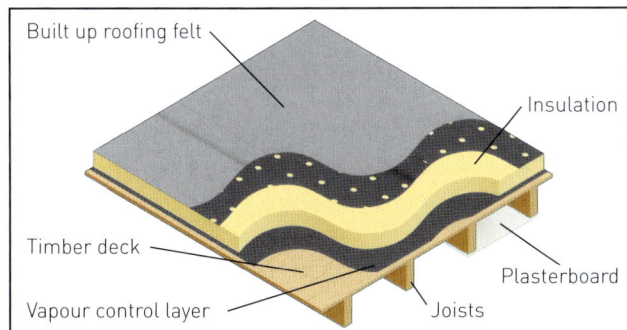

Fig 8.40: Over joists option A

Built up roofing felt
Insulation
Timber deck
Plasterboard
Vapour control layer
Joists

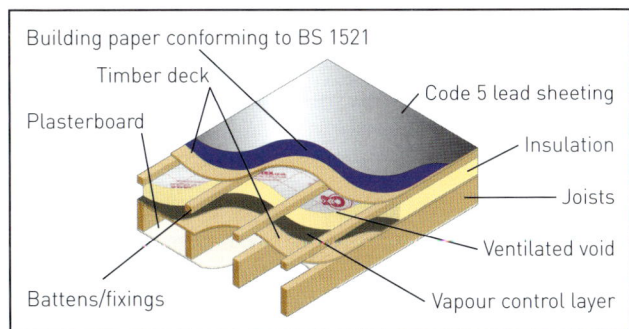

Fig 8.41: Over joists option B

Building paper conforming to BS 1521
Timber deck
Code 5 lead sheeting
Plasterboard
Insulation
Joists
Ventilated void
Battens/fixings
Vapour control layer

Material	Thickness of deck (mm)	
	Joist centres (mm)	
	450mm	600mm
Pre-treated plywood, WBP grade	15	18
Marine-plywood, WBP grade	15	18
Orientated Strand board Type OSB3	15	18
Pre-treated timber planking – tongue and grooved ('close boarded timber') Max. board width 100mm	19	19

Table 8.2: Thickness of decking material

Note 1:
The minimum plasterboard thickness is 12.5mm, except where plasterboard thermal laminates are used, in which case the plasterboard layer is 9.5mm.

Note 2:
For joists spaced at 450mm centres, 38mm x 38mm treated timber battens/firrings should be used.

Note 3:
For joists spaced at 600mm centres, 38mm x 50mm treated timber battens/firrings should be used.

Note 4:
In general a flat roof has a maximum slope of 10 degrees from the horizontal. This can be achieved through firrings, sloping joists or tapered insulation.

Note 5:
Where two layers of insulation are provided, the layer with the greater thermal resistance should be to the cold side to prevent interstitial condensation.

Note 6:
For full details on the use of lead, visit the Lead Sheet Association at: **www.leadsheetassociation.org.uk**.

8.9 PITCHED ROOF – RAFTER LEVEL

Insulation between rafters

8.9.1 Figures 8.42 - 8.45 are generic details outlining four methods for insulating between the rafters. Unless your rafters are 150mm deep (the minimum for high performance insulation) or greater this option will not achieve the 'minimum standard' required to meet the Building Regulations.

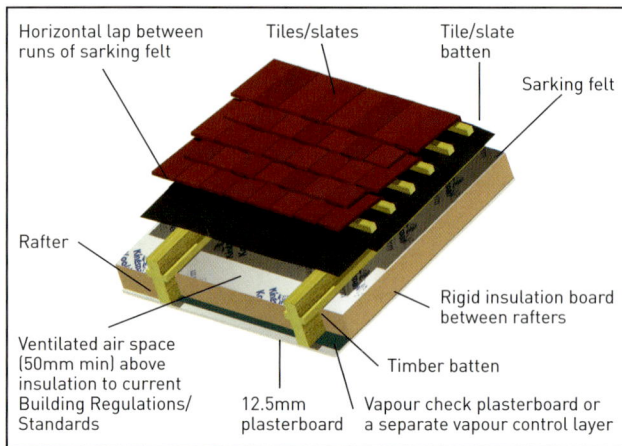

Fig 8.42

Horizontal lap between runs of sarking felt
Tiles/slates
Tile/slate batten
Sarking felt
Rafter
Ventilated air space (50mm min) above insulation to current Building Regulations/Standards
12.5mm plasterboard
Timber batten
Vapour check plasterboard or a separate vapour control layer
Rigid insulation board between rafters

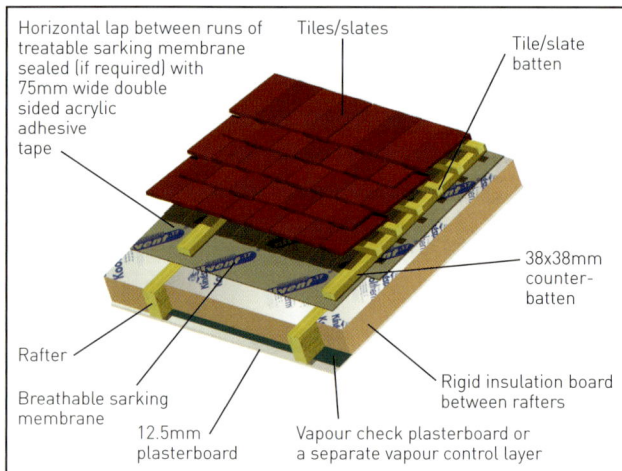

Fig 8.43

Horizontal lap between runs of treatable sarking membrane sealed (if required) with 75mm wide double sided acrylic adhesive tape
Tiles/slates
Tile/slate batten
Rafter
Breathable sarking membrane
12.5mm plasterboard
Vapour check plasterboard or a separate vapour control layer
Rigid insulation board between rafters
38x38mm counter-batten

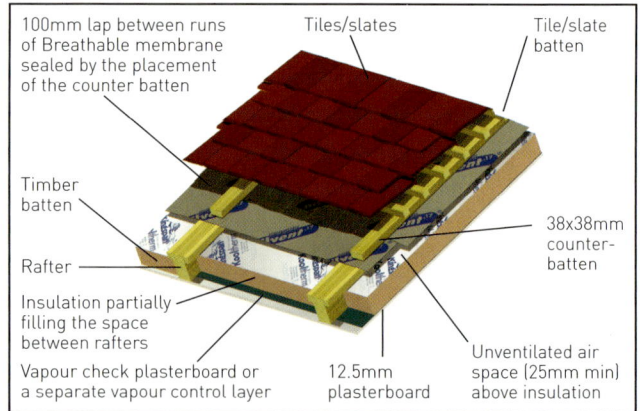

Fig 8.44

100mm lap between runs of Breathable membrane sealed by the placement of the counter batten
Tiles/slates
Tile/slate batten
Timber batten
Rafter
Insulation partially filling the space between rafters
Vapour check plasterboard or a separate vapour control layer
12.5mm plasterboard
38x38mm counter-batten
Unventilated air space (25mm min) above insulation

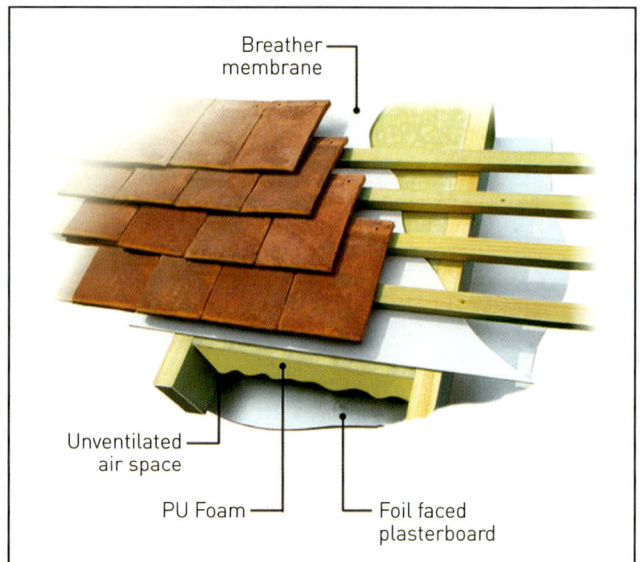

Fig 8.45:

Breather membrane
Unventilated air space
PU Foam
Foil faced plasterboard

Note:

In the unventilated options, the plasterboard ceiling and any penetrations of ceiling and vapour control layer must be well sealed.

Insulation between and under rafters

8.9.2 Figures 8.46 - 8.48 are generic details outlining three methods for insulating between and under rafters.

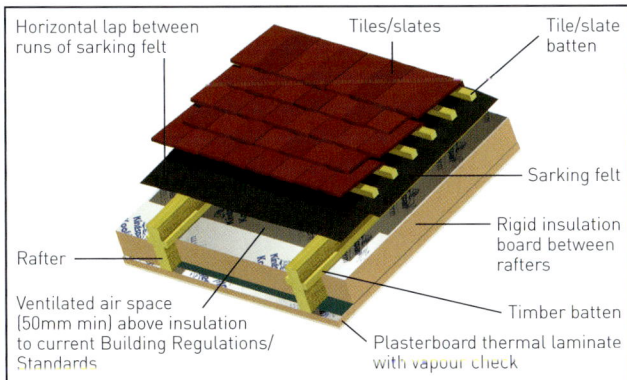

Fig 8.46

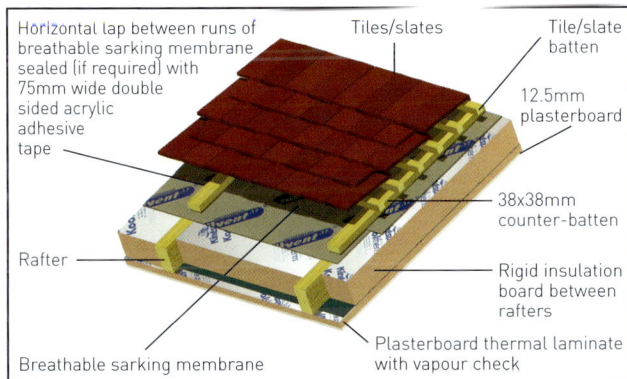

Fig 8.47

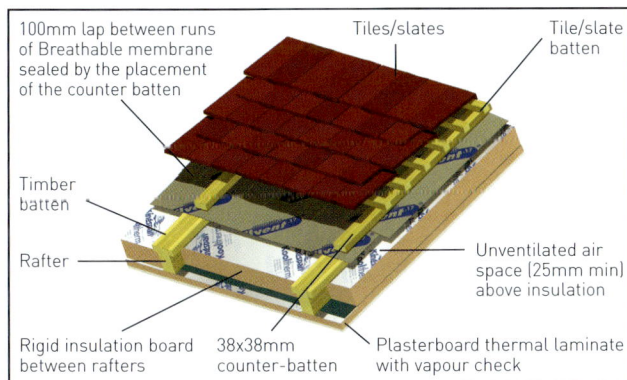

Fig 8.48

8.9.3 Insulation can be installed in two other locations on a pitched roof; however, these are generally not used in a loft conversion unless the roof structure is stripped. Therefore no details have been provided. For information, the other two locations are:

• Between and over rafters

• Over rafters.

8.10 PITCHED ROOF – CEILING LEVEL

Insulation between and over joists

8.10.1 Figures 8.49 - 8.50 are generic details outlining two methods for insulating between and over joists.

Single layer of insulation laid between joists

Fig 8.49

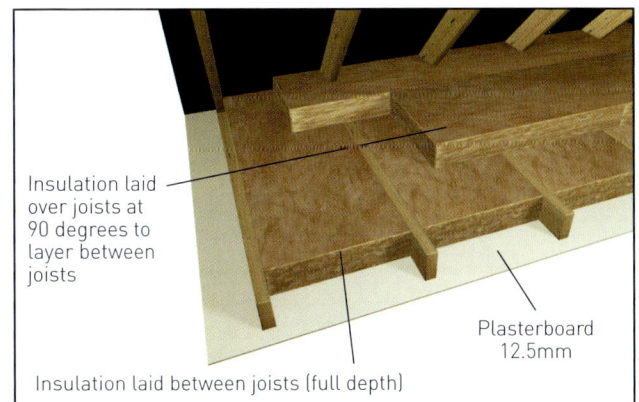

Insulation laid over joists at 90 degrees to layer between joists

Plasterboard 12.5mm

Insulation laid between joists (full depth)

Fig 8.50

9. SOUND

9.0 INTRODUCTION

9.0.1 This chapter provides information on the need to prevent sound transmission through areas which include the existing structure, separating wall, new floor and new internal walls.

9.1 This is an area that requires care and attention to detail. Although not all the proposals within the Building Regulations are compulsory with regard to sound transmission, when you are creating a loft conversion, the materials required to achieve the standards are normally already on site and, if they are installed correctly, the end result improves the living environment once the work is completed. Acoustic engineers are available and their expert advice should be sought if required.

9.2 A factor that should be considered is the age of the property that you are converting. Any new home constructed post July 2003 will have been constructed in accordance with Approved Document E of the Building Regulations and all elements of the existing home will conform; therefore the conversion work should also comply because any additional work to the property must be no worse than the standard in the existing home.

9.3 An advantage here is that the separating wall will have been constructed to the suggested standards within the guidance document or through a third-party scheme called 'Robust Details Ltd'. The property's Home Information Pack will hold this information. (Further information on HIPs can be found in Chapter 13.)

9.4 This chapter is divided into four sections and covers in detail:

- Existing structure.
- New floor.
- New separating wall.
- New internal walls.

9.5 EXISTING STRUCTURE

9.5.1 There are not many alterations that can be made to the existing structure to improve impact and airborne sound without extensive refurbishment work taking place. However, there are areas that should be considered when creating the loft conversion if you live in a semi-detached or terraced property.

- The new staircase in most instances will be fixed to the existing separating wall. This will increase the sound transmission through the wall into the adjacent property. Careful consideration should therefore be given to provisions to decrease this sound transmission.

- The end bearings to steel beams should not be installed into or from the separating wall. However, where this has been justified by design to support the proposed loft conversion there will be an increase in the sound transmission through the separating wall if appropriate measures are not taken.

- Where a chimney breast is removed, the remaining masonry may only be a half-brick thick. This will form a pathway to sound and should be given special attention.

9.6 NEW FLOOR

9.6.1 This element of construction can be easily upgraded to a standard similar to that required for new-build properties through the following:

- In normal circumstances loft insulation will already be present. To meet the requirements, maintain 100mm of this insulation within the void between the floor joists but replace it if its density is less than 10kg/m^3. A 25mm gap should be left between the underside of the new joists and the existing ceiling.

- The floor finish is new; therefore provide a floor surface of timber or wood-based board with a minimum mass per unit area of 15kg/m^2 (normally 22mm tongued and grooved boards).

- Impact sound can be improved further with the addition of a suitable underlay/absorbent material and soft covering.

- Unless new attic trusses have been installed the existing plasterboard ceiling will still be in place and cannot be improved unless you wish to re-board or board over the existing ceiling. This would generally not be necessary, and therefore would not be practicable or cost-effective to carry out. The only time this will normally be done is if the ceiling requires upgrading to meet the minimum requirements for fire protection. (Further information on fire safety can be found in Chapter 7.)

9.6.2 Figure 9.1 illustrates how to achieve suitable protection against airborne and impact sound.

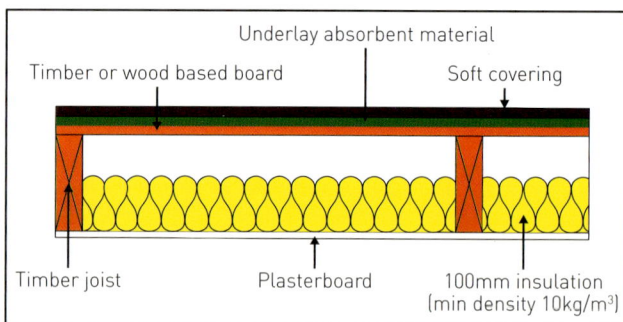

Fig 9.1: Upgrading a floor for sound insulation

9.7 SEPARATING WALL

9.7.1 As previously stated, if the property that is being converted was built post July 2003 the separating wall will have been constructed in accordance with the regulations and no further action is required. The guidance below is divided into two sections according to whether or not a separating wall is present.

Note:

It is advisable to confirm with the local Building Control Department that the property was constructed following the 2003 version of Approved Document E as in some instances Building Regulations approval may have been granted prior to the regulation change.

Separating wall present

9.7.2 Where a separating wall is present in the loft space, the work to bring the wall up to a suitable standard is quite straightforward. The following guidance may be of assistance:

- Make good the existing separating wall, filling all open bed and perp. joints with mortar.

- Where the separating wall meets the underside of the roof it is advisable to provide a layer of mineral wool to act as a fire-stop.

- Steel beams should not be installed into the separating wall. However, where this has been justified by design, they should be 'made good' around.

- The separating wall should then be insulated in accordance with the recommendations in Chapter 8, with a plasterboard finish such as Figure 9.2.

No separating wall present

9.7.3 It is common in Victorian terraces for the separating wall to be absent in the loft space. If this is the case, a new separating wall will need to be constructed. Another situation where a new wall would be required is when steel work cannot be designed other than by being built into the separating wall, but the wall is of poor construction or only a single skin thick (100mm or less).

9.7.4 To construct the separating wall to a suitable standard, the following guidance may be of assistance:

- Build the new separating wall straight off the existing separating wall, either in blockwork or timber studding, to the standard set out in section 2 of Approved Document E to the Building Regulations. The use of timber is either the choice of the individual or may be predetermined because following the structural survey the foundations of the separating wall are deemed unsatisfactory for additional loading. (For further information on property surveys, see Chapter 2.)

- Care should be taken at the intersection of the existing separating wall and new wall construction as this connection detail of all elements (block/studwork, insulation, plasterboard, etc.) can have a detrimental effect on the performance of the wall if installed incorrectly.

- Where the separating wall meets the underside of the roof it is advisable to provide a layer of mineral wool to act as a fire-stop.

- Any new steel beams that have been installed into the separating wall (where permitted) should be 'made good' around.

- The separating wall should be insulated with a plasterboard finish in accordance with the recommendations in Chapter 8.

9.8 NEW INTERNAL WALLS

9.8.1 If new timber- or metal-frame internal walls are constructed either within the loft conversion itself or to accommodate the protected staircase below, for example, there are two straightforward methods that can be adopted to achieve the minimum requirements. These are detailed below.

9.8.2 Option 1:

- This is achieved by providing two or more layers of plasterboard to each side of the frame with all joints well sealed. Each sheet of plasterboard should have a minimum mass per unit area of 10kg/m^2 (normally 15mm plasterboard).

- If the frame is of timber construction it should be a minimum 75mm wide.

- If the frame is of metal construction it should be a minimum 45mm wide.

9.8.3 Option 2:

- This is achieved by providing a single layer of plasterboard to each side of the frame with all joints well sealed. Each sheet of plasterboard should have a minimum mass per unit area of 10kg/m^2 (normally 15mm plasterboard).

- An absorbent layer of unfaced mineral wool batts or quilt (minimum thickness 25mm, minimum density 10kg/m^3), which may be wire reinforced, is suspended in the cavity.

- If the frame is of timber construction it should be a minimum 75mm wide.

- If the frame is of metal construction it should be a minimum 45mm wide.

9.8.4 Figures 9.2 and 9.3 illustrate the above options.

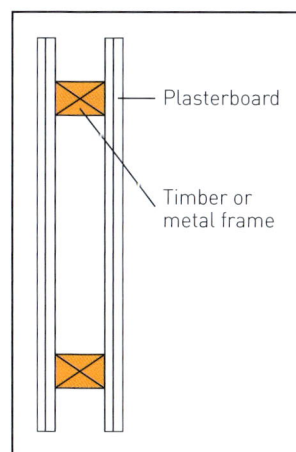

Fig 9.2 Option 1   *Fig 9.3: Option 2*

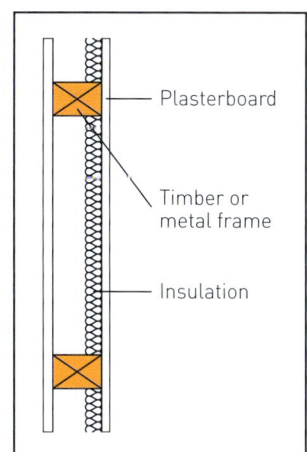

Options for internal walls

10.0 INTRODUCTION

10.0.1 This chapter provides good practice techniques and information on the need to provide ventilation to areas including the converted roof, habitable rooms and wet rooms.

10.1 When carrying out a loft conversion, ventilation is a very important issue. Depending on the planned use of the converted loft, you will need to consider ventilation to either two or three locations. The first and most obvious location that will be covered within this chapter is ventilation to the converted roof itself; second, the chapter will discuss how to ventilate a habitable room; and third, the ventilation requirements if a bath/shower or WC is to be installed.

10.2 ROOF

10.2.1 The majority of existing roofs will be cold roofs, designed with insulation laid along the ceiling joists and well ventilated to offer maximum air flow in the roof space to avoid timber decay and mould growth through dampness from condensation and rain. A loft conversion will move this insulation from the ceiling joists to between the rafters; therefore the free-flowing air will be restricted and requires careful consideration.

10.2.2 To provide adequate ventilation to a roof space you first need to be aware of the roofing felt/underlay that is currently in place, if at all, and its type and condition.

10.2.3 There are normally two types of underlay used: high resistance (HR) (which has a vapour resistance greater than 0.25 MN.s/g), or low resistance (LR) (which has a vapour resistance less than or equal to 0.25 MN.s/g).

10.2.4 The following information and diagrams detail minimum ventilation requirements depending on the type of underlay used and position of insulation, roof lights, intersections, etc.

Type HR underlay with a ventilated void beneath

10.2.5 To minimise the risk of interstitial condensation occurring, it is necessary to provide a well-sealed ceiling and to ensure that 50mm deep vented voids (at least 25mm deep at the centre of the drape) are maintained between the insulation and the underlay. It is important that these air paths remain unobstructed during the life of the building.

10.2.6 Ventilation openings should be provided to each void, at both high and low level, to allow free air movement through the gap between the insulation and the underlay. The following information applies for each of these locations:

a. Low-level openings should be equivalent in area to a continuous opening of not less than 25mm x length at eaves.

b. High-level openings should be equivalent in area to a continuous opening of not less than 5mm x length at the ridge or hips.

Note:
Where there is no cross communication between each roof slope, 5mm should be provided on both sides of the ridge.

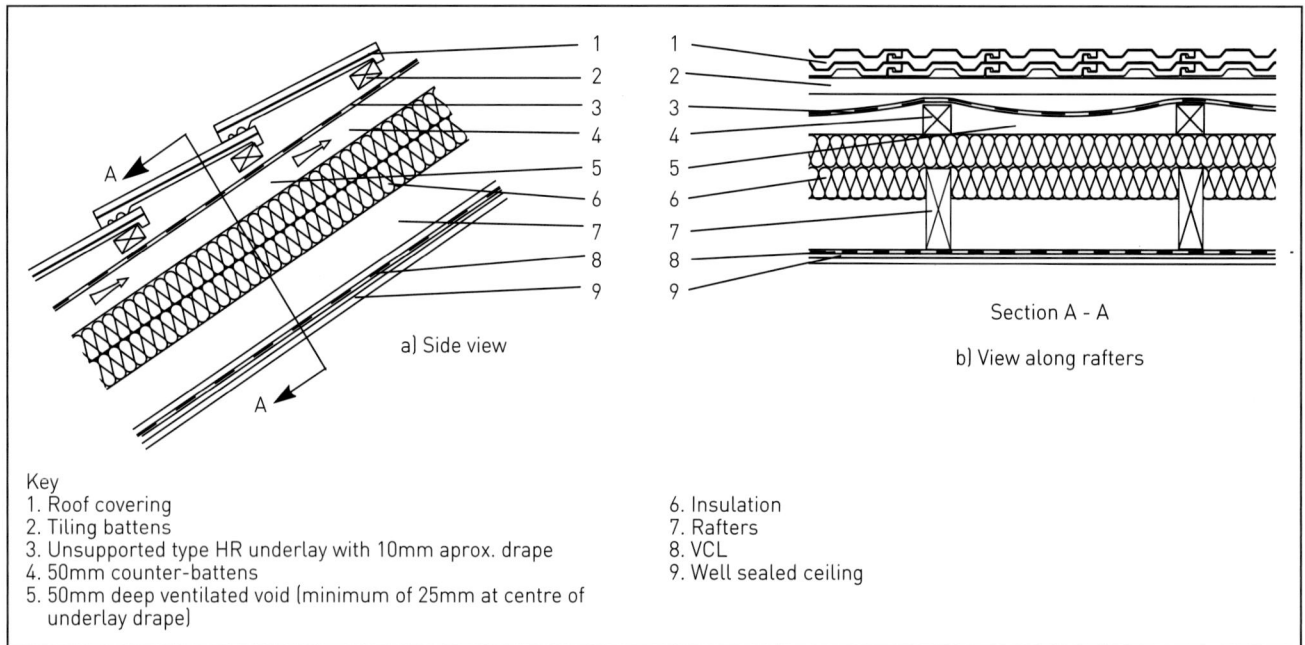

Fig 10.1: Details of roof with HR underlay

Key
1. Roof covering
2. Tiling battens
3. Unsupported type HR underlay with 10mm aprox. drape
4. 50mm counter-battens
5. 50mm deep ventilated void (minimum of 25mm at centre of underlay drape)
6. Insulation
7. Rafters
8. VCL
9. Well sealed ceiling

a) Side view

Section A - A

b) View along rafters

10.2.7 Particular attention must be paid to potential restrictions at eaves, at changes in roof slope, at valleys and hips, and at changes in construction details where such a void may be difficult to achieve. Obstructions such as dormers, roof windows, compartment walls, fire barriers or changes in pitch create separate voids in the roof slope. Where this occurs the roof void should have additional ventilation openings:

a. Immediately below the obstruction equivalent to 5mm x length of obstruction

b. Immediately above the obstruction equivalent to 25mm x length of obstruction.

10.2.8   Figures 10.2 - 10.5 detail the ventilation positions for loft conversions in a number of situations.

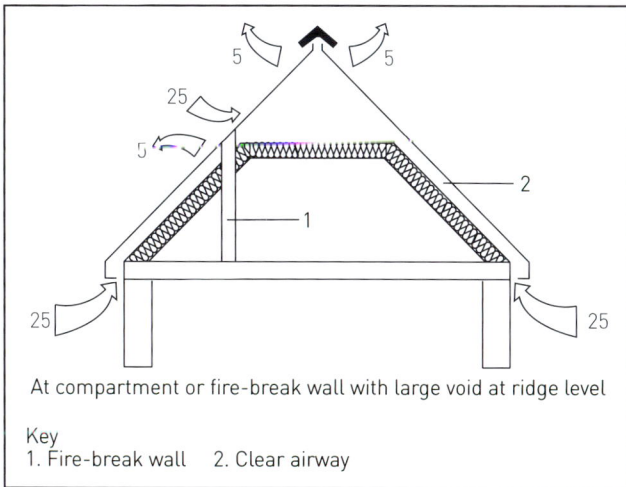

At compartment or fire-break wall with large void at ridge level

Key
1. Fire-break wall   2. Clear airway

Fig 10.2

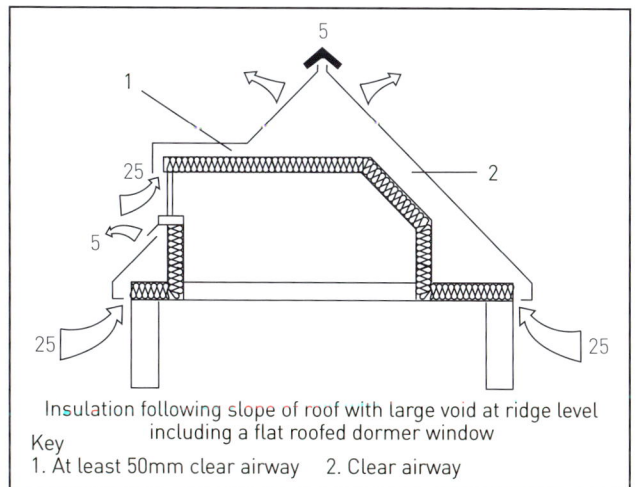

Insulation following slope of roof with large void at ridge level including a flat roofed dormer window

Key
1. At least 50mm clear airway   2. Clear airway

Fig 10.4

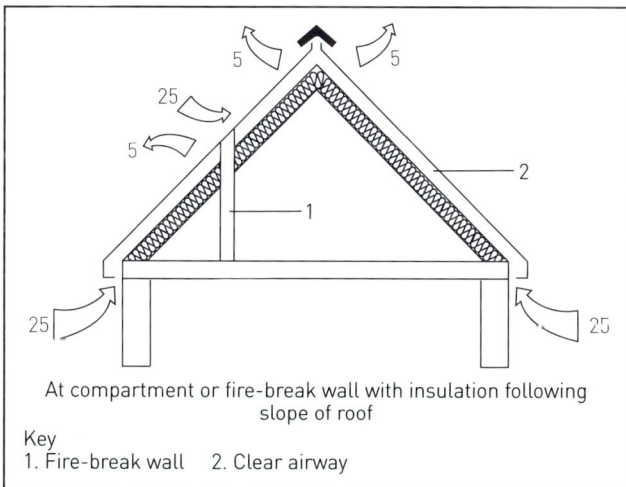

At compartment or fire-break wall with insulation following slope of roof

Key
1. Fire-break wall   2. Clear airway

Fig 10.3

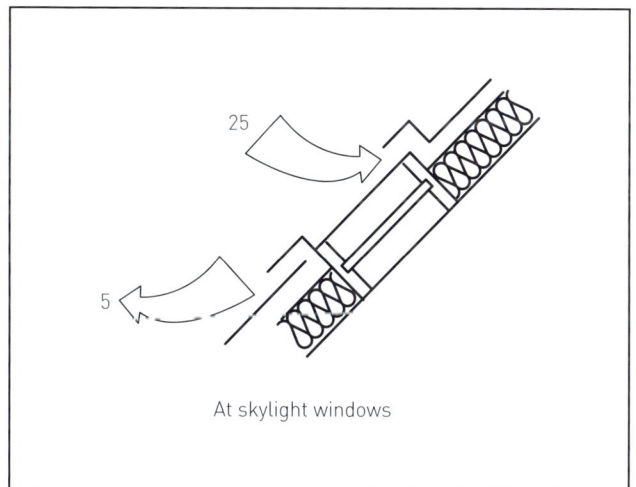

At skylight windows

Fig 10.5

Figs 10.2 - 10.5: Ventilation positions for various configurations

Type LR underlay fully supported on the insulation (no void)

10.2.9 It is not necessary to provide a void beneath the underlay in roofs of this type, but a vapour control layer (VCL) should be provided below the insulation. Where joints are present in the VCL, they should have at least 100mm laps and be well sealed. A VCL is generally 500 gauge (120 micron) polyethylene sheet.

10.2.10 To minimise the risk of interstitial condensation occurring, it is necessary to provide a well-sealed ceiling and ensure that there is sufficient air movement between the underlay and the roof covering to allow moist air to migrate to the atmosphere. For air-open outer coverings no specific provision for batten-space ventilation is required, but for tight outer coverings batten-space ventilation should be provided. In this instance you should make available either:

a. Ventilation openings to the batten space which are equivalent to a continuous slot 25mm wide in the eaves and 5mm wide at the ridge and 25mm at counter battens; or

b. Ventilation openings to the roof void or air void below the underlay at:

1. Low-level equivalent in area to a continuous opening of not less than:

   i. 25mm x length at eaves for pitches of 15 degrees or less.

   ii. 10mm x length at eaves for pitches of more than 15 degrees.

2. High-level equivalent in area to a continuous opening of 5mm in:

   i. Roofs where the pitch exceeds 35 degrees.

   ii. Roofs of any pitch with a span greater than 10m.

   iii. Lean-to and mono-pitch roofs.

Note:
Most traditional unsealed slating and tiling methods are sufficiently air-open.

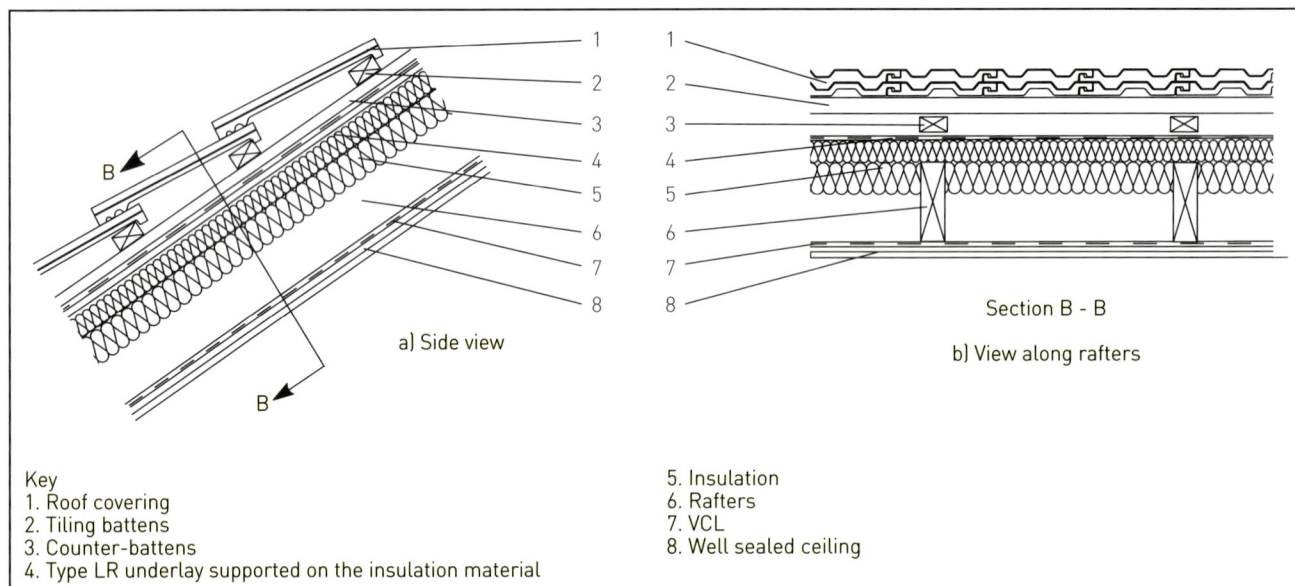

a) Side view

Section B - B

b) View along rafters

Key
1. Roof covering
2. Tiling battens
3. Counter-battens
4. Type LR underlay supported on the insulation material
5. Insulation
6. Rafters
7. VCL
8. Well sealed ceiling

Fig 10.6: Details of roof with LR underlay (no void)

Type LR underlay unsupported (small void)

10.2.11 There are many forms of roof where, for constructional reasons, there is a small void above the insulation. To minimise the risk of interstitial condensation occurring, it is necessary to provide a well-sealed ceiling and ensure that there is sufficient air movement between the underlay and the roof covering to allow moist air to migrate to the atmosphere. For air-open outer coverings no specific provision for batten-space ventilation is required, but for tight outer coverings batten-space ventilation should be provided (as outlined above for Type LR underlay fully supported on insulation with no void).

10.2.12 If the integrity of the roof and wall vapour control layer can be maintained, there is no need to provide ventilation in the void between the insulation and the LR membrane. If there is any doubt about the ability to provide and maintain an effectively sealed vapour control layer, ventilation openings should be provided to each void, at both high and low level, to allow free air movement through the gap between the insulation and the underlay.

a. Low-level openings should be equivalent in area to a continuous opening of not less than 25mm x length at eaves.

b. High-level openings should be equivalent in area to a continuous opening of not less than 5mm x length at the ridge or hips. Where there is no cross communication between each roof slope, 5mm should be provided on both sides of the ridge.

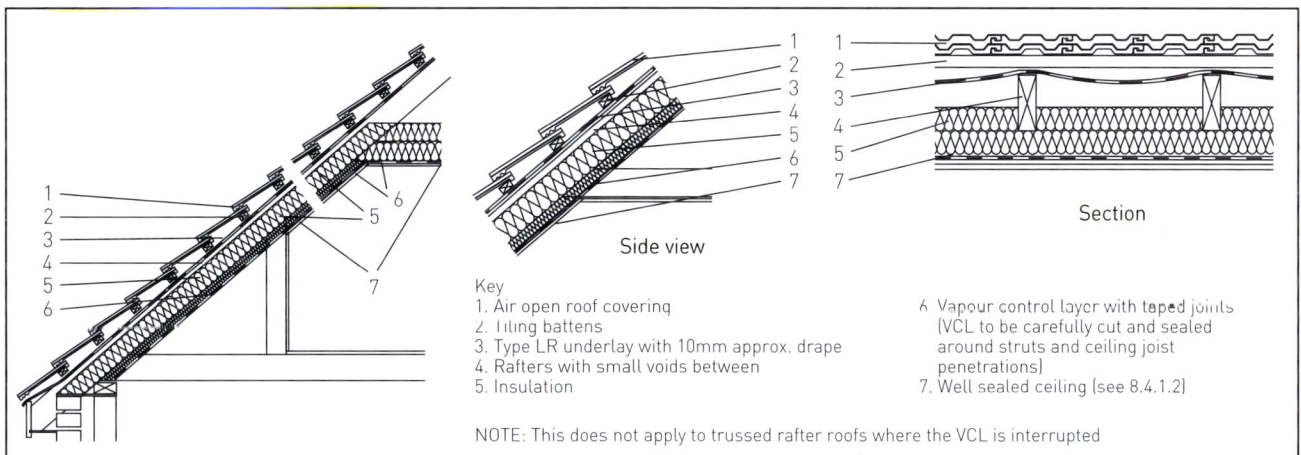

Key
1. Air open roof covering
2. Tiling battens
3. Type LR underlay with 10mm approx. drape
4. Rafters with small voids between
5. Insulation
6. Vapour control layer with taped joints (VCL to be carefully cut and sealed around struts and ceiling joist penetrations)
7. Well sealed ceiling (see 8.4.1.2)

NOTE: This does not apply to trussed rafter roofs where the VCL is interrupted

Side view

Section

Fig 10.7: Details of roof with LR underlay (small void)

10.3 HABITABLE ROOMS

Habitable room with window to outside air

10.3.1   The majority of loft conversions will create at least one habitable room. In normal circumstances the easiest and most cost-effective method of providing ventilation to this space will be provided. This is outlined below.

10.3.2   To comply with the regulations, the habitable room should have a background ventilator capable of at least $8000mm^2$ equivalent floor area. Figure 10.8 shows a selection of background ventilators available.

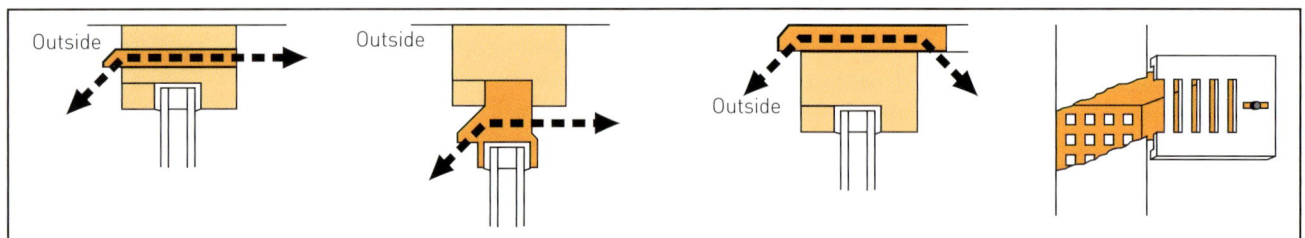

Fig 10.8: Selection of background ventilators

10.3.3   A habitable room also requires purge ventilation, which can be achieved by the use of openable windows and/or external doors. If the room contains more than one openable window, the areas of all the opening parts may be added to achieve the required proportion of the floor area. The required proportion of the floor area is determined by the opening angle of the largest window in the room.

10.3.4   When using a window the requirement will be met if:

- A hinged/pivot window opens 30 degrees or more; or with sliding sash windows, the height x width of the opening part is at least 1/20 of the floor area of the room.

- A hinged or pivot window opens between 15 degrees and 30 degrees; the height x width of the opening part is at least 1/10 of the floor area of the room.

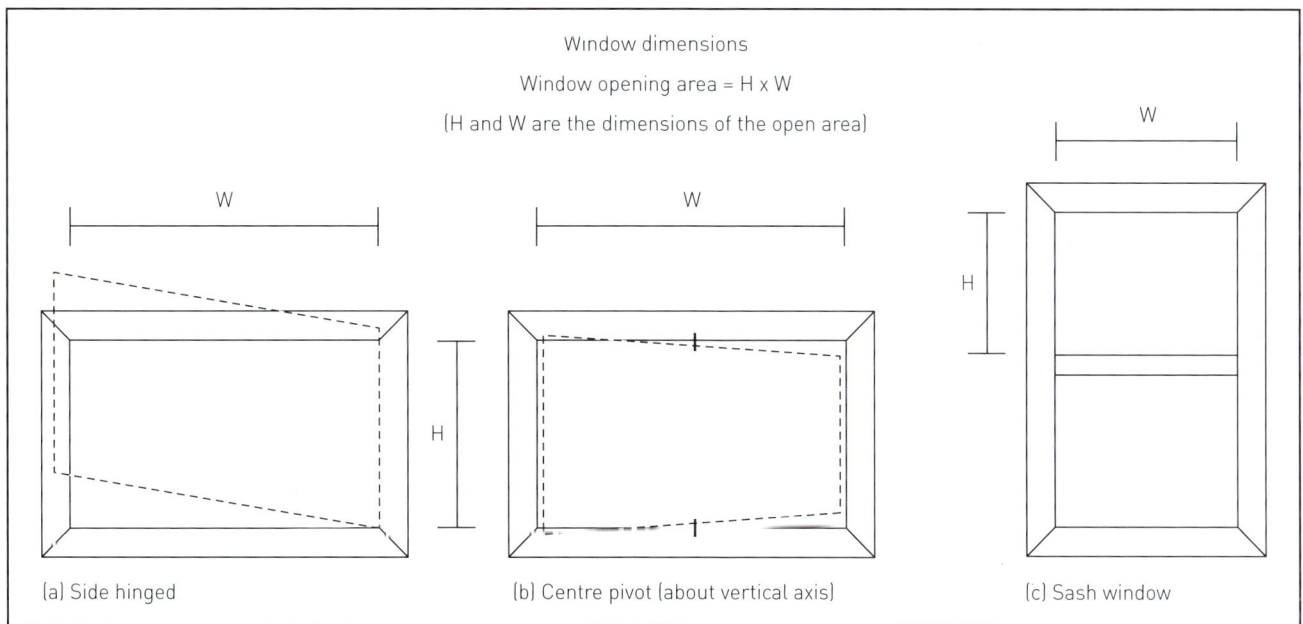

Fig 10.9: Measuring opening dimensions of windows

Window dimensions

Window opening area = H x W

(H and W are the dimensions of the open area)

(a) Side hinged

(b) Centre pivot (about vertical axis)

(c) Sash window

10.3.5 When using an external door (including patio doors) the requirement will be met if:

- For an external door, the height x width of the opening part is at least 1/20 of the floor area of the room.

- The room contains more than one external door and the areas of all opening parts can be added to achieve at least 1/20 of the floor area of the room.

- The room contains a combination of at least one external door and at least one openable window and the areas of all the opening parts can be added to achieve at least 1/20 of the floor area of the room.

Habitable room without window to outside air

10.3.6 There are occasions where more complex arrangements are required, for example where a new first floor is constructed and includes an inner room. (An inner room is defined as a room from which escape is possible only by passing through another room.) In this scenario ventilation to the inner room should be provided using the following guidance.

10.3.7 A habitable room that does not contain an openable window may be ventilated through another habitable room if:

- There is a background ventilator capable of at least 8000mm² equivalent floor area; and

- There are one or more ventilation openings that will achieve the purge ventilation requirements explained under 'habitable room with window to outside air', with a total area based on at least the combined floor of the habitable rooms; and

- There is an area of permanent opening between the two rooms of at least the same area as required for purge ventilation.

Figure 10.10 relates to the above three points.

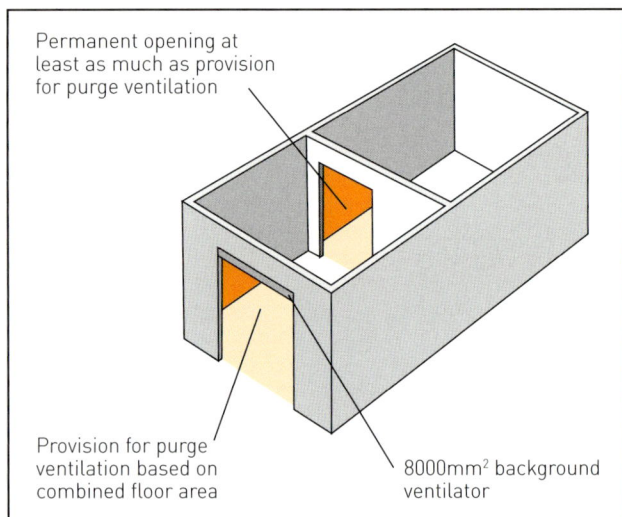

Fig 10.10: Requirements for inner rooms

10.4 BATH/SHOWER OR WC

10.4.1 Where a bath/shower or WC is provided in the converted loft, the same principle exists as for habitable rooms; the easiest, most cost-effective method will be used.

10.4.2 Bath/shower or WCs normally come in two forms:

a. A room that contains a wash-hand basin (WHB) and toilet (WC); or

b. A room that contains a bath and/or shower and a WHB, with or without a WC.

The different scenarios and compliance methods are outlined below.

Wash hand basin and WC; with window to outside air

10.4.3 To comply with the regulations, all that is required is an openable window of any size. In addition, there should be a minimum undercut area of 7600mm^2 in any internal doors between the wet room and the existing building (equivalent to an undercut of 10mm above the floor finish for a standard 760mm width door*).

Wash hand basin and WC; without window to outside air

10.4.4 Where no window is provided to the outside air, a continuous or intermittent mechanical extract fan with a 15-minute overrun with a rate equal to 6 l/s is necessary. In addition, there should be a minimum undercut area of 7600mm^2 in any internal doors between the wet room and the existing building (equivalent to an undercut of 10mm above the floor finish for a standard 760mm width door*).

Bath/shower and wash hand basin with or without WC; with window to outside air

10.4.5 To comply with the regulations, the wet room should have a background ventilator capable of at least 2500mm^2 equivalent floor area and an intermittent mechanical extract fan with a rate equal to 15 l/s or a continuous mechanical extract fan with a rate equal to 8 l/s. In addition, there should be a minimum undercut area of 7600mm^2 in any internal doors between the wet room and the existing building (equivalent to an undercut of 10mm above the floor finish for a standard 760mm width door*).

Note:
Background ventilators and extract fans should be kept a minimum of 0.5m apart.

10.4.6 Figure 10.8 shows a selection of background ventilators available.

*If the floor finish is in place. If the floor finish is not in place, then the undercut should be 20mm.

Bath/shower and wash hand basin with or without WC; without window to outside air

10.4.7 Where no window is provided to the outside air, an intermittent mechanical extract fan with a rate equal to 15 l/s incorporating a 15-minute overrun or a continuous mechanical extract fan with a rate equal to 8 l/s is necessary. In addition, there should be a minimum undercut area of 7600mm^2 in any internal doors between the wet room and the existing building (equivalent to an undercut of 10mm above the floor finish for a standard 760mm width door*).

10.5 ADDITIONAL GUIDANCE

10.5.1 In all but one of the above cases, mechanical fans are provided to extract air from the wet room to the outside. For these fans to work effectively it is essential that they are installed correctly. The following guidance illustrates how this should be carried out:

- Fans and ducting placed in or passing through unheated voids or loft spaces should be insulated to reduce the possibility of condensation forming.

- Where the duct rises vertically it may be necessary to fit a condensation trap in order to prevent backflow of any moisture into the product.

- Horizontal ducting, including ducting in walls, should be arranged to slope slightly downwards away from the fan to prevent backflow of any moisture and should be pulled taught and straight, with as few bends and kinks as possible to minimise resistance.

- Where ducting passes through a fire-stopping wall or fire compartment, the required measures to ensure compliance with Part B of the Building Regulations must be taken.

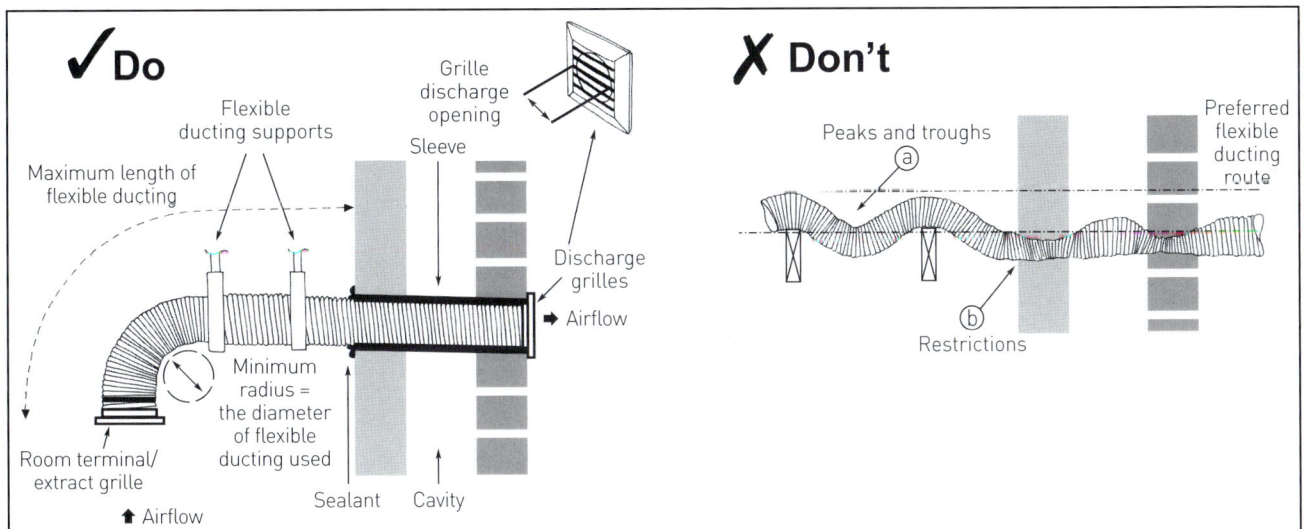

Fig 10.11: Duct installation

10.6 ALTERNATIVE METHODS

10.6.1 There are alternative methods available to provide ventilation to habitable rooms and wet rooms. A brief description of two of these methods is provided below:

1. **Single room heat recovery ventilator:** Heat recovery room ventilators provide a continuous air change, replacing stale moisture-laden unhealthy air with filtered, fresh, warmed air from outside the dwelling. The continuous controlling of relative humidity levels ensures that conditions will not exist in which condensation or mould growth problems can develop and thrive.

2. **Passive stack ventilator:** A passive stack ventilation system uses a duct running from a ceiling to a terminal on the roof to remove any moisture-laden air. It operates by a combination of natural stack effect, i.e. the movement of air due to the difference in temperature between inside and outside temperatures and the effect of wind passing over the roof of the building.

10.6.2 Examples of each product are provided in Figures 10.12 - 10.15.

Fig 10.12: Extractor fan

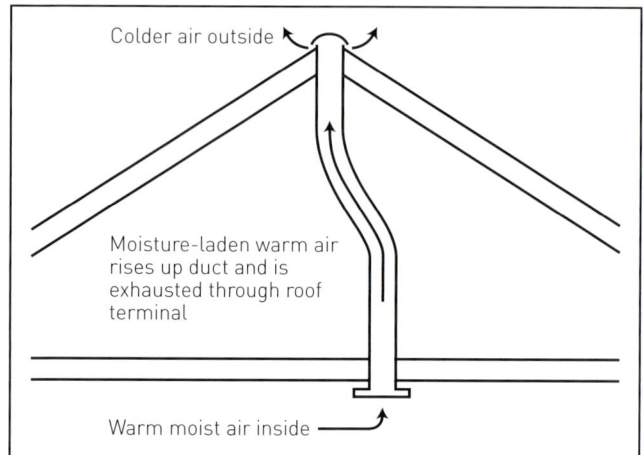

Colder air outside

Moisture-laden warm air rises up duct and is exhausted through roof terminal

Warm moist air inside

Fig 10.13: Passive stack arrangement

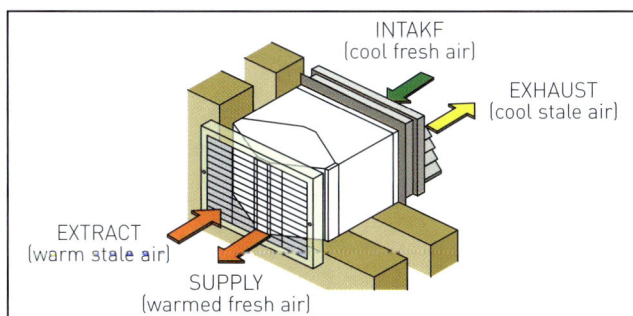

Fig 10.14: Single room heat recovery ventilator

Fig 10.15: Ceiling extractor cover

10.6.3   If you intend to use these alternative methods or would like further guidance and detailed information, refer to Approved Document F of the Building Regulations, 2010 edition and *Domestic Ventilation Compliance Guide* 2010 Edition.

11. HEATING, ELECTRICAL AND LIGHTING

11.0 INTRODUCTION

11.0.1 This chapter provides information on the dwelling's heating system whether gas fired, oil fired, electric or solid fuel. Guidance is given for electrical and lighting installations including the minimum allowable light fittings and socket outlets per room.

11.1 Creating additional space with a loft conversion requires extending your heating system and electrics. This will provide an added strain on them and, depending on their age and performance, they may need replacing or upgrading. The following information is for guidance only.

11.2 HEATING

11.2.1 The four types of heating used within homes are gas-fired, oil-fired, electric and solid fuel. When these heating/water systems are replaced or extended they require the following:

- To achieve an efficiency not less than that recommended in the *Domestic Building Services Compliance Guide*.
  See: **www.planningportal.gov.uk/uploads/ br/domestic_building_compliance_ guide_2010.pdf**.

- To have minimum control requirements as stated in the *Domestic Building Services Compliance Guide* for the particular type of appliance and heat distribution system: **www.planningportal.gov.uk/uploads/ br/domestic_building_compliance_ guide_2010.pdf**.

- To be commissioned and certified by a competent person.

11.2.2 Tables 11.1 and 11.2 provide an example of how to satisfy the requirement for a gas-fired central heating system.

Gas-fired wet heating	New systems	Replacement systems	Supplementary information
1.0 Efficiency	a. The boiler SEDBUK 2005 efficiency should be not less than 90% (or 88% as rated by SEDBUK 2009). b. In existing dwellings, in the exceptional circumstances defined in the CLG *Guide to the condensing boiler installation assessment procedure for dwellings*[1], the boiler SEDBUK 2005 (or SEDBUK 2009) efficiency should be not less than 78% if natural gas-fired, or not less than 80% if LPG-fired. c. The boiler efficiency for heating boilers that are combined with range cookers should be as defined in Section 2.3 *Gas-fired range cookers with integral central heating boiler*.	**Replacements not involving a fuel or energy switch** a. The boiler seasonal efficiency should be as defined for new systems; and b. not worse than two percentage points lower than the seasonal efficiency of the controlled service being replaced. If the efficiency of the system or appliance to be replaced is not known, efficiency values may be taken from Table 4a or 4b of SAP 2009. **Replacements involving fuel or energy switch** a. If the new heating system or heat generating appliance uses a different fuel, the efficiency of the new service should be multiplied by the ratio of the CO_2 emission factor of the fuel used in the service being replaced to that used in the new service before making the checks in a. and b. above. The CO_2 emission factors should be taken from Table 12 of SAP 2009.	*The SEDBUK method for determining efficiency has been revised in SAP 2009. SEDBUK 2009 values are different from SEDBUK 2005. The Boiler Efficiency Database at www.sedbuk. com gives both, together with separate winter and summer (i.e. hot water) efficiencies for boilers that are used by SAP 2009 to calculate the carbon dioxide emission rate for dwellings. If the SEDBUK efficiency given in a boiler manufacturer's literature does not give a date, it should be assumed to be the SEDBUK 2005 value.* *The CLG "Guide to the condensing boiler installation assessment procedure for dwellings" sets out the approved procedure for establishing the exceptional circumstances in which boilers may be of the non-condensing type.* *Where condensing boilers are fitted, systems should be designed so as to provide low primary system return temperatures, preferably less than 55 degC, which maximise condensing operation. Low temperature heat emitters such as underfloor heating and weather compensation are examples of techniques which provide low return water temperatures.*
2.0 System circulation	a. Space heating systems and domestic hot water primary circuits should have fully pumped circulation. b. If the boiler manufacturer's instructions advise installation of a bypass, an automatic bypass valve should be provided and the manufacturer's instructions on minimum pipe length followed.	a. As for **new systems**. b. When boilers are replaced, existing systems with semi-gravity circulation should be converted to fully pumped circulation.	
3.0 Hot water storage	a. Vented copper hot water storage cylinders should comply with the heat loss and heat exchanger requirements of BS 1566:2002 Part 1. b. Copper hot water storage combination units should comply with BS 3198:1981. c. Primary storage systems should meet the insulation requirements of the Hot Water Association *Performance specification for thermal stores*. d. Unvented hot water storage system products should comply with BS EN 12897: 2006 or an equivalent standard as set by an accredited test body such as the British Board of Agrément, the Water Research Council, or KIWA. e. The standing heat loss for all hot water storage vessels in a, b, c and d above should not exceed $Q = 1.15 \times (0.2+0.051V^{2/3})$ kWh/day, where V is the volume of the cylinder.	a. As for **new systems**, but b. for replacement copper vented cylinders and combination units, the standing loss should not exceed $Q = 1.28 \times (0.2+0.051V^{2/3})$ kWh/day, where V is the volume of the cylinder.	*If a vented cylinder is made from an alternative material to copper then the heat loss and heat exchange characteristics should be tested in accordance with BS EN 12897:2006. The HWA thermal storage specification is available for free download from www.hotwater.org.uk.* **British Standards** *BS 1566: 2002 "Copper indirect cylinders for domestic purposes. Open vented copper cylinders. Requirements and test methods".* *BS EN 12897 "Water supply. Specification for indirectly heated unvented (closed) storage water heaters".* *BS 3198 "Copper hot water storage combination units for domestic purposes".*

Table 11.1: Recommended minimum standards for efficiency, system circulation, hot water storage, system preparation and commissioning for gas-fired wet central heating systems
Source: Domestic Building Services Compliance Guide 2010 Edition

1. *Guide to the condensing boiler installation assessment procedure for dwellings*, CLG, 2005. Available from www.planningportal.gov.uk/approveddocuments

Gas-fired wet heating	New systems	Replacement systems	Supplementary information
3.0 Hot water storage (*continued*)	f. All hot water vessels should carry a label with the following information: i. type of vessel (vented, unvented, combination unit or thermal store); ii. nominal capacity in litres; iii. standing heat loss in kWh/day; iv. heat exchanger performance in kW; v. reference to product compliance with relevant standard (e.g. BS 1566, BS 12897) and logos of accreditation bodies as required. For labelling requirements for other heat inputs, see relevant sections (e.g. Section 11 for solar).		
4.0 System preparation and water treatment	a. Central heating systems should be thoroughly cleaned and flushed out before installing a new boiler. b. During final filling of the system, a chemical water treatment inhibitor meeting the manufacturer's specification or other appropriate standard should be added to the primary circuit to control corrosion and the formation of scale and sludge. c. Installers should also refer to the boiler manufacturer's installation instructions for appropriate treatment products and special requirements for individual boiler models. d. Where the mains total water hardness exceeds 200 parts per million, and if required by the manufacturer, provision should be made to treat the feed water to water heaters and the hot water circuit of combination boilers to reduce the rate of accumulation of limescale. e. For solar thermal systems, see Section 11.	a. As for *new systems*.	*Inhibitors should as a minimum be BuildCert approved. Limescale can be controlled by the use of chemical limescale inhibitors, combined corrosion and limescale inhibitors, polyphosphate dosing, electrolytic scale reducers or water softeners.* *The relevant standard for water treatment is BS 7593:2006 "Code of practice for treatment of water in domestic hot water central heating systems".* *BS 7593 notes that soft water has an increased potential for corrosion, and this may influence the choice of corrosion inhibitor. Where water is artificially softened, it is advisable to feed unsoftened water not only to drinking water taps, but also to the boiler primary circuit. In soft water areas, the boiler manufacturer should be consulted for advice.* *In order to avoid loss and consequent replacement of circulating fluid and water treatment when removing radiators for service or maintenance, it is advisable to install radiator valves that can isolate not only the heating circuit but also seal off the radiators.*
5.0 Commissioning	a. On completion of the installation of a boiler or hot water storage system, together with associated equipment such as pipework, pumps and controls, the equipment should be commissioned in accordance with the manufacturer's instructions. These instructions will be specific to the particular boiler or hot water storage system. b. The installer should give a full explanation of the system and its operation to the user, including the manufacturer's User Manual where provided.	a. As for *new systems*.	***The Benchmark System*** *The Benchmark Commissioning Checklist can be used to show that commissioning has been carried out satisfactorily. Benchmark licenceholders provide a checklist with the appliance for completion by the persons commissioning the system so that they can record that all the checks have been made and the results show efficient operation of the equipment in compliance with building regulations. The Benchmark checklist should be provided to the builder, or the householder in the case of work in existing dwellings, an appointed agent, or the end user.* *A Benchmark Commissioning Checklist will be included in all HHIC gas boiler manufacturer members' installation manuals to help installers record information about the installation in order to assist with servicing and repairs. For example, details of system cleaners and inhibitors can be recorded.* *Only manufacturing companies who hold a Benchmark licence will be eligible to use the Benchmark logo and the approved log book wording and layout. (Benchmark is registered as a European Collective Mark by the Heating and Hot Water Industry Council and the content is copyright.)*

Table 11.1: Recommended minimum standards for efficiency, system circulation, hot water storage, system preparation and commissioning for gas-fired wet central heating systems

Source: Domestic Building Services Compliance Guide 2010 Edition

Gas-fired wet heating	New systems	Replacement systems
1.0 Boiler interlock	a. Boiler-based systems should have a boiler control interlock in which controls are wired so that when there is no demand for either space heating or hot water, the boiler and pump are switched off. b. The use of thermostatic radiator valves (TRVs) alone does not provide interlock.	a. As for *new systems*.
2.0 Space heating zones	a. Dwellings with a total usable floor area up to 150m² should be divided into at least two space heating zones with independent temperature control, one of which is assigned to the living area. b. Dwellings with a total usable floor area greater than 150m² should be provided with at least two space heating zones, each having separate timing and temperature controls. c. For single-storey open-plan dwellings in which the living area is greater than 70% of the total floor area, sub-zoning of temperature control is not appropriate.	a. As for *new systems*.
3.0 Water heating zones	a. All dwellings should have a separate hot water zone in addition to space heating zones. b. A separate hot water zone is not required if the hot water is produced instantaneously, such as with a combination boiler.	a. As for *new systems*.
4.0 Time control of space and water heating	a. Time control of space and water heating should be provided by: i. a full programmer with separate timing to each circuit; or ii. two or more separate timers providing timing control to each circuit; or iii. programmable room thermostat(s) to the heating circuit(s), with separate timing of the hot water circuit. b. For dwellings with a total usable floor area greater than 150m², timing of the separate space heating zones can be achieved by: i. multiple heating zone programmers; or ii. a single multi-channel programmer; or iii. programmable room thermostats; or iv. separate timers to each circuit; or v. a combination of (iii) and (iv) above. c. Where the hot water is produced instantaneously, such as with a combination boiler, time control is only required for space heating zones.	a. As for *new systems* unless only the hot water cylinder is being replaced and separate time control for the hot water circuit is not present. In this case it is acceptable to have a single timing control for both space heating and hot water.
5.0 Temperature control of space heating	a. Separate temperature control of zones within the dwelling should be provided using: i. room thermostats or programmable room thermostats in all zones; and ii. individual radiator controls such as thermostatic radiator valves (TRVs) on all radiators other than in reference rooms (with a thermostat) and bathrooms.	a. As for *new systems*.*
6.0 Temperature control of domestic hot water	a. Domestic hot water systems should be provided with a cylinder thermostat and a zone valve or three-port valve to control the temperature of stored hot water. b. In dwellings with a total usable floor area greater than 150m² it would be reasonable to provide more than one hot water circuit, each with separate timing and temperature controls. This can be achieved by: i. multiple heating zone programmers; or ii. a single multi-channel programmer; or iii separate timers to each circuit. c. Non-electric hot water controllers should not be used. Also, in some circumstances, such as with thermal stores, a zone valve is not appropriate; a second pump could be substituted for the zone valve.	a. As for *new systems* for planned replacement of hot water cylinders on all fully pumped installations, and on gravity circulation installations. b. In exceptional circumstances, such as emergency replacement or where the cylinder or installation is of a type that precludes the fitting of wired controls, either a wireless or thermomechanical hot water cylinder thermostat would be acceptable.

Supplementary information

More details on control systems can be found in manufacturers' literature and on The Association of Controls Manufacturers (TACMA) website at www.heatingcontrols.org.uk. Controls may be provided by any boiler management control system that meets the specified zoning, timing and temperature and boiler interlock control requirements.
*When an individual system component – such as the boiler or a room thermostat – is being replaced, it is not necessary to upgrade the whole system. However, while not essential for compliance with building regulations, in the case of a boiler replacement, because the system has to be drained down, it would be good practice to install thermostatic radiator valves (or equivalent) on all radiators other than in the room with the main thermostat, provided the radiators are suitable and pipework does not need to be altered.

Table 11.2 Recommended minimum standards for control of gas-fired wet central heating systems
Source: Domestic Building Services Compliance Guide 2010 Edition

Note: The Domestic Building Services Compliance Guide covers other systems as well as the four mentioned above, including:

- Under-floor heating systems.

- Heat pump systems.

- Solar water heating.

- Individual domestic (micro) combined heat and power.

11.2.3   When extending the heating system, modern practices have seen copper pipework being replaced with plastic. There is no problem with this practice; however, it is advisable to make this pipework identifiable so that when DIY work is carried out it does not become damaged. A simple way to achieve this is to provide metallic tape either directly behind or to the side of the plastic pipes. It is currently not advisable to 'wrap' the pipework with the tape as the adhesive may, over time, have an adverse effect on the pipe.

Fig 11.1: Positions for metallic tape by plastic pipes

Fig 11.2: Positions for metallic tape by plastic pipes

11.2.4   Depending on the age of the property, hot water storage cylinders and cold water storage cisterns may be present in the roof space. In general these will have to be relocated if the system is not upgraded to accommodate the conversion, and in such cases the following guidance should be followed:

11.2.5   Hot water storage:

- Cylinders should be fully supported in accordance with manufacturer's recommendations.

- Cylinders should be installed vertically, unless designed otherwise.

- Cylinders should remain accessible.

- Cylinders should be insulated.

11.2.6   Cold water storage:

- Where the water tank is supported by roof trusses, the load should be transferred to the node points of the trussed rafter and spread over the trussed rafters in accordance with BS 5268-3. This is illustrated in Figures 11.3 - 11.6.

- To prevent the cistern bottom becoming deformed use a suitable material as a support platform, e.g. softwood boarding, marine plywood, chipboard Type P5 to BS EN 312 or oriented strand board Type OSB3 to BS EN 300 laid with stronger axis at right angles to bearers, as shown here.

- Water tanks should remain accessible with boarding provided to the cistern location. An area of 1m² of boarding should be provided next to cisterns to permit routine maintenance; care should be taken to ensure that the ceiling insulation is not compressed.

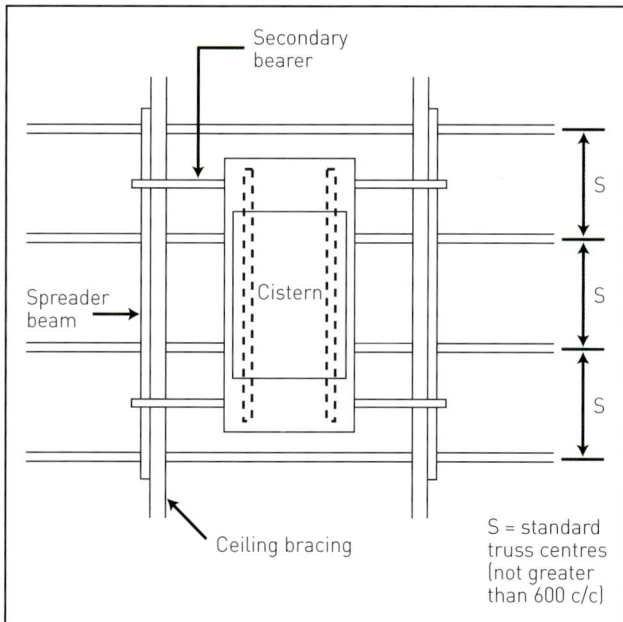

Fig 11.4: Tank capacity not more than 230 litres supported on three trusses

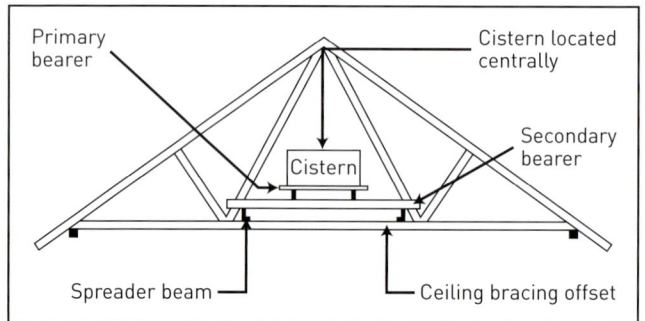

Fig 11.5: Tank position in the roof

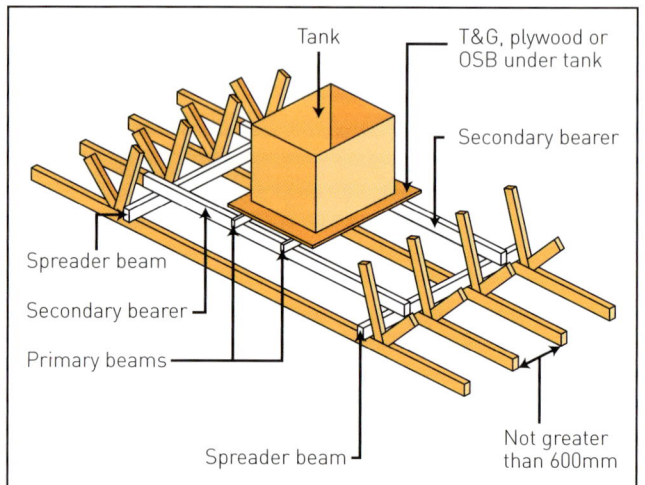

Fig 11.3: Tank capacity not more than 300 litres supported on four trusses

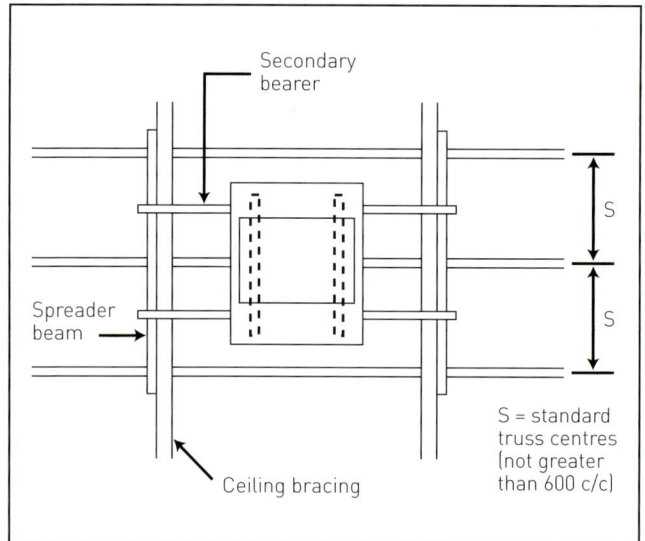

Fig 11.6: Materials for supporting the tank

Thermal insulation of water services

11.2.7   Water services in unheated spaces, including cisterns and vent pipes, should be insulated against freezing:

- Insulation should not be placed beneath a cold water tank where it can benefit from heat from below.

- Raised tanks should be insulated on all sides in an unheated roof space.

- Where lapping the loft insulation with the tank insulation is not possible, the underside of the tank should be insulated and the ceiling insulation should be continuous below the tank while maintaining an air gap between these two layers of at least 200mm.

- All bends and junctions should be fully insulated.

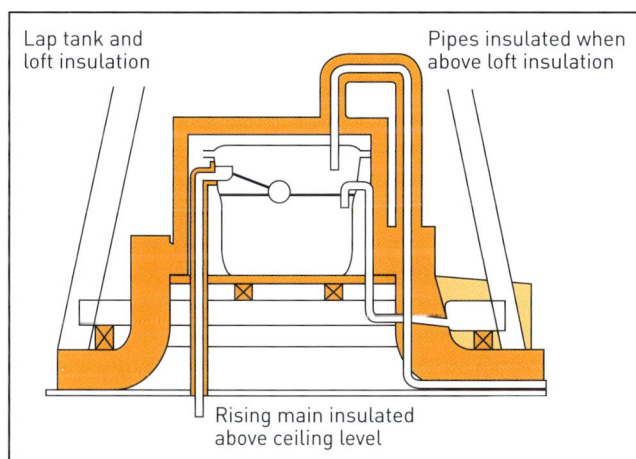

Fig 11.7: Insulating pipes and tanks

11.2.8   Consideration needs to be given to existing flue outlets that terminate through the roof space. The outlet from a flue should be above the roof of a building in a position where the products of combustion can discharge freely and also, if a balanced flue, the intake of air, while not presenting a fire hazard, whatever the wind conditions. The main concern here is the addition of dormer windows, roof lights and other openings. Where this situation occurs the following guidance should be followed:

- Where a window is provided in the roof space near the outlet for a gas appliance, the flue should not penetrate the shaded area shown on the left in Figure 11.8.

- Where a window is provided in the roof space within 2.3m of a flue outlet for a solid fuel appliance, the flue should terminate at least 1m above the highest point of the opening, as shown on the right in Figure 11.8.

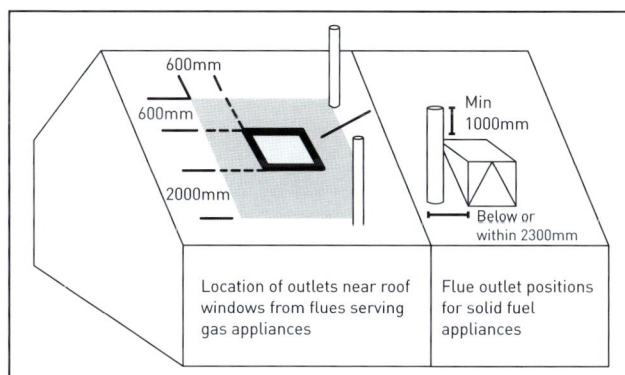

Fig 11.8: Positioning flues on a roof

11.3 ELECTRICAL

11.3.1 Converting the loft space will require the electrical circuit to be extended to provide power to the new usable space. This will require all electrical installations to comply with BS 7671 Requirements for electrical installations or equivalent standards to ensure that they are designed, suitably enclosed and separated by appropriate distances to provide mechanical and thermal protection, so that they afford appropriate protection for persons against the risk of electric shock, burn or fire injuries.

11.3.2 Electrical installations should be inspected and tested as necessary and appropriate during and at the end of installation before they are taken into service, to verify that they are safe to use, maintain and alter, and that they comply with Approved Document P of the Building Regulations and with any other relevant parts of the Building Regulations.

11.3.3 Approved Document P of the Building Regulations categorises electrical work as notifiable or non-notifiable for the purposes of Building Control. Non-notifiable work should still be carried out in accordance with BS 7671:2008 or alternative standard. For guidance, Tables 11.3 and 11.4 and the additional notes that follow have been provided and give general rules for determining whether or not electrical installation work is notifiable.

Work consisting of:
Replacing any fixed electrical equipment (for example, socket-outlets, control switches and ceiling roses) which does not include the provision of any new fixed cabling.
Replacing the cable for a single circuit only, where damaged, for example, by fire, rodent or impact[a]
Re-fixing or replacing the enclosures of existing installation components[b]
Providing mechanical protection to existing fixed installations[c]
Installing or upgrading main or supplementary equipotential bonding[d]

Work that is not in a kitchen or special location and does not involve a special installation[e] and consists of:
Adding lighting points (light fittings and switches) to an existing circuit[f]
Adding socket-outlets and fused spurs to an existing ring or radial circuit[f]

Work not in a special location, on:
Telephone or extra-low voltage wiring and equipment for the purposes of communications, information technology, signalling, control and similar purposes.
Prefabricated equipment sets and associated flexible leads with integral plug and socket connections.

Notes:
(a) On condition that the replacement cable has the same current-carrying capacity and follows the same route.
(b) If the circuit's protective measures are unaffected.
(c) If the circuit's protective measures and current-carrying capacity of conductors are unaffected by increased thermal insulation.
(d) Such work will need to comply with other applicable legislation, such as the Gas Safety (Installation and Use) Regulations.
(e) Special locations and installations are listed in Table 2.
(f) Only if the existing circuit protective device is suitable and provides protection for the modified circuit, and other relevant safety provisions are satisfactory.

Table 11.3: Work that need not be notified to Building Control Bodies Source: Approved Document P

Special locations
Locations containing a bath tub or shower basin
Swimming pools or paddling pools
Hot air saunas

Special installations
Electric floor or ceiling heating systems
Garden lighting or power installations
Solar photovoltaic (PV) power supply systems
Small scale generators such as microCHP units
Extra-low voltage lighting installations, other than pre-assembled, CE-marked lighting sets.

Notes:
(a) See IEE Guidance Note 7 which gives more guidance on achieving safe installations where risks to people are greater.

Table 11.4: Definition of special locations and installations Source: Approved Document P

Note 1:
Notifiable jobs include new circuits back to the consumer unit and extensions to circuits in kitchens and special locations (bathrooms etc.) and associated with special locations (garden lighting and power installations etc.).

Note 2:
Replacement, repair and maintenance jobs are generally not notifiable, even if carried out in a kitchen or special location or associated with a special installation.

Note 3:
Consumer unit replacements are, however, notifiable.

Note 4:
In large bathrooms, the location containing a bath or shower is defined by the walls of the bathroom.

Note 5:
Conservatories and attached garages are not special locations. Work in them is therefore not notifiable unless it involves the installation of a new circuit or the extension of a circuit in a kitchen or special location or associated with a special installation.

Note 6:
Detached garages and sheds are not special locations. Work within them is notifiable only if it involves new outdoor wiring.

Note 7:
Outdoor lighting and power installations are special installations. Any new work in, for example, the garden or that involves crossing the garden is notifiable.

Note 8:
The installation of fixed equipment is within the scope of Part P, even where the final connection is by a 13A plug and socket. However, work is notifiable only if it involves fixed wiring and the installation of a new circuit or the extension of a circuit in a kitchen or special location or associated with a special installation.

Note 9:
The installation of equipment attached to the outside wall of a house (for example, security lighting) is not notifiable provided that there are no exposed outdoor connections and the work does not involve the installation of a new circuit or the extension of a circuit in a kitchen or special location or associated with a special installation.

Note 10:
The installation of a socket outlet on an external wall is notifiable, since the socket outlet is an outdoor connector that could be connected to cables that cross the garden and requires RCD protection.

Note 11:
The installation of prefabricated, modular systems (for example, kitchen lighting systems and armoured garden cabling) linked by plug and socket connectors is not notifiable, provided that products are CE-marked and that any final connections in kitchens and special locations are made to existing connection units or points (possibly a 13A socket outlet).

Note 12:
Work to connect an electric gate or garage door to an existing isolator is not notifiable, but installation of the circuit up to the isolator is.

Note 13:
The fitting and replacement of cookers and electric showers is not notifiable unless a new circuit is needed.

Note 14:
New central heating control wiring installations are notifiable even where work in kitchens and bathrooms is avoided.

11.3.4 If notifiable work, the installation should be in accordance with one of the following options:

    a. **Registered with an electrical self-certification scheme.** In these cases the person is responsible for ensuring compliance with BS 7671:2008 or an equivalent standard and all relevant Building Regulations requirements and should complete and provide a copy of the BS 7671 installation certificates to the homeowner.

    b. **Not registered but qualified to carry out inspection and testing and completing the appropriate BS 7671 installation certificates.** In this instance the installer should notify the Building Control Body (BCB) prior to commencement of work. They can then inspect, test and complete the appropriate BS 7671 installation certificate. A copy of this certificate should be given to the BCB. The BCB will then decide whether to request additional testing of the electrical work. They may ask for evidence that installers are qualified.

11.3.5 **Neither of the above, e.g. DIYers.** The BCB should be notified prior to commencement of the electrical work. The BCB will decide on the level of inspection and testing required and will either carry out the inspection and testing themselves or through an independent body, with no additional cost to the homeowner.

Note:
A BS 7671 certificate will not be issued with this option as they can only be issued by those carrying out the work.

11.3.6 The guidance that follows will assist when electrical works are being installed.

11.3.7 All socket outlets should be protected by a residual current device (RCD). To meet with this regulation, all power circuits supplying sockets should be protected by a residual current device to BS EN 61008. Other areas where RCD protection is required include:

- A cable installed in a wall or partition that includes metal parts and is not protected by steel conduit or trunking.

- A cable installed in a wall or partition at a depth of less than 50mm and not enclosed in steel conduit.

11.3.8 If installing a kitchen, a minimum 30A electricity supply, suitably switched and terminated, should be provided to the cooker space. If a cooker panel is provided it should be located to the side of the cooker space.

11.3.9 Rooms should be provided with no fewer than the number of 13A outlets shown in Table 30. Dual outlets count as two.

Room	Outlets	Notes
Kitchen/utility	8	Where homes have separate areas, the kitchen should have a minimum of 4 outlets, and the utility room 4. Where appliances are provided, at least 3 outlets should be free for general use.
Dining room	4	
Living or family room	8	At least 2 outlets should be near the TV aerial outlet.
Bedrooms	6 (4)	6 for main bedroom. 4 for other bedrooms.
Landing	2	
Hall	2	

Table 11.5: Guidance on numbers of 13A outlets
Source: NHBC

11.3.10 Where a gas appliance is installed and requires an electricity supply, a suitable fixed spur or socket outlet should be provided.

11.3.11 The location of electric cables will need consideration. Cables without special protection, such as an earthed metal conduit, should be positioned as follows (see also paragraph 11.3.5):

- Vertically from the outlet or switch being served; or

- Horizontally from the outlet or switch being served; or

- Within the shaded zone in Figure 11.9; or

- Not less than 50mm from the surface of a wall; or

- Not less than 50mm from the top or bottom of a timber joist or batten in a floor or ceiling.

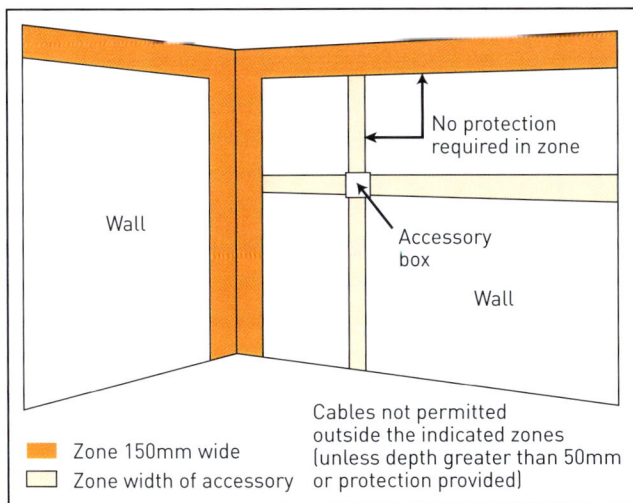

Fig 11.9: Location of electric cables

Conductor	Colour
Protective conductor	Green-and-yellow
Neutral	Blue
Phase of single phase circuit	Brown
Phase 1 of 3 phase circuit	Brown
Phase 2 of 3 phase circuit	Black
Phase 3 of 3 phase circuit	Grey

Table 11.6: Identification of conductors in ac power and light circuits
Source: Approved Document P

Examples of cable colours

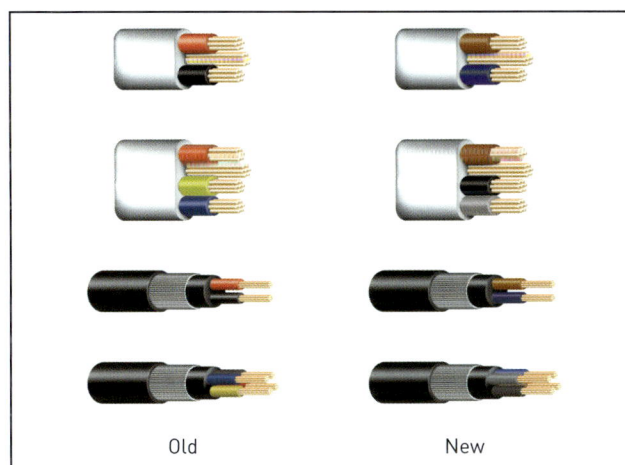

Fig 11.10: Examples of cable colours

11.3.12 Where the position of switches or sockets can be determined from the reverse side of the wall or partition, the zone on one side of the wall or partition also extends to the reverse side.

11.3.13 Cables should not be placed under, against or within thermal insulation, unless they have been appropriately sized. For further information and guidance, refer to the BRE Report 'Thermal insulations: avoiding the risks'.

11.3.14 PVC-covered cables should not be in contact with polystyrene insulation.

11.3.15 Since 31 March 2006 new (harmonised) cable core colours only are permitted to be used. For single-phase installations in domestic premises the new colours are the same as those for flexible cables to appliances, namely green-and-yellow, blue and brown for the protective, neutral and phase conductors respectively.

11.3.16 Table 11.6 and Figure 11.10 are provided for reference and to aid identification. Table 11.6 gives the new cable core colours for ac power circuits and Figure 11.10 shows examples of flat and armoured single-phase and three-phase ac power cables with the old and the new harmonised colours.

11.3.17 Wall-mounted socket outlets, switches and consumer units should be located so that they are easily reachable. The Building Regulations are only enforceable on new-build dwellings; however, good practice would be to follow Figure 11.11. Accessible consumer units should comply with BS EN 60439-3.

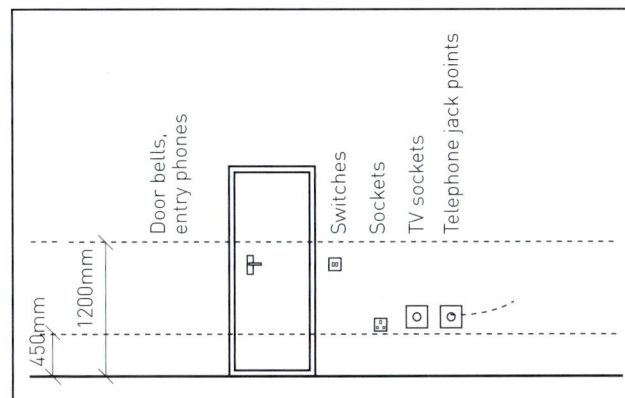

Fig 11.11: Heights of switches, sockets, etc.

11.4 LIGHTING

11.4.1 When extending a dwelling, efficient electric lighting should be provided in accordance with the table 11.7 below.

Lighting	New and replacement systems	Supplementary information
Fixed internal lighting	a. In the areas affected by the building work, provide low energy **light fittings** (fixed lights or lighting units) that number not less than three per four of all the **light fittings** in the main dwelling spaces of those areas (excluding infrequently accessed spaces used for storage, such as cupboards and wardrobes). b. Low energy **light fittings** should have lamps with a luminous efficacy greater than 45 lamp lumens per circuit-watt and a total output greater than 400 lamp lumens. c. **Light fittings** whose supplied power is less than 5 circuit-watts are excluded from the overall count of the total number of light fittings.	**Light fittings** may be either: • dedicated fittings which will have separate control gear and will take only low energy lamps (e.g. pin based fluorescent or compact fluorescent lamps); or • standard fittings supplied with low energy lamps with integrated control gear (e.g. bayonet or Edison screw base compact fluorescent lamps). **Light fittings** with GLS tungsten filament lamps or tungsten halogen lamps would not meet the standard. The Energy Saving Trust publication GIL 20, "Low energy domestic lighting", gives guidance on identifying suitable locations for fixed energy efficient lighting.

Fixed external lighting	Where fixed external lighting is installed, provide **light fittings** with the following characteristics:
	a. Either:
	  i. lamp capacity not greater than 100 lamp-watts per light fitting; and
	  ii. all lamps automatically controlled so as to switch off after the area lit by the fitting becomes unoccupied; and
	  iii. all lamps automatically controlled so as to switch off when daylight is sufficient.
	b. Or
	  i. lamp efficacy greater than 45 lumens per circuit-watt; and
	  ii. all lamps automatically controlled so as to switch off when daylight is sufficient; and
	  iii. light fittings controllable manually by occupants.	

British Standards BS EN 15193:2007 "Energy performance of buildings – Energy requirements for lighting". **Other related documents** E80 "Domestic lighting innovations", Energy Efficiency Best Practice in Housing. CE61 "Energy efficient lighting – guidance for installers and specifiers", Energy Saving Trust. EP84 "Housing for people with sight loss", Thomas Pocklington Trust Design Guide. IP412 "Making the most of your sight: Improve the lighting in your home", RNIB and Thomas Pocklington Trust. **Energy Saving Trust best practice standards** The Energy Saving Trust sets best practice "Energy Saving Recommended (ESR)" standards for lamps that cover not only energy efficiency, but also other aspects of quality including colour rendering, warm-up time, product life and power factor. It is advisable to install only ESR low energy lamps in dwellings.		

Table 11.7: Recommended minimum standards for fixed internal and external lighting

Source: Domestic Building Services Compliance Guide 2010 Edition

11.4.2   It is not just energy-efficiency that you need to be aware of when selecting light fittings. The rise of the downlighter has caused many a headache for the Building Control officer; however, following the simple guidance given here should aid compliance.

11.4.3   The detail in Figure 11.12 prevents:

- The loss of heat and the movement of water vapour from the rooms below into the roof space.

- The downlighter from becoming damaged through overheating where insulation has been laid directly over the lamp fitting.

Note:
Sealed downlighters are available on the market. Where these are not used the detail in Figure 11.12 should be provided through the use of hoods or boxing.

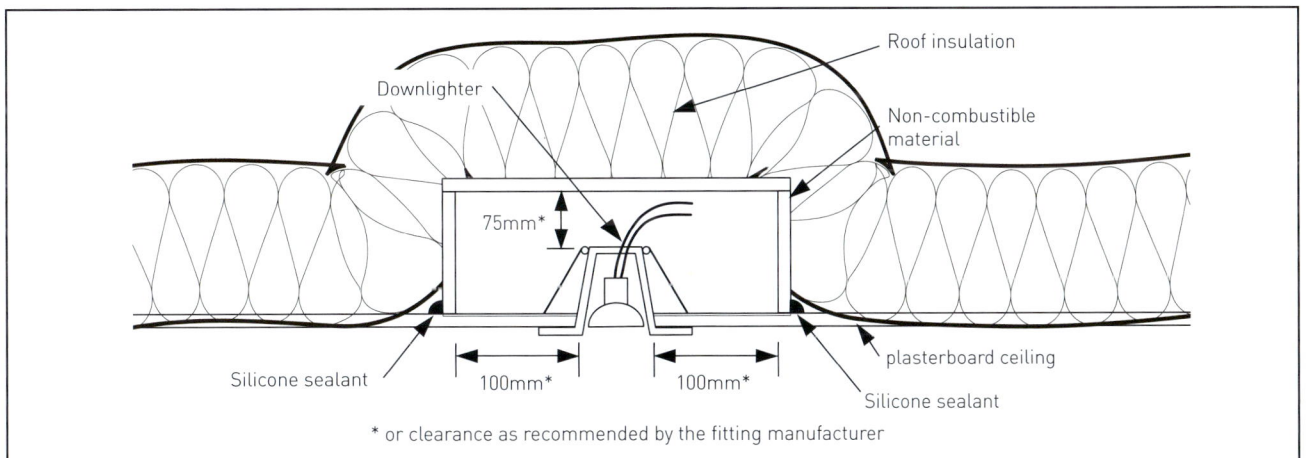

Fig 11.12: Detailing downlighters when not sealed

12. SUSTAINABILITY

12.0 INTRODUCTION

12.0.1 This chapter provides advice and directs the reader to tools and guidance currently available that offers support to those wishing to improve the energy efficiency of their existing home and contribute to a low carbon economy. It also mentions biodiversity and other sustainability issues.

12.1 Although many of the environmental and economic aspects of sustainability have already been covered, it is useful to briefly summarise all the relevant issues that people generally understand by sustainability:

- Energy efficiency

- Energy generation.

- Water efficiency.

- Surface water management.

- Materials selection – both efficient use of materials through good design, and/or choosing lower-impact materials.

- Waste reduction during construction and waste management during house occupation.

- Health and well-being – such as indoor air quality, sound insulation, daylighting.

- Biodiversity and ecology – such as improving bird and bat habitat with green roofs or nest boxes.

12.2 Our homes account for around 27% of the UK's carbon emissions, a major cause of climate change. Many consumers want to increase their energy efficiency and contribute to a low carbon economy. The information provided in this chapter offers an insight into how this can be achieved and a selection of the methods available.

12.3 ENERGY PERFORMANCE CERTIFICATES

12.3.1 To reduce your home's energy usage it is advisable to obtain an Energy Performance Certificate (EPC). This certificate gives homeowners, tenants and buyers information on the energy efficiency of their property. It gives the building a standard energy and carbon emission efficiency grade from A to G, where A is the most efficient.

12.3.2 EPCs are measured using the same calculations for all homes, so you can compare the energy efficiency of different properties. Part of the EPC is a report which will list the potential rating that your home could achieve if you made the recommended changes. The report lists:

- Suggested improvements (such as fitting loft insulation).

- Approximate cost.

- Possible cost savings per year if the improvements are made.

- How this would change the energy and carbon emission rating of the property.

12.3.3 You can use this information to improve energy performance in your home, which will cut your fuel bills and at the same time help cut carbon emissions.

12.3.4 If you decide to act on the recommendations contained in the recommendation report, you could make your property more attractive for sale or rent by making it more energy efficient. An example of pages from an EPC has been provided in Figures 12.1 and 12.2.

Energy Performance Certificate

S·A·P
© Crown copyright 2005

17 Any Street,
Any Town,
County,
YY3 5XX

Dwelling type:	Detached house
Date of assessment:	02 February 2007
Date of certificate:	[dd mmmm yyyy]
Reference number:	0000-0000-0000-0000-0000
Total floor area:	166 m²

This home's performance is rated in terms of the energy use per square metre of floor area, energy efficiency based on fuel costs and environmental impact based on carbon dioxide (CO_2) emissions.

Energy Efficiency Rating

Current: 37
Potential: 73

Very energy efficient - lower running costs
(92-100) A
(81-91) B
(69-80) C
(55-68) D
(39-54) E
(21-38) F
(1-20) G
Not energy efficient - higher running costs

England & Wales — EU Directive 2002/91/EC

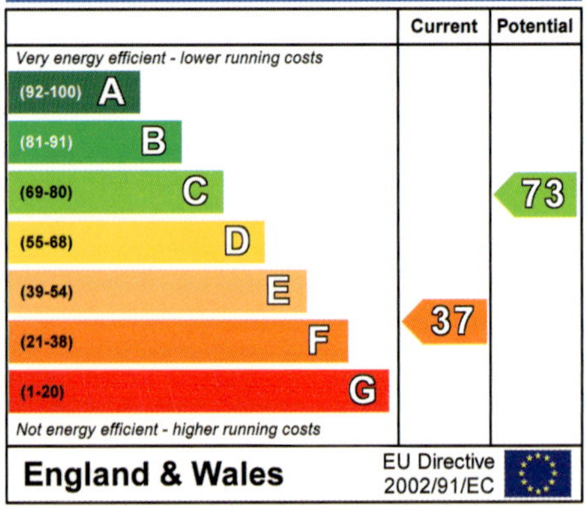

The energy efficiency rating is a measure of the overall efficiency of a home. The higher the rating the more energy efficient the home is and the lower the fuel bills will be.

Environmental Impact (CO_2) Rating

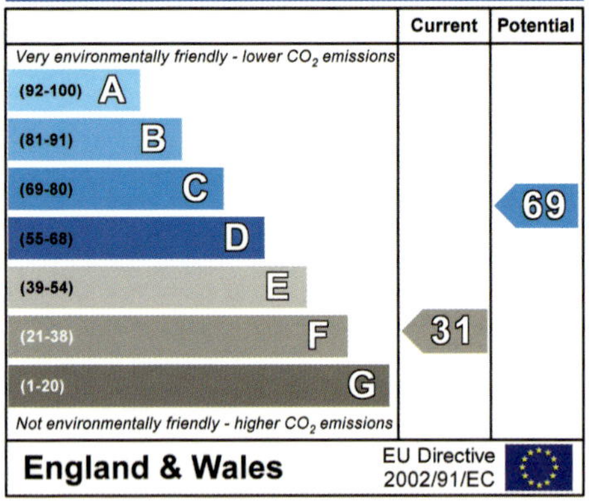

Current: 31
Potential: 69

Very environmentally friendly - lower CO_2 emissions
(92-100) A
(81-91) B
(69-80) C
(55-68) D
(39-54) E
(21-38) F
(1-20) G
Not environmentally friendly - higher CO_2 emissions

England & Wales — EU Directive 2002/91/EC

The environmental impact rating is a measure of a home's impact on the environment in terms of carbon dioxide (CO_2) emissions. The higher the rating the less impact it has on the environment.

Estimated energy use, carbon dioxide (CO_2) emissions and fuel costs of this home

	Current	Potential
Energy Use	453 kWh/m² per year	178 kWh/m² per year
Carbon dioxide emissions	13 tonnes per year	4.9 tonnes per year
Lighting	£81 per year	£65 per year
Heating	£1173 per year	£457 per year
Hot water	£219 per year	£104 per year

Based on standardised assumptions about occupancy, heating patterns and geographical location, the above table provides an indication of how much it will cost to provide lighting, heating and hot water to this home. The fuel costs only take into account the cost of fuel and not any associated service, maintenance or safety inspection. This certificate has been provided for comparative purposes only and enables one home to be compared with another. Always check the date the certificate was issued, because fuel prices can increase over time and energy saving recommendations will evolve.

To see how this home can achieve its potential rating please see the recommended measures.

energy saving recommended — Certification mark

Remember to look for the energy saving recommended logo when buying energy-efficient products. It's a quick and easy way to identify the most energy-efficient products on the market.

For advice on how to take action and to find out about offers available to help make your home more energy efficient, call **0800 512 012** or visit **www.energysavingtrust.org.uk/myhome**

Fig 12.1: Energy Performance Certificate 1

Recommended measures to improve this home's energy performance

17 Any Street,
Any Town,
County,
YY3 5XX

Date of certificate: [dd mmmm yyyy]
Reference number: 0000-0000-0000-0000-0000

Summary of this home's energy performance related features

The following is an assessment of the key individual elements that have an impact on this home's performance rating. Each element is assessed against the following scale: Very poor / Poor / Average / Good / Very good.

Element	Description	Current performance Energy Efficiency	Environmental
Walls	Cavity wall, as built (no insulation)	Poor	Poor
Roof	Pitched, 250 mm loft insulation	Good	Good
Floor	Solid, no insulation (assumed)	–	–
Windows	Partial double glazing	Poor	Poor
Main heating	Boiler and radiators, mains gas	Average	Average
Main heating controls	Programmer, room thermostat and TRVs	Average	Average
Secondary heating	None	–	–
Hot water	From main system, no cylinderstat	Poor	Poor
Lighting	Low energy lighting in 75% of fixed outlets	Very good	Very good
Current energy efficiency rating		**F 37**	
Current environmental impact (CO$_2$) rating			F 31

Fig 12.2: Energy Performance Certificate 2

12.4 MICROGENERATION CERTIFICATION SCHEME

12.4.1   Once you know what needs to be done to your home, you may wish to learn more about new technologies and available products. One scheme that has been established to help you do that is the Microgeneration Certification Scheme (MCS), designed to independently certify microgeneration products and services in accordance with consistent standards. The MCS places a requirement on products and installers to be certified in order to carry the MCS 'mark', and for installers to sign up to a code of practice in line with the Office of Fair Trading's Consumer Code of Approval Scheme.

12.4.2   Microgeneration offers a range of technically advanced low carbon and renewable technologies that will help to:

- Provide consumers with energy sources that use existing natural resources.

- Contribute to the future security of our energy supply.

- Contribute to a low carbon economy.

- Reduce reliance on energy imports.

- Address fuel poverty by reducing the cost of energy.

12.4.3   For further information on this scheme, visit the website www.microgenerationcertification.org.

12.5 T-ZERO WEB TOOL

12.5.1   T-ZERO is a website tool set up to help homeowners upgrade their existing dwelling to increase its energy efficiency and reduce its carbon emissions. The web tool allows the user to input characteristics of a home to establish its carbon footprint. The web tool will then recommend measures that could reduce this footprint, with suggested packages of improvement measures that can be applied to the user's home. It illustrates quantitatively and graphically how these improvements perform, allowing the user to determine the relative importance of the criteria used to judge the suggested packages. Once the user has determined their preferred package, T-ZERO can put them in touch with suppliers of the component measures in the Solutions Marketplace. Users will be able to request a quotation through the site, and suppliers will then have all the details on the house type they are quoting for. The web tool can be accessed at www.tzero.org.uk.

12.6 NHBC FOUNDATION

12.6.1   The NHBC Foundation in partnership with the BRE Trust facilitates research and development, technology and knowledge sharing, and the capture of industry best practice. It has delivered a programme of practical, high-quality research, targeting areas where it is needed most and in particular addressing the sustainability and zero carbon agendas.

12.6.2   *A Review of Microgeneration and Renewable Energy Technologies* is one of the research papers that have been published. The work in this paper focuses on how these technologies will work in, and impact on, homes and homeowners and considers the energy implications of building design, fabric and services systems. It outlines the different types of technology currently available, detailing issues they present and their carbon-saving benefits.

12.6.3   For further information and to access all the papers published by the Foundation, see the website www.nhbcfoundation.org.

12.7 ENERGY AND WATER EFFICIENCY

12.7.1 A brief description of energy and water efficiency measures has been provided below to summarise the type of measures that can easily be carried out on existing homes.

Cavity wall insulation

12.7.2 This is the easiest and cheapest type of wall insulation, and one of the most cost-effective energy improvement measures. Cavity wall insulation works by filling the air space in a cavity wall with an insulating material. In the UK the material is usually mineral wool, though other systems are also available. The insulation is installed by drilling holes into the wall (to a set pattern) and injecting (or 'blowing') the material into the cavity through these holes. See Chapter 8 for further information.

Solid wall insulation

12.7.3 Solid walls are typically found in pre-1930s houses. External wall insulation is more effective than internal insulation, but is typically more expensive. Internal wall insulation products and techniques are well developed and are sometimes also used to reduce internal condensation and mould growth. Mineral wool can be used within a timber frame or rigid internal insulation boards with plasterboard lining. Both applications reduce room size and are disruptive as re-decoration is required. External wall insulation provides a continuous thermal barrier around the vertical perimeter of the entire property, thereby improving air tightness and reducing thermal bridging. It also allows solid walls to act as thermal mass, helping to retain heat in the winter and coolness in the summer. See Chapter 8 for further information.

Roof insulation

12.7.4 See Chapter 8 for information.

Floor insulation

12.7.5 Floor insulation is effective but potentially disruptive. It will usually only be cost-effective as part of refurbishment work. Floor insulation can be applied to any floor:

- Suspended timber floors: either above or below the floor boards, i.e. between the floor joists. A common way is by lifting the floorboards and laying mineral wool insulation supported by netting between the joists or fitting rigid boards between the joists supported on battens.

Windows and doors

12.7.6 See Chapter 5 for information.

Draught-proofing

12.7.7 Air leakage is a fundamental problem, even with comparatively new housing. A significant amount of energy can be wasted through air leakage. The average UK dwelling leaks as much air as if a 300mm x 400mm window were continuously left open. Draughts can cause occupants to feel significant discomfort. Draught-proofing measures aim to fill gaps in the building envelope, thus decreasing the heat escaping from the home and the amount of cold air entering the building. There are several types of materials available, from brushes, foams and sealants to strips and shaped rubber or plastic.

Boilers and controls

12.7.8 With the right controls, a replacement high-efficiency condensing gas or oil boiler can save up to 25–35% on heating bills. Condensing boilers have lower running costs since they recover as much energy as possible from waste heat, which is normally lost through the flue of conventional boilers. Good controls include a hot water tank thermostat, boiler interlock, room thermostat, thermostatic radiator valves, etc. See Chapter 11 for further information.

Lighting and appliances

12.7.9 Provide low-energy light bulbs; consider installing low-energy light fittings; install A-rated appliances. It should be noted that incandescent light bulbs are currently being phased out and will not be available from 2011. See Chapter 11 for further information.

12.7.10 Water shortages are likely to increase with growing pressure on demand, making reducing water consumption more and more important. This can be achieved through collection of rainwater, recycling of grey water and reducing the amount of water taken from the mains for use externally. Measures to reduce consumption include the following.

Low-flush toilets

12.7.11 Modify all toilets in the dwelling to have a flush of no more than 6 litres.

Low-flow taps

12.7.12 Modify all taps in the dwelling to be fitted with either flow regulators, aerating and/or auto shut-off valves.

Low-flow showers

12.7.13 Modify showers in the dwelling to have a flow rate of 9 litres per minute or less.

Small or standard baths

12.7.14 Install standard or small baths. A standard bath is 1500–1700mm (L) x 650–800mm (W) x 450–580mm (H).

External water use

12.7.15 Provide water butts to collect rainwater for garden use.

Grey water recycling

12.7.16 Grey water is defined as the waste water produced from baths, showers, clothes washers, and wash-hand basins. In simple terms this water is collected, treated and then reused in toilets and for outdoor use.

Rainwater harvesting

12.7.17 This is water collected from roofs via traditional guttering, through downpipes to an underground tank. It is then delivered on demand by an in-tank submersible pump for outdoor use, to flush toilets and in some instances for washing machines.

12.8 GREEN ROOFS

12.8.1 Climate change is a hot topic and will not go away. It is crucial that we reduce energy consumption in housing and therefore carbon emissions into the environment. Installing green roofs can have an effect on the way a building performs and could help to achieve zero or low carbon targets as they have considerable insulation properties, providing warmth in the winter and cooling in the summer.

12.8.2 Green roofs can be divided into two categories:

1. Intensive green roofs: these are roof gardens and require the intensive management of a ground-level garden. They are usually based on a thick soil or substrate layer and require irrigation. These are heavy systems and therefore have major structural implications for the building.

2. Extensive green roofs: these tend not to require substantial maintenance although they can be integrated with intensive systems. Based on a relatively thin layer of soil or substrate, they are lightweight with minimal structural implications for the building, are low maintenance and once established need no irrigation.

12.8.3 The following information details some of the benefits of green roofs. Consideration should be given to fire spread when they are used in loft conversions.

Storm water management

12.8.4   In many cities around the world it has been recognised that the most significant ecological advantage of roof planting is in storm water management. Development results in permeable ground being replaced by artificial surfaces through which rainwater cannot permeate. The result is that drainage systems in developed areas are unable to cope with the instant changes in flow rate and volume of storm water, resulting in flooding and water course contamination.

12.8.5   Since it is difficult to install water containment measures within urban areas where space is at such a premium and ground-based storage is expensive, keeping the water on the roof and returning it to the atmosphere is a cost-effective solution.

12.8.6   Rainwater retained on green roofs in the substrate and drainage layers is taken up by the plants and transported from the root to the leaf where it is lost through the leaf surface – a process known as transpiration. Water is evaporated from the substrate and plants by the sun. Both processes are accelerated by wind disruption. Any water that is not retained on the roof is released much more slowly into the drainage system, preventing flooding.

Space for wildlife

12.8.7   A green roof cannot replace a ground-based habitat for the complexity and diversity of species supported; however, some provision of natural areas for wildlife can be sustained through the use of green roofs. They should be viewed as complementary to the maintenance of 'green' corridors for flora and fauna within an urban setting. For certain species, green roofs could provide habitat stepping-stones in the city environment where any protected habitat is becoming increasingly island-like in nature. The advantage of green roofs is that they are undisturbed and free of predators such as the domestic cat. By careful plant selection and/or inclusion of 'brown' roof space, timber and stone they can also be constructed to encourage the colonisation of selected plant and animal species, and provide perching and nesting places for birds.

Cleaner air

12.8.8   Plants remove atmospheric carbon dioxide and emit oxygen during photosynthesis. This is the chemical reaction by which plants use the sun's energy to combine water and carbon dioxide to make sugars for growth. The only universal process that removes carbon dioxide from the atmosphere is photosynthesis. Plants also release water vapour by evaporation or transpiration to humidify the air, and remove airborne particulate pollutants which are deposited in the substrate, and trapped on the leaf surfaces of the plant layer and the moist internal surfaces of the leaf.

Cooler cities

12.8.9   The impervious surfaces of cities such as concrete, tarmac and the wide variety of roof surfaces soak up solar energy and re-radiate it as heat. The result of this is that cities are warmer both day and night than the surrounding countryside. This can have profoundly negative effects on air quality in the city. Production of some pollutants can be higher and the flushing out of others is reduced as the inflow of clean cool air is reduced by the thermal conditions. The strong heat sink effects seen on roofs in the UK can be greatly reduced by planting. With a collective approach to the issue, planting existing roof space would have a very significant and positive effect on air quality and temperatures within our cities.

13. OTHER ITEMS

13.0 INTRODUCTION

13.0.1 This chapter provides information and a useful list of necessary documentation that must be obtained or considered when carrying out a loft conversion.

13.1 BUILDING REGULATIONS

13.1.1 The following pages contain examples of:

- a Full Plans application form (Figures 13.1 and 13.2).

- an Initial Notice form (Figures 13.3 and 13.4).

THE INFORMATION ON
THIS FORM IS IN THE
PUBLIC DOMAIN

**FULL PLANS
SUBMISSION**
The Building Act 1984
The Building Regulations

Building Regulations Ref Number:
(office use only)

FP/20   /

This form is to be filled in by the person (or his/her agent) who intends to carry out building work. If the form is unfamiliar please read the notes on the reverse side or consult the office indicated below. Please type or use block capitals.

1 **Applicant's details** (see note 1)
Name:
Address:
Postcode: Tel: Mob/Fax:
e-mail :

2 **Agent's details** (if applicable)
Name:
Address:
Postcode: Tel: Mob/Fax:
e-mail:

3 **Location of building to which work relates**
Address:
Postcode: Tel: Mob/Fax:

4 **Proposed work**
Description:
Is the proposed work or any part of it subject to a current LABC Type Approval (see note 8)?   YES/NO

5 **Use of building**
1 If new building or extension please state proposed use:
2 If existing building state present use:
3 Is the building to be put, or intended to be used as flat accommodation or any other non-   YES/NO
   domestic use (see note 9)?

6 **Conditions** (see note 10)
Do you consent to the plans being passed subject to conditions where appropriate?   YES/NO

7 **Fees** (see notes 3 and separate Guidance Note on Fees for information)
1 If Schedule 1 work please state number of dwellings and types - Total: No of types:
2 If Schedule 2 work please state internal floor area: m^2
3 If Schedule 3 work please state the estimated cost of work excluding VAT: £
Plan fee: £   plus VAT (where applicable): £   Total: £

8 **Additional information**
Is this application a re-submission?   YES/NO   If so state previous FP reference no – FP/
Do you agree to an extension of time to consider your application (see note 13)?   YES/NO

9 **Electrical Work**
Are there any electrical controlled works to be carried out?   YES/NO
Is the person carrying out the electrical works registered under a competent person scheme?   YES/NO

10 **Statement**
This notice is given in relation to the building work as described, is submitted in accordance with Regulation 12(2)(b) and is accompanied by the appropriate fee. I understand that further fees will be payable following the first inspection by the local authority.
Name: Signature: Date:

Fig 13.1: Full Plans Submission 1

Notes

1. The applicant is the person on whose behalf the work is being carried out, eg the building's owner.

2. One copy of this notice should be completed and submitted with 2 copies of any plans and particulars in accordance with the provisions of Regulation 14 of The Building (Amendment) (2) Regulations 2004.

3. Subject to certain exceptions a Full Plans submission attracts fees payable by the person by whom, or on whose behalf, the work is to be carried out. Fees are payable in two stages. The first fee must accompany the deposit of plans and the second charge is payable after the first site inspection of work in progress. The second fee is a single payment in respect of each individual building, to cover all site visits and consultations, which may be necessary, until the work is satisfactorily completed.
Schedule 1 prescribes the plan and inspection charges payable for small domestic buildings. Schedule 2 prescribes the charges payable for the extensions to a dwelling home or the addition of a small detached garage. Schedule 3 prescribes the charges payable for all other cases.
The appropriate fee is dependent upon the type of work proposed. Fee scales and methods of calculation are set out in the Guidance Notes on Fees, which is available on request.

4. A block plan to a scale of not less than 1:1250 is required showing:-

   ∞ The size and position of the building, or the building as extended, and its relationship to adjoining boundaries;
   ∞ The boundaries of the land belonging to the building, or the building as extended and the size, position and use of every other building or proposed building within that curtilage;
   ∞ The width and position of any street on or within the boundaries of the curtilage of the building or the building as extended;
   ∞ The provision made for the drainage of the building or extension.

5. All plans, sections and elevations must be drawn to a scale of 1:20, 1:50, 1:100 or 1:200.

6. Where it is proposed to erect the building or extension over a sewer or drain shown on the relative map of public sewers, adequate precautions should be taken when building over a sewer or drain.

7. Subject to certain provisions of the Public Health Act 1936, owners and occupiers of premises are entitled to have their private foul and surface water drains and sewers connected to the public sewers, where available. Special arrangements apply to trade effluent discharge. Persons wishing to make such connections must give not less than 21 days notice to the appropriate authority.

8. LABC provides national type and systems approvals for a range of building types, building systems and major building elements where they are used repeatedly. If the work proposal, or any part of it, is subject to a LABC Type approval please answer YES and enclose a copy of the appropriate current certificate(s). If there is any variation in this proposal from that shown on the LABC Type approval plans attention should be drawn to it.

9. All non-domestic work except flats is subject to the Regulatory Reform (Fire Safety) Order 2005 and as such 2 additional copies of fire plans will be required to allow consultation with the Fire Authority.

10. Section 16 of the Building Act 1984 provides for the passing of plans subject to conditions. The conditions may specify modifications to the deposited plans and/or that further plans shall be deposited.

11. These notes are for general guidance only, particulars regarding the deposit of plans are contained in Regulation 14 of The Building (Amendment) (2) Regulations 2004.

12. Persons proposing to carry out building work, or make a material change of use of a building, are reminded that permission may be required under the Town and Country Planning Acts.

13. Further information and advice concerning the Building Regulations and planning matters may be obtained from your local authority.

14. You can agree to an extension of the 5 week period for checking your application up to a maximum of 8 weeks. This should assist you or your Architect in furnishing the Council with any additional information regarding your application and avoid an unnecessary rejection.

HAVE YOU ?

∞ **Entered the applicant's full name.**
∞ **Entered the full postcode.**
∞ **Enclosed the appropriate fee.**
∞ **Signed the form.**
∞ **Enclosed two copies of plans and details.**
∞ **Enclosed three copies of fire plans (if required).**

Fig 13.2: Full Plans Submission 2

Section 47 of the Building Act 1984 ("the Act")

The Building (Approved Inspectors etc.) Regulations 2000 ("the 2000

Regulations")

INITIAL NOTICE

To: **(1)**

1. This notice relates to the following work: **(2)**

2. The approved inspector in relation to the work is: **(3)**

3. The person intending to carry out the work is: **(3)**

4. With this notice are the following documents, which are those relevant to the work described in this notice **(4)**:

    a. In the case of a notice given by an inspector approved following an application under regulation 3(1) of the 2000 Regulations, a copy of the notice of approval,

    b. A declaration signed by the insurer that a named scheme of insurance approved by the Secretary of State applies in relation to the work described in the notice,

    c. In the case of the erection or extension of a building, a plan to a scale of not less than 1:1250 showing the boundaries and location of the site and a statement -

        I.   As to the approximate location of any proposed connection to be made to a sewer, or

        II. If no connection is to be made to a sewer, as to the proposals for the discharge of any proposed drain, including the location of any cesspool, or

        III. If no provision is to be made for drainage, of the reasons why none is necessary,

    d. Where it is proposed to erect a building or extension over a sewer or drain shown on the relative map of sewers, a statement as to the location of the building or extension and the precautions to be taken in building over the sewer or drain,

    e. A statement of any local enactment relevant to the work, and of the steps to be taken to comply with it.

5. The work [is]/[is not] **(5)** minor work **(6).**

6. I **(7)** declare that I do not, and will not while this notice is in force, have any financial or professional interest **(8)** in the work described.**(9)**

7. The approved inspector [will]/[will not] **(10)** be obliged to consult the fire authority by regulation 13 of the 2000 Regulations.

8. I **(7)** undertake to consult the fire authority before giving a plans certificate in accordance with section 50 of the Act or a final certificate in accordance with section 51 of the Act in respect of any of the work described above. **(9)**

9. I **(7)** am aware of the obligations laid upon me by Part II of the Act and by regulation 11 of the 2000 Regulations.

Signed	Signed
Approved Inspector	Person intending to carry out the work
Date	Date

Fig 13.3: Initial Notice

NOTES

(1) Name and address of local authority.

(2) Location and description of the work, including the use of any building to which the work relates.

(3) Name and address.

(4) The local authority may reject this notice only on grounds prescribed by the Secretary of State. These are set out in Schedule 3 to the 2000 Regulations. They include failure to provide relevant documents. The documents listed in paragraph 4 of the notice relevant to the work described above should therefore be sent with this notice. Any sub-paragraph which does not apply should be deleted.

(5) Delete whichever does not apply.

(6) "Minor work" has the meaning given in regulation 10(1) of the 2000 Regulations. If the work is not minor work, the declaration in paragraph 6 must be made.

(7) Name of the approved inspector.

(8) "Professional or financial interest" has the meaning given in regulation 10 of the 2000 Regulations.

(9) Delete this statement if it does not apply.

(10) Delete whichever does not apply. If the inspector is obliged to consult the fire authority, the declaration in paragraph 8 must be made.

Fig 13.4: Initial Notice notes

13.1.2 You should notify the BCB when construction work reaches certain stages. It is advisable to discuss with your Building Control Officer at the earliest opportunity the stages at which they would like to inspect on your loft conversion. To obtain a completion certificate, site inspections must be undertaken. The stages of inspection, generally, are outlined below (not all may be applicable):

- Commencement on site.
- Expose existing foundations and lintels for adequacy, including survey on all load-bearing elements.
- All structural alterations:
  - Underpinning, new timbers, steel beams, lintels.
  - Construction of new or re-building of the party wall.
  - Raising existing roof or elements, e.g. chimneys and party walls.
- New attic/RIR trusses.

- New staircase:
  - Headroom, pitch, balustrading, etc.
- Insertion of insulation.
- First and second fix:
  - Drainage, plumbing, heating, electrical.
- Completion inspection:
  - Means of escape:
    - Fire doors, smoke detectors, escape windows.
  - Ventilation:
    - Background, purge and extraction.
  - Drainage test.
  - Windows:
    - Safety glass, U-value check.
  - Certificates.
    - Plumbing, electrical, etc.

Fig 13.5: Trial hole for foundation inspection

Fig 13.7: Extension of space heating system

Fig 13.6: Testing smoke alarm

Fig 13.8: Completion of loft conversion

13.1.3   Failure to comply with the Building Regulations may result in the local authority Building Control Body issuing a section 35 – penalty for contravening building regulations, and/or a section 36 – removal or alteration of offending work under the Building Act 1984. An approved inspector cannot enforce this but they can cancel the Initial Notice and hand the project over to the local authority who will carry out enforcement action.

STANDARDS AND PUBLICATIONS REFERRED TO

British Standards

BS 476-3:2004	External fire exposure roof tests
BS 476-22:1987	Fire tests on building materials and structures
BS 1566:2002	Copper indirect cylinders for domestic purposes. Open vented copper cylinders. Requirements and test methods
BS 5268	Parts 1-7 Structural use of timber
BS 5268-3:2006	Structural use of timber. Code of practice for trussed rafter roofs
BS 5395-2:1984	Stairs, ladders and walkways: Code of practice for the design of helical and spiral stairs
BS 5410-1:1997	Code of practice for oil firing
BS 5446-2:2003	Fire detection and fire alarm devices for dwellings. Specification for heat alarms
BS 5482-1:2005	Code of practice for domestic butane
BS 5516-2:2004	Patent glazing and sloping glazing for buildings. Code of Practice for sloping glazing
BS 5534:2003	Code of practice for slating and tiling (including shingles)
BS 5628-1:2005	Code of practice for the use of masonry. Structural use of unreinforced masonry
BS 5839-1:2002	Fire detection and alarm systems for buildings. Code of practice for system design, installation and servicing
BS 5839-6:2004	Fire detection and fire alarm systems for buildings. Code of practice for the design, installation and maintenance of fire detection and fire alarm systems in dwellings
BS 6399-1:1996	Loading for buildings. Code of practice for dead and imposed loads
BS 6399-2:1997	Loading for buildings. Code of practice for wind loads
BS 6399-3:1988	Loading for buildings. Code of practice for imposed roof loads
BS 6891:2005	Specification for installation of low pressure gas pipework of up to 28 mm (R1) in domestic premises (2nd family gas)
BS 7593:2006	Code of practice for treatment of water in domestic hot water central heating systems
BS 7671:2008	Requirements for electrical installations. IEE Wiring Regulations. Seventeenth edition
BS 8103-1:1995	Structural design of low-rise buildings. Code of practice for stability, site investigation, foundations and ground floor slabs for housing
BS 8103-3:2009	Structural design of low-rise buildings. Code of practice for timber floors and roofs for housing
BS 8303-1:1994	Installation of domestic heating and cooking appliances burning solid mineral fuels. Installation of domestic heating and cooking appliances burning solid mineral fuels. Specification for the design of installations
BS 8303-2:1994	Installation of domestic heating and cooking appliances burning solid mineral fuels. Installation of domestic heating and cooking appliances burning solid mineral fuels. Specification for installing and commissioning on site
BS 8303-3:1994	Installation of domestic heating and cooking appliances burning solid mineral fuels. Recommendations for design and on site installation
BS 9251:2005	Sprinkler systems for residential and domestic occupancies. Code of practice
BS EN 300:2006	Oriented strand boards (OSB). Definitions, classification and specifications
BS EN 312:2003	Particleboards. Specifications
BS EN 572-3:2004	Glass in building. Basic soda lime silicate glass products. Polished wire glass
BS EN 572-6:2004	Glass in building. Basic soda lime silicate glass products. Wired patterned glass
BS EN 752:2008	Drain and sewer systems outside buildings

BS EN 845:2003	Specification for ancillary components for masonry
BS EN 1634-3:2004	Fire resistance and smoke control tests for door and shutter assemblies, openable windows and elements of building hardware. Smoke control test for door and shutter assemblies
BS EN 1991	UK National annex to Eurocode 1 – Actions on structures
BS EN 1995	UK National annex to Eurocode 5 – Design of timber structures
BS EN 12056:2000	Parts 1-5 Gravity drainage systems inside buildings
BS EN 12150:2000	Parts 1 & 2 Glass in building. Thermally toughened soda lime silicate safety glass.
BS EN 12600:2002	Glass in building. Pendulum test. Impact test method and classification for flat glass
BS EN 12828:2003	Heating systems in buildings. Design for water-based heating systems
BS EN 12831:2003	Heating systems in buildings. Method for calculation of the design heat load
BS EN 12897:2006	Water supply. Specification for indirectly heated unvented (closed) storage water heaters
BS EN 13024-1:2002	Glass in building. Thermally toughened borosilicate safety glass. Definition and description
BS EN 14179:2005	Parts 1 & 2 Glass in building. Heat-soaked thermally-toughened soda lime silicate safety glass
BS EN 14336:2004	Heating systems in buildings. Installation and commissioning of water based heating systems
BS EN 14449:2005	Glass in building. Laminated glass and laminated safety glass. Evaluation of conformity/product standard
BS EN 14604:2005	Glass in building. Laminated glass and laminated safety glass. Evaluation of conformity/product standard
BS EN 60439-3:1991	Specification for low-voltage switchgear and controlgear assemblies. Particular requirements for low-voltage switchgear and controlgear assemblies intended to be installed in places where unskilled persons have access to their use. Distribution boards
BS EN 61008-1:2004	Residual current operated circuit-breakers without integral overcurrent protection for household and similar used (RCCBs). General rules
BS EN ISO 12543-2:1998	Glass in building. Laminated glass and laminated safety glass. Laminated safety glass
BS EN ISO 8990:1996	Thermal insulation. Determination of steady-state thermal transmission properties. Calibrated and guarded hot box

Publications

Communities and Local Government

Building Regulations 2000

Approved Document A:
Structure (2004 edition incorporating 2004 amendments)

Approved Document B:
Fire Safety (volume 1) – Dwellinghouses (2006 edition)

Approved Document B:
Fire Safety (Volume 2) – Buildings other than dwellinghouses (2006 edition incorporating 2007 amendments)

Approved Document C:
Site preparation and resistance to contaminants and moisture (2004 edition)

Approved Document D:
Toxic substances (1992 edition incorporating 2002 amendments)

Approved Document E:
Resistance to the passage of sound (2003 edition incorporating 2004 amendments)

Approved Document F:
Ventilation (2010 edition)

Approved Document G:
Sanitation, hot water safety and water efficiency (2010 edition)

Approved Document H:
Drainage and waste disposal (2002 edition)

Approved Document J:
Combustion appliances and fuel storage systems (2010 edition)

Approved Document K:
Protection from falling, collision and impact (1998 edition incorporating 2000 amendments)

Approved Document L1A:
Conservation of fuel and power – New dwellings (2010 edition)

Approved Document L1B:
Conservation of fuel and power – Existing dwellings (2010 edition)

Approved Document L2A:
Conservation of fuel and power – New buildings other than dwellings (2010 edition)

Approved Document L2B:
Conservation of fuel and power – Existing buildings other than dwellings (2010 edition)

Approved Document M:
Access to and use of buildings (2004 edition)

Approved Document N:
Glazing – safety in relation to impact, opening and cleaning (1998 edition incorporating 2000 amendments)

Approved Document P:
Electrical safety – dwellings (2006 edition)

Approved Document to support regulation 7:
Materials and workmanship (1992 edition incorporating 2000 amendments)

Domestic Building Services Compliance Guide (2010 Edition)

Building Research Establishment
BR262 *Thermal insulation: avoiding the risks* (2002)
BR443 *Conventions for U-value calculations* (2006)
BR454 *Multi-storey Timber Frame Buildings: A Design Guide* (2006)

TRADA Technology Ltd
Span tables: for solid timber members in floors, ceilings and roofs for dwellings (2009), *Timber Frame Construction* (2007)

Glass and Glazing Federation
Guide to best practice in the specification and use of fire resistant glazed systems (2005)

Institute of Electrical Engineers
IEE Guidance Note 7: *Special locations* (2009)

BSRIA
Underfloor heating systems – an assessment standard for installations AG13 (2001)
Underfloor heating systems – the designers' guide AG12 (2001)

Legislation
Building (Approved Inspectors etc.) Regulations 2000
Building Act 1984
Building Regulations 2000
Conservation (Natural Habitats etc.) Regulations 1994
Construction (Design and Management) Regulations 2007
Gas Safety (Installation and Use) Regulations
Party Wall Act 1996
Wildlife and Countryside Act 1981

Websites
www.approvedinspectors.org.uk
www.bre.co.uk
www.bwf.org.uk
www.direct.gov.uk
www.ggf.co.uk
www.hse.gov.uk
www.labc.uk.com
www.leadsheetassociation.org.uk
www.microgenerationcertification.org
www.nhbcfoundation.org
www.planningportal.gov.uk
www.submit-a-plan.com
www.tzero.org.uk

INDEX

CREDITS

© Crown copyright material is reproduced with the permission of the Controller of HMSO and Queen's Printer for Scotland.

Permission to reproduce extracts from:
BS 5395-2:1984 *Stairs, ladders and walkways. Code of Practice for the design of helical and spiral stairs.*
BS 5268-3 *Structural use of timber. Code of practice for trussed rafter roofs.*
BS 5250:2002 *Code of practice for control of condensation in buildings.*
is granted by BSI. British Standards can be obtained in PDF or hard copy formats from the BSI online shop: **www.bsigroup.com/Shop** or by contacting BSI Customer Services for hardcopies only: Tel: **+44 (0)20 8996 9001**, Email: **cservices@bsigroup.com**.

Adapted from Approved Document B Vol 1. (2006) © Crown Copyright
Figs 7.1, 7.2, 7.3, 7.4, 7.5, 7.8, 7.9, 7.11, 7.12, 7.13, 7.14

Adapted from Approved Document E (2003) © Crown Copyright
Figs 9.1, 9.2, 9.3

Adapted from Approved Document F (2010) © Crown Copyright
Figs 10.8, 10.9, 10.10

Adapted from Approved Document H (2002) © Crown Copyright Fig 6.1

Adapted from Approved Document J (2010) © Crown Copyright Fig 11.18

Adapted from Approved Document K (1998) © Crown Copyright
Figs 4.5, 4.6, 4.7, 4.8, 4.10, 4.11

Adapted from Approved Document N (1998) © Crown Copyright
Figs 5.1, 5.2, 5.3, 5.8

Adapted from Approved Document P (2006) © Crown Copyright
Figs 11.9, 11.10, 11.11

Adapted from diagram courtesy of Celotex Figs 8.37, 8.39, 8.41

Adapted from diagram courtesy of Loft Shop Figs 1.1, 1.2, 1.3

Adapted from diagram courtesy of One Project Closer Fig 2.3

Adapted from diagram courtesy of Universal Forest Products Fig 3.5

Adapted from diagram courtesy of Velux Figs 2.1, 3.2, 3.3, 3.4

Adapted from diagrams courtesy of Kingspan Figs 8.17, 8.18, 8.19, 8.20, 8.21, 8.22, 8.23, 8.24, 8.25, 8.26

Adapted from images courtesy of BRUFMA Figs 8.15, 8.16

BS 5250:2002 Code of practice for control of condensation in buildings
Figs 10.1, 10.2, 10.3, 10.4, 10.5, 10.6, 10.7

BS 5268-3 Structural use of timber. Code of practice for trussed rafter roofs Figs 11.3, 11.4, 44.5, 11.6

Chris Derzypilskyj Figs 2.2, 3.1, 4.4, 7.15, 7.16, 7.17, 7.18, 7.19, 8.27, 8.28, 8.29, 8.30, 8.31, 13.3, 13.4

Courtesy of ADM Systems Fig 10.14

Courtesy of BM TRADA Fig 7.6

Courtesy of Celotex Figs 8.1, 8.38, 8.40

Courtesy of Dunelm Geotechnical & Environmental Ltd Fig 13.5

Courtesy of E A Higginson & Co Ltd. Figs 4.1, 4.2

Courtesy of I D Steel Wrought Iron Fig 5.4

Courtesy of Jablite Ltd. Fig 8.5

Courtesy of Kingspan Figs 8.6, 8.7, 8.10, 8.11, 8.14, 8.32, 8.33, 8.34, 8.35, 8.42, 8.43, 8.44, 8.45, 8.46, 8.47, 8.48

Courtesy of Knauf Insulation Figs 8.2, 8.12, 8.13, 8.36, 8.49, 8.50

Courtesy of LABC Figs 13.1, 13.2

Courtesy of Monodraught Ltd. Figs 5.14, 5.15, 5.16

Courtesy of Neno Lennard BSc Dip Arch Figs 8.8, 8.9

Courtesy of NHBC Figs 3.6, 3.7, 3.8, 3.9, 3.10, 4.9, 5.5, 5.6, 5.7, 7.10, 7.20, 11.1, 11.2, 11.12, 12.1, 12.2

Courtesy of Passivent Ltd. Figs 10.13, 10.15

Courtesy of the British Woodworking Federation Fig 7.7

Courtesy of Velux Figs 5.9, 5.10, 5.11, 5.12

Courtesy of Jablite Ltd. Fig 8.5

Courtesy of Web Dynamics Ltd. Fig 8.4

Image of Xpelair LoVolt XHR 150 single room heat recovery ventilator courtesy of Applied Energy Fig 10.12

Thermal and air leakage: Robust construction details for dwellings and other similar buildings, DEFRA, 2001 © Crown Copyright Fig 5.13